———— Delirio ————

The Fantastic, the Demonic, and the Réel

THE BURIED HISTORY OF NUEVO LEÓN

Delírio

The Fantastic, the Demonic, and the Réel

Marie Theresa Hernández

UNIVERSITY OF TEXAS PRESS

Austin

An earlier version of Chapter 3 was previously published by the
University of Chicago Press in PARA-SITES, © 2000 by The University
of Chicago Press. All rights reserved.

Requests for permission to reproduce material from this work should be
sent to Permissions, University of Texas Press, P.O. Box 7819, Austin, TX
78713-7819.

⊗ The paper used in this book meets the minimum requirements of
ANSI/NISO Z39.48-1992 (R1997) (Permanence of Paper).

Library of Congress Cataloging-in-Publication Data

Hernández, Marie Theresa, 1952–
Delirio—the fantastic, the demonic, and the réel : the buried
history of Nuevo León / Marie Theresa Hernández.
p.   cm.
Includes bibliographical references and index.
ISBN 0-292-73129-9 (hardcover : alk. paper) — ISBN 0-292-73462-X
(pbk. : alk. paper)
1. Ethnology—Mexico—Nuevo León (State)   2. Folklore—Mexico—
Nuevo León (State)   3. Indigenous peoples—Mexico—Nuevo León
(State)—History.   4. Nuevo León (Mexico : State)—History.   5. Nuevo
León (Mexico : State)—Social life and customs.   I. Title.
GN560.M6 H47 202
305.8′00972′13 — dc21

2002000336

IN MEMORY OF

Don J. Aquiles Sepúlveda

Born in San Isidro del Potrero, Nuevo León, 1936
Died in Monterrey, Nuevo León, 2000

Don Gregorio Tijerina

Born in General Bravo, Nuevo León, 1902
Died in Wharton, Texas, 1991

Contents

List of Illustrations

Acknowledgments

My most sincere appreciation goes to George Marcus, James Faubion, Patricia Seed, and Stephen Tyler for sharing their knowledge with me and for their unfailing support as I studied Nuevo León and wrote *Delirio*. I also thank Kathleen Stewart for her guidance and encouragement regarding my work on poetics; José Aranda for his knowledge of Monterrey and his enthusiasm for my project; Carole Speranza for guiding me through the bureaucratic maze of graduate funding; Richard Tapía for his support and encouragement throughout my graduate program; José Limón for suggesting northern Mexico as a field site; Theresa May for her foresight and commitment to this project while it was still truly in a state of delirium; Shannon Leonard for her invaluable comments upon reading *Delirio;* and Rachel Jennings for her patience and expertise in the final copy edit.

My fieldwork was made possible by financial support from the Ford Foundation Fellowship for Minorities, whose assistance provided ongoing travel to my field site for a period of three years. I thank Licenciado Horacio Alvarado Ortiz, Don Ventura González and Doña Soledad Villagómez de González and their family, Yolanda and Rosalba González, Ana Sáenz, Profesor Artemio Villagómez Lozano, Don Maximiliano Villagómez and his daughter Blanca Villagómez and their family, Don Hector and Doña Margarita Villagómez and their family, the late Profesor Felipe Hernández, Profesora Guadalupe Rosales de Hernández, Profesora Citlalli Hernández, Doña Magdalena Vásquez and Don Jesús Villegas and their family, Rosie Vásquez, Don Quechú and Doña Petrita Vásquez and their family, Doña Juanera Domínguez and her children, Marta Garza, Jenny, Lili, and Pati Reséndiz, Cristóbal López, Sr. Abraham Nuncio, Loretta Pisegna, and Rosie Alméndarez. I thank Heriberto

Villagómez for introducing me to the world of Nuevo León. I appreciate the support of Rice students and alumni: Laura Helper, Cecilia Balli, Jae Chung, Tarra Drevet, Lamia Karim, and Brian Riedel. Visiting researcher Silvana de Paola was also instrumental in the early part of my research and fieldwork. I also want to thank Agustín Loredo and his family for letting me into their lives in Houston and in Monterrey.

Most of all I appreciate Doña Pepita, Señorita Ofelia, and the late Aquiles Sepúlveda for their assistance and affection.

I appreciate the support from my parents, José F. Hernández and María de la Luz Hernández; my father for his love of stories, my mother for her adventurous nature and advice to always have a packed suitcase; my aunts, Irma and Laura Hernández, who provided not only meals and a bed to sleep in during my numerous crossings back and forth through the United States–Mexican border, but also their comments on the information I brought with me and their endless opinions on Mexico from the perspective of being "border people." Those that I must acknowledge most are my children, Gregory and Belén Tijerina. They lived with me, through the travel, the adventures, and the writing. I thank Belén especially, for living with me in Monterrey. I will always remember her driving my little white car in circles around the dirt roads of Potrero, waving to Juanera Domínguez and me as she sped by.

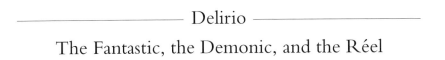

Delirio

The Fantastic, the Demonic, and the Réel

Map of Nuevo León.

Introduction

Delirio

> Modern Western history revolves around a deep split in the secret in which truth's dependence on untruth is ethnically and geographically divided between north and south. (Taussig 1999: 78)

While the centers of Mexican power and government are in Mexico City to the south, the economic force of Mexico is in the northern city of Monterrey, Nuevo León. When *regios* (residents of Monterrey) learned that I was writing on Nuevo León, they quickly told me that the north was very different from the south. They told me that people in the south do not have a work ethic and expect the benefits of nature to fall from the trees.[1] They do not work hard because their land is so abundant. In contrast, the northern landscape gives little to the *norteño;* the fruit on the tree limb often dries before maturity, due to the extreme temperatures and limited rainfall characteristic of the north. *Norteños* have to work for everything they have. Within these descriptions are allusions to a north that produces a more responsible and resourceful individual. In Mexico, the divisions between north and south have become conduits of the production of history.[2]

Nuevo León encompasses 65,000 square kilometers of territory in northeastern Mexico. It is bordered by the states of Tamaulipas, Coahuila, San Luis Potosí, and Zacatecas. The original territory of El Nuevo Reino de León (the new kingdom of León) is a portion of the original expanse of land that was given in a concession from Felipe II of Spain to Luis Carvajal y de la Cueva in 1579. Local narratives describe the Nuevo

Reino as a separate sovereignty from Spain. Carvajal had also been given the right of naming his own successor. This sense of separation became a constant in the history of Nuevo León. Its geographic distance from the nation's capital created a schism that led to a polemic regarding *nuevoleneses'* (residents of Nuevo León) lack of identification as citizens of *la patria* (the Mexican nation). Given their distance, could they really be considered Mexicans? Paradoxically, this gap provided a space of freedom for *norteños* to create a world that became strikingly different and prosperous compared to the rest of Mexico. This trend was facilitated by the realignment of the U.S.-Mexico boundary after the War of 1846-1848. Further pushed to the margin, now that the United States was only 200 kilometers north of Monterrey, it also allowed for the migration of American cultural practices (and capitalism) into Nuevo León, creating a world that in many ways appropriated a quasi-Protestant way of life inside of a loosely held Catholicism.

The broad expanse of desert and mountain range that encompasses the Mexican state of Nuevo León has a complex existence. In my fieldwork I found many avenues that facilitated a broader and possibly more understanding view of the region. There are numerous possibilities for explanation using geographic and cultural landmarks or minutiae of popular culture to describe the lives of the *nuevoleneses*. Such complexity created a dilemma in the development of a focus or central argument with regard to this project. Ultimately, the common thread located in the work appeared to be the concept of the hidden narrative.[3] Although the idea of secrecy and the idea of the occulted were present from the beginning of my fieldwork, the idea of the "hidden" did not appear as salient until I encountered the stories of *la ciudad subterránea* (the underground city), which I describe in Chapter IX, "La Sultana." This impressive "urban legend" evoked narratives of numerous events in Nuevo León's history. From the Indian raids to the revolution to the "malignant" role of the church, the stories evoked the issue of hiding either people or bodies. Stories told to me regarding occulted activities in the present day speculate that tunnels used for narcotics traffic, such as the tunnels in San Diego, California, and Nogales, Arizona, have been used in this manner.[4] These numerous stories formed a larger trajectory about the "repressed."

There have been many texts published regarding Nuevo León, all produced within the Mexican academy. As of this writing, there has been no ethnography written by an American anthropologist on Nuevo León. In addition, with the exception of Eugenio de Hoyo's *Historia de Nuevo*

León and the brief but concise work of Abraham Nuncio in *Visión de Monterrey,* existing works have often focused on information presented with the flavor of government propaganda. Most of the texts are written more like pronouncements than descriptions.

Genesis / Beginning

As often happens in the plan for one's research, there have been turns, stops, and regroupings within this project. Initially, my interest was in the Imaginary as Michael Taussig treated it in *Shamanism, Colonialism, and the Wild Man* (1987) or as Stefania Pandolfo treated it in *Impasse of the Angels* (1997). Taussig and Pandolfo write of the Imaginary as a space for the location of the unexplained and the uncanny. It is the place of the *réel,* which can be slightly disorienting to the observer if he or she is not acquainted with these types of events or experiences, the *réel* being the moment or space between the symbol and the conceptualization of what has been seen or heard. For Taussig the Imaginary is the spiritual dimension of healing and witchcraft. For Pandolfo it is the space of the demonic and the ethereal presence of death in the everyday life of the people in the Qsar. The quotidian use of the Imaginary and the *réel* serves as a vehicle for entering the space of the unexplained. There is a certain aspect to Taussig's and Pandolfo's narratives that places the ethnographer and the reader into the space of the story, yet decreases the sense of the exotic. Theirs is a trope that tugs at the space between subject and object, reality and unreality, reason and the fantastic.

For my own work, using the locus of Nuevo León, I saw the Imaginary as experienced through regional practices of folk healing. Many of the first stories I heard when I began traveling to Nuevo León were about folklore and magic. This search led to the television program *Reportajes de Alvarado,* which focused on the particular folklore of the north and its history. It was produced and directed by Horacio Alvarado Ortiz, whom I met through a series of contacts that began in Texas. Licenciado Ortiz was the first television announcer in Nuevo León. He had worked in television for over forty years. Through his television program on the history and culture of Nuevo León, he introduced me to the landscape and topography of the state. From Alvarado, I learned about the region from a certain panoramic perspective. I also learned about local norms of communication and comportment. He advised me on how to pursue certain issues and how to "de-code" the information I subsequently obtained. He assisted me in meeting many people from Monterrey and surrounding communities who were instrumental in providing information about the history and practices of the north. I came to know Alvarado as an icon of power in northern Mexico. I see my collaboration with him as a nexus that created numerous avenues of study. These interactions proved to be of significant assistance and support during the three years I traveled in Nuevo León.

The first year of my fieldwork was in a sense a transition. It became more than a quest for stories. A sense of history pervaded the search. During this year of traveling with Alvarado, I found that the stories of folkloric practices were inexplicably tied to an ambivalently experienced historical space that lurked inside the persona of the north. Narratives of "primitive" rural people, "barbarous" Indians, and the "first" Jews fell into many of the conversations I had with *nuevoleneses*. Narratives relate that the rural man/woman from Nuevo León fought the "barbaric Indian" under the most impossible of conditions and preserved the traditions and hard work of the region. It was also (in the fantasy of the illusion) the rural *nuevoleneses* who had once been Jews escaping from the dangers of the Inquisition and who had hidden the "original" story of a Jewish heritage.

While the stories I heard of witches and spells were fascinating and exotic, the history of the region became even more compelling as I learned of the narratives of Luis Carvajal, Diego Montemayor, and the other Portuguese who founded the Nuevo Reino de León. With regard to these stories, meeting Aquiles Sepúlveda was pivotal in the development of my project. His constant noting of traces still alive from the era of Carvajal and Montemayor made me aware of the unfathomable depth of narrative and memory that lurked behind the facade of the new industrial city that believes itself to be an active member of the First World. The exotic stories have not disappeared. In fact they remain in this text. Yet they are not central to the work. I show them as an integral part of a world that has chosen not to erase them completely and/or maintain them merely as superstition. They are ingredients still active in a place that has moved swiftly into modernity, yet has chosen not to occlude all of its past life. In a symbolic sense, these practices are used as methods of imaginative travel, allowing the *nuevoleneses* to move between the alternating identities and moments that characterize their world.

Thus what began as a view into the exotic ultimately cast this ethnography into the hidden recess of history that attached itself to these stories and practices. The work of Michel de Certeau provides a grounding for the intersection between the fantastic stories and the receding or hidden histories. Two concepts of interest to de Certeau are used as beacons in this work. I begin with the idea of a "Scriptural Economy." In *The Practice of Everyday Life* (1984), de Certeau writes of the modern disparity between the idea of the "Word" and of the "Text." This disparity is related to the uneven circulation of narratives. The mechanisms of the Scriptural Economy are used by sources of power to enhance, occlude, or diminish narratives that describe the history and personality of a place. What is diminished is ambivalently referenced in texts. What is occluded is vehemently denied in "official texts" and "official pronouncements" by government-sponsored academics and historians. In Nuevo León, the "Word" that did not become "Text" was lost to "formal history." This loss encompassed what is described in this book as the Jewish narratives. In addition, what was diminished was the presence of an indigenous population. These "reductions" of the "Word" have been transformed into phantasmic stories. The Scriptural Economy of Nuevo León has allocated a certain hidden corner (or underground tomb) for them. The narratives that have been displaced by the Scriptural Economy are no longer considered valid. They are now fiction and ancient legends.

The surviving narratives are legitimated and controlled by governmental and ecclesiastic powers. This exertion of control solidifies the current hegemonic narrative in Nuevo León. The "legitimate" stories assist in creating and maintaining the official identity of the *nuevolenese,* which is that of the fervent Catholic who in the first three centuries of Nuevo León's history "valiantly" battled the "barbarous" Indians. In contrast, the stories that continue to circulate in oral narratives or folktales exist on the fringe of Nuevo León's Scriptural Economy. As my descriptions of conversations with Aquiles Sepúlveda will attest, these oral snippets of history are generally located in private conversations, with some secrecy and intrigue associated with their circulation. While I do not agree with de Certeau that oral narratives and everyday stories are necessarily indications of "resistance," I believe the stories that are told among the *nuevoleneses* are a way of saying, "This is our history, this is who we are, regardless of what the government and the church decree." The telling of these stories may be a resistance to the official Scriptural

Economy, yet it is also the expectable counter-circulation of narratives. The choice to voice the narratives is conscious and determined. There are no imagined phantasms or pathology associated with the telling of these stories. They are simply part of a stream of information that has traveled through generations. They coalesce along with the framework of history provided by the government and the church.

In describing the structure of circulation of the narratives, I continue to use the concept of Scriptural Economy. This explanation as a map of telling is a structural diagram of where the indigenous, Jewish, and "barbaric" narratives have traveled; who has pushed them; and who has silenced them. After this phase of explanation, I go further into the reasoning and meaning of the narratives. The use of the psychoanalytic position intensifies the power of the subject. The emphasis on the "unconscious" betrays the limitations set by Freud and his peers. It could be argued that there is no connection between Freud and the "bald mountains" of Nuevo León (referred to in Chapter II). Yet there is something that is "not quite there" that provides an intriguing connection to Freud's concept, "the return of the repressed." The stories are repressed, erased, put aside, yet they continuously erupt. The confusion between fact and fiction lies in every chapter of this ethnography. The title of this text, which lists the fantastic, the demonic, and the *réel*, is a corollary to Jacques Lacan's three concepts, the imaginary, the symbolic, and the *réel*. The imaginary is the fantastic, the symbolic is demonic (the evil church and state that occlude popular narratives that people believe are True), and the *réel* is somewhere between what is imagined and what is proscribed. The appearance of theoretical inconsistency may be placed in the level of analysis. Scriptural Economy is about behavior, and the Return of the Repressed is about the *réel,* which in actuality cannot be defined.

In using the word *Imaginary* I am working within a continuum. The definition varies according to the context of my narrative. The Imaginary is associated with illusions, which Lacan tells us are the only way to understand the symbolic (Gallop 1985). We must fall into the illusion, travel with it, in order to understand how the symbolic (the power, the government, those in control) has determined the "register of language and social exchange" (ibid. 59).

The less dramatic use of *imaginary* is simply how the narrator/interlocutor envisions the way "things are." The movement of these visions provides informative insights into how a group of people perceive their universe, and how they believe those in power see the universe. The spaces between these two thoughts, greater or smaller, produce intriguing evidence regarding their quotidian existence.

As I traveled to Nuevo León, I concurrently searched and analyzed the literature and periodicals published on northern Mexico. The parallel study of oral and written practices assisted me in tracing the circulation of historical events, religious beliefs, and the everyday occurrence of what I came to see as *delirio* in the north. I rarely scheduled formal interviews, which were done only in the initial stages of contact. I often did not ask questions, unless it was to clarify a narrative I had heard from another person. The information, therefore, took on a quality and a flow that led itself into areas that I had not expected to explore.

My first encounters confronted "stories" I had heard "back home in Texas." I began my fieldwork in Nuevo León with many preconceived notions that emanated from what my relatives had told me. There was a fear (that continues) in my family that I was putting myself in danger by traveling in Mexico. I was told that most of the information given to me by *nuevoleneses* would be inaccurate because of their supposed penchant for telling untruths. While there are perhaps some risks, I found myself generally "safe" while in Nuevo León, though cautious about traveling anywhere else in Mexico, which I avoided during the project. I also found that the issue of "the lie" was not a lie in the American sense. The idea was best described by José Cárdenas (Televisa cameraman). He told me it was related to the use of a "different code." People do not lie—they only tell things in a different way, with different meanings for different concepts, in what is perceived as different from the American way of communicating verbally. Ultimately, these warnings appear as indicators of a fluctuating tension and ambivalence between those who have immigrated to the United States and those who have stayed behind.

I encountered numerous surprises while doing this work. One was the possibility of maneuvering so easily in Nuevo León among varying social groups and institutions. Such facility I can only believe is a result of the familial connection of my parents, who were from the Texas-Mexican border and were from families that cherished the presence of a person who is *educado*. Being *educado* is a form of social practice, a set of social skills that promote respect towards anyone at any time, regardless of the other person's social class or status.[5] One who is *educado* is expected to indicate a sincere interest in "listening to the stories" of those who are generous enough to offer their time and energy to explain something about life or the space in which they live. A person who is not *educado* is a *pelado,* an offensive term discussed by Octavio Paz in *The Labyrinth of Solitude* (1986). According to Paz, a *pelado* is common and vulgar. The class designations associated with these terms lead me to believe that presenting oneself as *educado* is not necessarily an altruistic practice. However, within what was "expected," there was an enjoyable "making do," to use de Certeau's term (1988), in which people find a way to create their own satisfying environment even as they are "conforming" to the rules of society. When I recall my aunts and grandmothers interacting with others, there seemed to be a quality of talking "for enjoyment." What may have seemed like altruism might really have been a desire to interact and live among people for the mere enjoyment of "talking." On my father's side of the family, the Hernández-Nietos, the women were (and still are) notorious for staying up half the night having interesting (and funny) conversations. On my mother's side, the Hernández-Paredes family would not stay up so late, but I do recall that every evening, after the work was done and the sun had just set, my grandmother Petra Paredes Hernández would sit in her green metal rocking chair on her porch and talk to her neighbor, Cecilia Ramírez, and my mother about whatever seemed interesting at the moment. It was the late 1950s. The grandchildren ran all over the neighborhood chasing fireflies and what we thought were ghosts while the adult women talked on Petra's porch.

The beauty of this practice lends itself perfectly to the development of a field project and a readable (and perhaps interesting) ethnography. It is about talking, conversing, listening, and relating to another person's story.

The other surprise was truly unexpected. I was adopted as an infant. Through my association with the Sepúlvedas I came to meet the family of my biological maternal grandfather, Felipe Vásquez Guzmán. The connection to the Vásquezes of Potrero added an interesting dimension to my definition of kinship under the most unusual of circumstances. The revelation of this connection (I did not know the Vásquez family before this time) provided an imaginary connection between myself and the Sepúlvedas. Aquiles Sepúlveda, my most significant informant, often told me that I looked like I was from Nuevo León.[6]

Traveling

According to the "rules" of the academic discipline of anthropology, what appears to be the necessary mode for fieldwork is one to two years in a foreign country that has little connection with the background of the ethnographer in training. Such has happened in the past, as George Marcus traveled to Tonga, Renato Rosaldo to the Philippines, Michael Taussig to Colombia, and Margaret Mead to Samoa. I chose to make alterations to my project in this respect. I did not carve out the block of two or three years consecutively. I began traveling to Nuevo León in January 1997. The reality of my familial obligations provided a plan that included numerous trips of varying duration, including two summers, to an area that is considered "somewhat" close geographically, and significantly close culturally, to my home in Houston. The area of Monterrey, Nuevo León, in northern Mexico has considerable cultural, economic, and migratory ties to Houston. These links actually provided an additional frame for understanding Nuevo León and how it relates and is connected to the United States, Texas, and the First World. Late twentieth-century developments in technology allowed for very frequent contact by telephone and Internet with the people I worked with in Nuevo León, whether I was in Mexico or in Houston. When I ultimately stayed there for a longer period (eight months in 1999), the relationships were solid and fairly intimate. I learned about the daily lives of my interlocutors and also learned of the greater social world that hovers around them as Monterrey becomes an international city.

Migration / Borders

The concept and feeling of migration/moving is constant in this ethnography. Like the narratives told to me by people in Nuevo León and the texts that I read on the past, my experiences while passing through the international border heavily influenced my perspectives and my writing. Highway 59 from Houston to Laredo; the stops at my aunt's before crossing the border; the encounter with the Mexican Federales as I crossed the bridge; the Aduana Checkpoint, which is fifty kilometers inside Mexico—all of these experiences are part of this ethnography. As are the return, again dealing with the Aduana, the occasional search for drugs inside my car, the U.S. Border Patrol officer at the bridge who checked my license plate number, the questions about the purpose of my research and my destination in Texas, and the doubt that at moments registered clearly in the officer's voice. Most impressive was the time Yolanda González was not allowed to enter the United States while she was traveling with me in my car. The Border Guards said she lacked documentation certifying she was gainfully employed in Mexico. Or the time that my cousin Citlalli was almost not allowed into the United States. The officers demanded documentation regarding her husband's employment. All Citlalli had was his business card and a photo. The demand was comical since Jesús is an attorney, who was employed at the time by the office of the Governor of the State of Nuevo León. One officer purposefully called Citlalli *retardada* (retarded) when she indicated *retirada* (retired). She is a retired schoolteacher. She and I both knew better than to confront him regarding his vulgarity. The movie *Born in East L.A.* kept coming to my mind. I could imagine both of us getting thrown back to Mexico.[7]

These and other experiences while passing through the U.S.-Mexican border assisted me in understanding the world of the *norteño* who goes back and forth, as so many do. The border feels like a war zone.

In this position as migrant, my role of ethnographer perhaps closely assumes the position of the modern-day, turn-of-the-millennium traveler, either Mexican or American, who travels from Nuevo León to Texas to Nuevo León, thus crossing the border repeatedly in search of connection to family, tradition, and identity. Perhaps if a sense of "unevenness" appears, it is a reflection of the ebb and flow of migration that creates an undulation of culture and practice between Texas and northern Mexico.

A Map of Writing

What we have here, therefore, is not only the makings of a theory of corruption, but one which emphasizes the power of fiction in the makeup of social reality. Indeed, why not see these as one and the same, reality itself being always honored "in the breach," a corruption of itself? (Taussig 1999: 61)

The focus of this text is the "making *of* history." De Certeau uses this phrase in explaining the premise for his work in *The Writing of History*

Left to right: Heriberto Garza, Carlitos Martínez, Baldemar Elizondo, Don Maximiliano Villagómez, and Juanito Rodríguez. All of the men in the photograph are originally from Hacienda San Pedro in General Terán, Nuevo León (not the same as the ex-Hacienda San Pedro educational center in Zua Zua). They all immigrated to Texas in the 1940s and 1950s. They are standing in front of a vintage El Dorado Cadillac convertible owned by Don Chanito's son. The occasion is Don Chanito's eighty-seventh birthday party. Houston. March 1998.

Photograph by the author.

(1988). The phrase is not necessarily about history as it occurs but about the process by which certain events are laboriously embedded in the story of a region or nation, in this case the Mexican state of Nuevo León. It also concerns how other events or narratives become phantasms that only surface at disparate moments when the text and the "argument" are not finely tuned. For the sake of establishing and maintaining the identity and ideology of a place, these phantasms are moved "in the direction of fiction or of silence through the law of 'scientific' writing" (ibid. xxvii). The materials chosen by the historian for documentation and their subsequent "scientific writing" are decided upon by the dogma that "our words are adequate to the real" (ibid. xxvii). De Certeau writes of this as an illusion of the veracity of written words.

The work of Michel Foucault is also relevant to this project. In Fou-

cault's *History of Sexuality* (1990) the discourse on sexuality and its relation to power has a strong connection with the narratives I have found
in Nuevo León. These include his focus on sex as a political issue, politics as another form of war, the regulation of populations, surveillance,
the rigid ordering of space, the improvement of blood lines, and, most
importantly for Nuevo León, the protection of the purity of blood.

The politics of "breeding" enters into almost every aspect of the discourse surrounding the history of Nuevo León. The separation of the
"whites" and the Indians became a war that produced thousands of deaths,
while keeping alive the myth of separation. The space was marked for the
white settlers through regulation, which meant the elimination of the indigenous population. Separation, which prohibited marriage and formal
social interaction, was severely enforced in these spaces in that a transgression produced a disappearance into a wall or an underground tunnel
or into the Inquisition. The transgressor in such discourse is usually a
"white woman" or an indigenous man. The discourse has continuously
been about the "purity of blood," *limpieza de sangre*.

In this study on Nuevo León I go a step further than de Certeau and
Foucault and focus on those phantasms that have been pushed to the
margin. If the scriptural creates a scientific history, what is the economy
of the fantastic text? How do allegories of writing and oral narrative that
exist in the liminal region of the *réel* explain history? De Certeau writes
that the "return of the repressed," narratives pushed aside for political
reasons, are later manifested in "mystical expression." The stories described in this ethnography border on the mystical and the fantastic. It is
quite possible that the surreal quality of what was told to me is related to
the lack of structured, documented history regarding certain strategic aspects of Nuevo León's history. What is left is delirium. Yet this is not the
delirium defined by the First World as related to madness or the actual
loss of lucidity. It is about the de-centering and de-territorializing of the
person inside a particular space. The ambiguity about identity and safety
in Nuevo León has left a residual delirium. This is not as much manifested in confusion on the part of the *nuevoleneses*. It is located more intensely in the attitude of those outside of northern Mexico who speak or
write about the north.

De Certeau supports Lacan's thesis that a "lack" of something is reme-
died by an overflow of something else, something perhaps fantastic or
unexplainable. I agree in part with this explanation, yet I believe that the
stories of the fantastic that I heard repeated in Nuevo León have several

sources. The emptiness of the archival narratives leads to projections of all sorts.[8] The storyteller can conjure whatever comes to mind, whatever may have a faint connection with the original issue.

In the numerous conversations I had with *nuevolenese* historian Cristóbal López, we discussed the idea that Nuevo León does not have a story of origin. Before I proceed further, I need to clarify that my presenting this question does not intimate that I believe in "stories of origin." Foucault, in *The Order of Things* (1974), proposes that the search for origins is futile, in that it is an endless pursuit that cannot be resolved. However, in a surviving rationale that speaks of the purity of blood and the genealogy of nobility, the issue of origins, especially the "correct" origin, continues to be strikingly salient at the beginning of the twenty-first century.

In Mexico, the ideology of the *mestizo* is central to the conceptualization of the nation-state. This discourse is rarely disputed publicly, although anthropologist Claudio Lomnitz Adler (1996) writes of the farcicality of the *mestizo* ideology within Mexico. Lomnitz Adler's statement is that the Mexican elite is still "white" and the value of the *mestizo* is in name only. Such a statement is rare in stories about the origin of the Mexican people that detail the first union between Spanish and Indian, the colossal pre-conquest culture of the Aztecs, the relationship between Hernán Cortez and Malintzin, and the ever-present image of the *mestiza* Virgin of Guadalupe. All these stories attest to the living intensity of this ideology. In a brilliant political move, Mexican national leaders promoted this historical production, which made *mestizos,* who are the majority of the national population, the symbol for the authentic Mexican.

The narratives of origin circulated in the rest of Mexico, however, do not fit Nuevo León. In the north, there was no spectacular indigenous culture: the Indians lived more like the Apache and Comanche in the United States. They were nomadic and moved about in small bands. There is no certainty to their numbers, but the intense thrust of genocide that was authorized and promoted by the state of Nuevo León in the latter part of the nineteenth century left a narrative of a "miniscule" Indian population that did not "mix" with the "white" settlers.

In addition, in the north, there is no story of a "blending" of the conqueror and the conquered. The stories circulating about the first Spanish settlers tell of converted Jews, an overactive Spanish Inquisition, and a deposed first governor. The "Jewish" families were known for their endogamy; therefore, the assumption of "mixing" with the Indians is not contained in the narratives. According to official documentation, the "Jewish" settlers disappeared after Governor Luis de Carvajal y de la Cueva died in the Inquisition's prison.

The narratives that were pressed out as "fiction" and given the status of wild or impossible stories became the expression of the "lack." An illicit explanation is given for an origin that cannot be traced. The elite proudly tell their clandestine stories of Jews in order to accentuate their present economic success. These stories also negate the possibility of being "mixed." This emphasis separates them from other Mexican stories by suggesting that Nuevo León is a First World region. What mixing occurs is forced and violent. The stories unfold as accounts of kidnappings, rapes, murders, or threats of cannibalism. It is against the will of the "white" *nuevoleneses* to become *mestizo*.

Ultimately, the illicit and hidden stories join together in an underground economy of the fantastic. Denied legitimacy by textual history, they are embedded in walls, tunnels, and under the foundations of houses. Stories of people buried alive (perhaps holding secrets) erupt repeatedly in my conversations with *regiomontanos*. It is possible that the "origins" of Nuevo León have been narrated into spaces that cannot be accessed, leaving the imagination to produce a *réel* that assists the *nuevoleneses* in formulating the beginnings of their existence using whatever fantastic means are available.

Finally, although Nuevo León is strikingly different from the rest of Mexico, it is not totally separated. It is still part of the nation-state. It is a center of industry and commerce, containing a spectacular wealth that cannot be imagined in the rest of the country. There is frequent movement between the center of the nation and this periphery. People are constantly traveling or migrating to this rich area. This phenomenon is not new.[9] Even when Nuevo León was seen as a desert wasteland, people came from southern Mexico to settle in the northern region of the country. This history has allowed a semblance of practices and conceptions of the *réel* to transport themselves into Nuevo León. The stories and explanations of the fantastic are related not only to a history that has been lost but also to a history that has moved north. The myths and legends that proliferate in Latin American culture exist in Nuevo León. Perhaps their influence lacks the intensity that is seen in the south, yet they remain alive. This live movement of the phantasmic has joined with the empty space of *nuevolenese* history to create multiple narratives of other worlds that coalesce, intermingle, and perhaps collaborate with modern Monterrey and its surroundings. It is in these mythical environs that Nuevo León remains tightly joined with *la patria*.

Time, Narrative, and Trope

> Instead of proceeding with a chronological reconstruction overly obedient to the fiction of a linearity of time . . . , it seemed preferable to bring into view the *present* site in which this investigation took its form. (de Certeau 1988: xxvi)

This story is told in a nonlinear manner, in keeping with its subject—the hauntings and differences related to history, blood, and purity located in northern Mexico that make themselves known in ways that do not follow linear time. The expected correspondence of nonlinear to "circular time" is not in this book. I do not use the term "circular time" because the time that I refer to does not return neatly to its beginning. Rather, I refer to "nonlinear time" in order to convey the sense of spiraling time, which may return but not to the point of origin.

The narratives are not temporal in the sense that they can be located in a specific moment in time. They seem to travel through lives, centuries, and settlements. This discourse is outside of time. It is about "time" inside of "memory." De Certeau writes that memory "has no general and abstract formulation, no proper place" (1984: 82). It "designates a presence to the plurality of times and thus is not limited to the past" (218). While I present the stories with the designated times (assigned by their authors), I do not seek to question the validity or discredit the chronological time associated with the events described. Instead, I seek to study how different events form a hierarchy of knowledge. In his chapter "History: Science and Fiction" in *Heterologies,* de Certeau explains that the place of the event as maintained by the subject/storyteller introduces "an experience of time" (1986: 217). The "nonlinear" approach to time presented in this project creates a doublet of exegesis and experience. The back-and-forth, fragmentary presentation of the narratives (and their analysis) is an attempt at re-creating the particular experience of time at the moment the story was told, or read, or written.

The stories link themselves together by themes, remembrances, and places that subtly correspond to the past and to the present. The archaeological field contains events and narratives from numerous epochs. The pieces of the past come together and form a "tableau," to use the words of Foucault (1972). In the traditional ethnographic text, chronology and text become a place of "ordering" related to the Scriptural Economy, which is where stories have been put in a certain order, written according to the wishes of those in power (de Certeau 1984). Temporal chronology reorganizes these, providing the subject with what is seen as a more rational and logical understanding of "when" things happened. In such reorganization, the narratives emanating from the interstices between each piece are occluded, leaving time as primary. The tableau would be bare, no longer having narratives to tell of the different moments, spaces, pieces, and stories that have fallen onto its broad mass of existence. In contrast, the tableau of this ethnography has become time as "memory," a counter-narrative to the normalized sequence expected by most readers of ethnographic documents.

Manners of Speaking: The Temporality of Meaning[10]

These turns of phrase . . . later "museographied" in dictionaries, but also gathered and carried (like old battle scars?) within the tireless memory that is any language itself, are primarily the effects of operations that connect historical circumstances to linguistic practices. (de Certeau 1992: 114)

Irony—A figure of speech in which the intended meaning is the opposite of that expressed by the words used; usually taking the form of sarcasm or ridicule in which laudatory expressions are used to imply condemnation or contempt. (Oxford English Dictionary, Second Edition)

The spiral of time that moves along the past of Nuevo León also *presents* a trope of irony. This choice is related to the discrepancy between the narrative flavor concerning stories regarding the barbarians and the Jews and my actual objective in making apparent the inconsistency in the stories. Their circulation orchestrated by the "Scriptural Economy" of Nuevo León and the reasoning behind the normalizing factor inherent in these stories are what I seek to reveal. Narratives of "barbaric Indians" and "rich Jews" are presented with mimetic flavor, reminiscent of how these words may have been expressed by historians and other interested and curious *nuevoleneses*. The repetition of these words belies the reality of the phantom Indian, who is represented as barbaric in texts that are crumbling in the poorly maintained libraries of Nuevo León. My use of the words *barbarous* and *diabolic* in this book represents an ironic attempt to present the impossible nature of the offensive terms. There is no way of knowing who may have been barbarous or diabolic. The difficulty of dealing with this "manner of speaking" is that presenting the narratives "as they are repeated" produces a flavor of believing. Perhaps the narrators who told me the stories believe that there is indeed an "essential" Jew for whom making money becomes an obsession. It certainly became an issue as I continued my conversations with Aquiles Sepúlveda regarding what he believed to be a "Jewish Conspiracy." It is my hope that the repetition of what Americans perhaps would describe as "old" and "obsolete" descriptive terms leaves the reader with the notion that mimesis embeds its traces within the structure of power.

The use of these "archaic" descriptors indicates the presence of explanations that are continuously juxtaposed with the designated identity of modern-day *norteños*. This form of mimesis leaves polluted traces of past narratives. What remain to be studied are these leftover words inside the texts and the soft murmurs of an embarrassed past that eliminated the stories and the existence of entire groups of people.

Complexities

The modernist ethnography recognizing such properties of discourses as dominance, residualness and emergence (or possibility), would map the relationships of these properties in any site of enquiry . . . by exposing, to the extent possible, the quality of voices by means of metalinguistic categories (such as narrative, trope, etc.). (Marcus 1998: 66)

Following the trajectory of George E. Marcus, the voices in this ethnography are not "seen as products of local structure . . . alone, or as privileged sources of perspective" (ibid.). The voices emanate from a web of relationships, history, and purpose. Even in this post–"writing culture" era, this approach continues to be contrary to the ongoing norms of ethnographic writing. While structured methodology continues to reign in the academic world of anthropology, I have chosen to risk a deviation.

While I met the goals of acquiring knowledge and establishing relationships with people from my field site, these tasks were, as previously mentioned, accomplished in a manner that varied from the usual plan of fieldwork. Although I had familial obligations that limited my geographic movement, this fact was not the solitary determining factor in my choice of approach. Placing this ethnography in the realm of "voice/discourse" as described by Marcus (1998), I delimit the traditional boundaries of anthropological description and exegesis. This book is an indication of the permeability of thought and practices within the region of northern Mexico, which are parallel to the blurring boundaries of early twenty-first-century world systems. Just as Marcus writes of "transcultural process and historical perspective" (ibid.), I find that this ethnography weaves itself through both history and practice. As I traveled through different parts of Nuevo León's culture, I became very aware of the intermingling of the American with the Mexican. Perhaps a striking example of this intermingling occurred the day I was sitting on the front porch of the home of *curandera* Fela Hernández in the Acapulco subdivision of General Escobedo, a working class suburb of Monterrey. As I waited for Fela I was eating some Lay's Potato Chips. Inside the bag I found a two-by-three-inch sticker of Pope John Paul II. The sticker was a commemoration of his 1999 visit to Mexico, a most profoundly Catholic country. Yet the type of food and brand of chips was American. This experience reminded me that the issue of historical perspective is naturally embedded in the transcultural process. The role of the church has been central to the formation of Mexico as a nation. Nuevo León's embattled attitude towards the church, as will be detailed here, is symbolized in the photograph of the Pope, which has been affixed to a sticker, then hidden in a bag of potato chips, as if it were a Pokémon or some similar child's toy.

The explanations that I provide of narratives I heard as I met people, waited for them, ate their food, shopped with them, and lived with them do not necessarily present an examination of "how they live" in the strict ethnographic sense. What is reported here is the quality and subtlety of the interaction between them, *nuevoleneses* who happen to be my informants, and myself, the ethnographer who is (for the most part) awkwardly trying to live in their world for a specified period of time. The encounter between the two of us is a transnational process in itself. Historical perspective, also, undoubtedly affects how we view each other, how we interact, and what we do not say to each other. The comical and the uncanny enter into the exegesis with this mode of study. The story of a sticker with an image of the Pope inside of a bag of potato chips becomes important in the overall project that looks at the microcosms of practice that exist in the interchange between the insider and the outsider, namely my informants and myself.

In my fieldwork, I moved from city to village to city and from family to family just as the narratives circulated between these places and people. My descriptions follow the movement of the stories, representing the "traveling discourse" which may seem at first glance fragmented and inconsistent. Yet, as Foucault speaks of history as a series of ruptures (1974), stories are also full of ruptures, inconsistencies, stops and starts. In this manner, as with other issues (such as the concept of time), this book seeks to be descriptive and analytic, while simultaneously creating a mimetic moment that attempts to reproduce the experience of a traveling discourse that has appropriated words along the way, and has stopped abruptly in shock or in awe of the stories that it comes to hear.

Methodology

My work was conducted in a manner that allowed daily interaction with my interlocutors, whether I was in Nuevo León or Houston. My connection with the González Villagómez family in Monterrey provided an ongoing circuit of communication. In addition to my staying in their home during much of my fieldwork in Nuevo León, their twenty-two-year-old granddaughter, Ana Sáenz González, came to live in my home in Houston for fifteen months. During this time (May 1998–August 1999) she studied English at the University of Houston. Ana has since returned to Monterrey and is now employed by a subsidiary of El Grupo Monterrey, Nuevo León's conglomerate of Fortune 500 companies.

My association with Ana helped me in understanding the position of the young educated people of Monterrey, their issues of "independence" regarding their families, their ambition in the face of an overwhelming American culture that continuously influences their lives in Mexico, seductively pulling them toward the United States, yet creating boundaries that can be crossed only if one is wealthy or willing to enter into a state of "non-legality" (becoming an illegal alien). While I do not refer specifically to Ana elsewhere in this book, the influence of our conversations can be found in every chapter.

Geography

The geography described in this ethnography is that of four municipalities, two rural, one suburban, and one urban: General Bravo, Potrero,
Villa de Santiago, and Monterrey, Nuevo León.

In the middle of the twentieth century, General Bravo became known
as a modern-day Wild West in which men killed each other for minor
transgressions. The town is only fifty kilometers from the Texas border.
The mythology of the town incorporated stories of violence and revenge
that are still circulating throughout Nuevo León.

San Isidro del Potrero is much older than Bravo. Potrero is a village
in the northwest section of the state. It is actually considered a part of the
municipality of Villaldama, eight kilometers to the north. During the
seventeenth and eighteenth centuries, Potrero was maintained as an hacienda that produced foodstuffs that supported nearby mining settlements. It now has few inhabitants, little farming, and no industry.

Villa de Santiago is a city south of Monterrey that was fairly isolated
until affluent corporate executives discovered its spectacular scenery and
cheap real estate prices in the last part of the twentieth century. Among
las quintas (the estates of the rich) is the sanctuary of the Medalla Milagrosa, which for over thirty years has served as a religious site for Nuevo
León's poor and working class.

Monterrey, "la Sultana del Norte," is presently considered the wealthiest industrial city in Latin America.[11] Horacio Alvarado Ortiz, the first
newscaster in Monterrey, describes the city: "*la Capital Industrial de México, la ciudad ejemplar que ha llevado tantas veces el nombre de nuestro país en
plan de triunfo por todos los ámbitos del mundo, con sus productos industriales,
comerciales*" (the industrial capital of Mexico, the model city, that has
placed the name of Mexico in triumph throughout the world, with its
industrial and commercial products) (1994: 207; my translation).[12]

Schemata

This book is divided into four parts. Part One focuses on three issues that
are discussed in two chapters. The first is my own family history, which
provided the impetus for this project. The first stories I heard of Nuevo
León were about the area where my father-in-law was born. Dramatic

narratives resembling those of Appalachia's Hatfield-McCoy wars sparked my interest. The second chapter deals with the indigenous history or, rather, non-history. This chapter traces out the demarcation created by the "whites" in El Nuevo Reino as they encircled and eliminated the indigenous population in a war so fierce and bloody it can hardly be compared to any other conflict between the colonizers and the colonized in Mexico. The second chapter, also, concerns the story of Luis de Carvajal y de la Cueva, the ill-fated first governor of El Nuevo Reino de León.

Part Two, "Landscape and Narrative," is a quasi-topography, an account of my preliminary work in Nuevo León and my first year of working with television producer Horacio Alvarado Ortiz, who provided me with an introduction to the region. This section has the semblance of a travel narrative in that I recount the film crew's travels from town to town as we were in pursuit of the Nuevo León that Alvarado believed was disappearing. The next chapter, titled "Spaces In-between," is about a group of Dominican nuns from Mina, whom I met while filming with Alvarado and his crew. My later work with Alvarado and my visits to Mina comprise an ethnographic in-between, not indicating the beginning of my study, yet not at the core of my thematic.

Part Three, "Ethnographic Imaginaries," consists of ethnographic accounts of my work in Potrero, Nuevo León, and Villa de Santiago, Nuevo León. The title "Imaginaries" emanates from the stories and legends that I was told in these places, the interplay between the ethnographic search and the actual "evidence" found. The surreal quality I encountered was often conflated with the imaginary that contained the history and everyday life of Potrero and Santiago.

Part Four, "Locations of the *Réel*," concerns narratives emanating from the city of Monterrey. Chapters VII and VIII detail the "unsubstantiated" stories of Jews who settled in northern Mexico and the current polemic regarding the authenticity of these stories. In Chapter IX are set the multiple stories of people being underground and in walls, of a fantastic underground city, and of tunnels that have been actually seen and filmed. Chapter X is about the Sepúlveda home near the Alameda in downtown Monterrey.

I conclude with a chapter titled "Delirio," which is also the title of the book, which argues that the instability of the ambivalent and ambiguous narratives creates a delirium that places the *nuevoleneses* in a *réel* that is never secure and is constantly transposing itself to suit the current rule of history.

The People

There are many people whom I describe in this ethnography. In this book I choose against anonymity for my informants. I realize this anonymity is a standard aspect of anthropological convention. However, I favor using their real names for several reasons. I believe that if I use pseudonyms and write about issues they would not want published, there is still a significant possibility that they could be recognized. From the beginning, the Sepúlvedas stressed to me their need for privacy. Therefore, I give their names while at the same time omitting any information that I believe would compromise my agreement with them. I find it possible to write an ethnography about these families without divulging intimate details of their personal lives. For me to provide more information than they wish not only would damage our collaborative relationship but also would furnish the reader information that would exoticize and sensationalize the stories and further objectify my informants. Thus they remain real people with their true names and true stories. Their "dirty laundry," so to speak, is kept out of view. The "dirty laundry" of Monterrey and Nuevo León should suffice.

I offer here a brief description of the people I came to know well, how I met them, and how the relationships developed.

Horacio Alvarado Ortiz is a television producer from Nuevo León. He is in his seventies, lives near El Cerro de la Silla, and works in downtown Monterrey. Yolanda González facilitated the meeting. I worked with him in 1997 and the early part of 1998, accompanying his film crew to various locations in northern Nuevo León.

Juanera Domínguez, a widow from Potrero, is a *sobadora* (healer) in her mid-sixties. She is my second cousin, whom I did not know before doing my fieldwork. She lives several houses away from my great-aunt, Elena Vásquez. I would often visit Juanera while I was in Potrero because her wise conversation seemed to contain everything I wanted to know about the place.

Yolanda González Villagómez, a single woman in her fifties, originally from General Terán, is part owner of a small café. She introduced me to Alvarado and many others who were very helpful in my fieldwork. I stayed in her home which sits on el Cerro de la Silla. She lives and works in Guadalupe. She is first cousin to Artemio Villagómez and Heriberto Villagómez, my childhood friend. She has continued to be a good friend and fabulous collaborator. Several times per year she travels to Houston. I have maintained contact with her in Monterrey and in Texas.

Citlalli Hernández Rosales, my second cousin, is a retired schoolteacher, whom I used to visit in Monterrey in the late 1960s.

Cristóbal López, a young scholar in his early thirties, is a historian and lecturer at the Universidad de Monterrey. His particular interest is in Nuevo León's indigenous history and folklore. Cristóbal lives in General Escobedo and works in Santa Catarina. When I am not in Monterrey, we communicate frequently by email. He has been of great help when I have had questions regarding Nuevo León, its people, and its politics.

Don J. Aquiles Sepúlveda González was an artist and collector of antiquities in his sixties. Born in Potrero, Don Aquiles lived in downtown Monterrey. Aquiles, Irma, Pepita, and Ofelia Sepúlveda are siblings. I worked most closely with Don Aquiles. While I was in Houston, we had long telephone conversations every few weeks. When I traveled to Monterrey in 1999, I either met with him or spoke with him daily. He died in January 2000.

Irma Sabina Sepúlveda was a nationally recognized writer and dramatist. Born in Potrero, she lived in downtown Monterrey. I never met Irma. Yet her family spoke of her so often and there was so much of her life still present in the Sepúlveda home that I believe I came to know her. She was in her mid-fifties when she died in 1988.

Doña Josefa (Pepita) Sepúlveda, founder of the sanctuary of the Medalla Milagrosa in Villa de Santiago, Nuevo León, is possibly in her mid-seventies. Born in Potrero, Nuevo León, she now lives in Villa de Santiago. I met with her continuously (four or five times per week) in 1998. She took a strong interest in our association and viewed herself as my mentor.

Rosie Vásquez is a Certified Public Accountant in her twenties. She lives in General Escobedo, works in Monterrey, and returns to visit her parents every weekend in Potrero, where she was born. She is my third cousin. I often gave Rosie a ride to and from Potrero. We talked on the telephone regularly while I was in Monterrey.

Artemio Villagómez Lozano, librarian for Preparatoria 15, is a first cousin of Yolanda González Villagómez. Originally from General Terán, he lives and works in Monterrey. He is the librarian at the school my daughter attended while we lived in Monterrey. We came to be good friends and spoke every day for the months I was in Monterrey (in 1999). I often visited him in the library at school.

Heriberto Villagómez González is a computer systems supervisor. Born in Reynosa, Tamaulipas, he lives in Houston. A double cousin of Yolanda González, Heriberto is a childhood friend of mine. He accompanied me on my first field site visit to Nuevo León and kindly introduced me to his family. His initial assistance was fundamental to the success of my fieldwork.

Doña Soledad (Chole) Villagómez de González is a housewife, originally from General Terán. She lives in a house on the famous Cerro de la Silla in Guadalupe. I lived in her home during most of my fieldwork in Nuevo León. I spent scores of hours conversing with Doña Chole. Through our association I learned of the role "older" women have in northern Nuevo León and of marital relationships. We watched many old movies together. She taught me the most about telenovelas, on which she is quite an expert.

PART ONE

HISTORY

Doble realidad. . .un hecho histórico y ser una representación simbólica de nuestra historia subterránea o invisible. (Paz 1993: 291) (Double reality. . . a historical event and a symbolic representation of our subterranean or invisible history)

The representation of historical realities is itself the means by which the real conditions of its own production are camouflaged. . . . the situation is told to us in a story which is the product of a certain milieu, of a power structure, of contracts between a corporation and its clients. (de Certeau 1986: 206)

The following two chapters are stories about the history of Nuevo León. The reality is descriptive and even somewhat entertaining. Yet the conditions of "the telling" are as important as the stories themselves. The stories are, as de Certeau writes, a "product of a certain milieu." It is in these "representation[s] of historical realities" that the "conditions" of history's own production are camouflaged. They are shown in order to hide.

These narratives tell of the formation of "origins." They are stories that form the description of what it means to be a *nuevolenese.* Three originary narratives emanating from Nuevo León's history continue to resonate in the beginning of the twenty-first century. These narratives of the subaltern (the barbarous Indian, the persecuted Jew, the uncivilized "white man") have found their way either into an occulted area of history or to the foreground of the socially conscripted *nuevolenese* identity. In a parody that has followed the evolution of the *norteños'* persona, the trace of the subaltern has accompanied the elite capitalist that now rules over Latin America.

One story of origin is the twentieth-century *bárbaro* (barbarian), a rural-born *nuevolenese* who is portrayed as a Latinized American cowboy, guns and all, straight out of the nineteenth-century American West. The second is the barbaric Indian, the savage who practices cannibalism, worships no deities, and disrespects the sanctity of his own family; the barbaric Indian is the antithesis of the erudite Aztec who built civilizations. Third is the Jew who was initially persecuted by the Inquisition, yet within the last century has succeeded in building financial empires.

In this section I discuss the regional history that has helped form these three characters that Nuevo León has confronted in its pursuit of First World status. Meant as a grounding for this ethnography, they recall oral and textual sources that configure *el norteño bárbaro* (the barbaric *norteño*). As I proceed, I ask myself several questions: What is the purpose of these stories? What do they hide? Whom do they benefit?

CHAPTER I

Don Gregorio Tijerina:
General Bravo, Nuevo León

*General Bravo, es la cabecera de un municipio del Estado de Nuevo León.
Lo he tomado como referencia para mostrar ciertos acontecimientos que sin
duda ocurren en otras partes del norte . . . Algunos de estos fenómenos, sin
embargo, no son de ninguna manera comunes, de ahí el porqué los cito en
este trabajo.* (Solís Garza 1970: 103) (General Bravo is the head of a
municipality of the State of Nuevo León. I have referenced this city
to demonstrate certain practices that without a doubt occur in
other parts of the north. Some of these phenomena are surely not
at all common, which is why I cite them in this work)

The foundation for later research is sometimes made many years before
the fieldwork begins. As George Marcus writes, "The extended exploration of existing affinities between the ethnographer and the subject of
study is indeed one of the most powerful and interesting ways to moti-
vate a research design" (1998: 15). The student begins with some affiliation to the site and/or subject. Yet after a certain time she is to some extent able to retreat in order to create a distancing and to contextualize
the project within "the delineation of more generic social-cultural problems and issues" (ibid.). I begin with a description of General Bravo,
Nuevo León, and of Don Gregorio Tijerina. My interest is formed by a
connection of kinship that holds the genealogy of my two children. Don
Gregorio is their paternal grandfather. There are other histories in my
family that have left traces of narrative from Nuevo León; however,
those are much more distant.

Ultimately, it was because of my "affinity" with the Tijerinas and
General Bravo that I did not choose to do fieldwork in that community.

Painting of a cowboy on the window of a grocery story in China, Nuevo León.
January 1997.

Photograph by the author.

The need for distance and objectivity required me to search for a field-site that would be less "familial." Even so, I include this "pre-condition" of my fieldwork in this text because I believe it is exceedingly relevant to the ideological narratives that cling to the margins of *nuevolenese* society. Having "removed" myself to an extent from the history of General Bravo, what is presented here is a combination of narratives and experiences that tell of the town's history and beliefs. Intertwined with these stories are "texts" that follow the lead of the oral narratives and continue explaining the complicated view of this "wild man," the man from General Bravo. What follows is not based on fieldwork in General Bravo as such. This writing is based on a different confluence of information that has steadily moved northeast into South Texas with each wave of Mexican migration. The stories are those I heard from people who had already left Bravo. As I read more about Nuevo León, I found these narratives laced inside the writing of General Bravo's native sons who tell of secession, contraband activities, violence in the name of honor, and the stealing of women.

Wharton, Texas
1971

I first met Gregorio Tijerina when I was eighteen years old. By that time he was already in his seventies and was retired; he had migrated from Mexico some fifty years before. His presence and intelligence left an enduring impression on me. He came from a little town I had never heard of—General Bravo, Nuevo León—which was not on the highway between Laredo and Monterrey, the tourist route to Mexico. He was a transplanted example of what I came to know as a *norteño*. He was tall and fair-skinned; he worked hard and was very careful with his money. In his youth he was wild and liked to gamble. He supported his parents financially until they died. Even though he was illiterate, his children were college-educated. In his late eighties he continued to work on cars and fix everything he could. He was never one to sit around. He died in 1991 at the age of ninety.

I married into the family of Gregorio Tijerina in 1975, which is when I began to hear the wild stories of General Bravo. I have since learned of other families close to me that came from the same place. Pompeyo Arizpe, who knew my parents since before I was born, was also from Bravo, where the Arizpes lived next door to the Tijerinas; their properties were separated by a fence of *leña* (large tree branches). In Texas, Pompeyo's son Johnny and I took piano lessons from the same teacher. I learned to dance the twist at Johnny's tenth birthday party. He called me the night the Beatles first appeared on the Ed Sullivan show, wanting to make sure I did not miss the program.

The migration of Gregorio Tijerina and Pompeyo Arizpe to Texas is significant in that the world of Nuevo León was and is not static. As with any other social form, it constantly transforms itself. While the bulk of my fieldwork came to be in Nuevo León itself, much of the peripheral work was done in Texas with people who were originally from Bravo, Monterrey, and other municipalities. Like most other *norteños,* Tijerina and Arizpe maintained a solid connection with their originary homes and with the relatives they left behind. This binational influence strongly affected not only those who migrated, but also those who remained behind in Nuevo León.

I made only two trips to General Bravo. The first I made in 1981 as a member of the Tijerina family, and the second was a preliminary field site visit in early 1997. The stories that I heard and read about the people from Bravo greatly influenced the writing of this ethnography. I believe that General Bravo's continuously circulating narratives of *matones* (killers) and *bárbaros* (barbarians) constitute a significant aspect of Nuevo León's ideology. The material presented is from conversations I had mostly with people in Texas and from texts written by local authors.

The *Norteño* as Hero

The myth presents its theme in a majestic way; it carries spiritual force; and the divine is present and is experienced in the form of superhuman heroes. (Bettelheim 1977: 26)

"Did you marry one of the *matones* (killers) from Bravo?" (what people asked me when they found out I married a Tijerina from General Bravo, Nuevo León, 1975)

The labyrinth of conversations went further to the west and south of General Bravo. Even so, the stories that produced this ethnography began with a man named Gregorio Tijerina. Don Goyo, as he was often called, was born at the turn of the century in General Bravo, Nuevo León. He was the only son of Agustín Tijerina and Rosalia Garza. During the 1920s, Goyo left Bravo for a small town in Texas by the name of New Gulf, more than three hundred miles from his home. For the next sixty years, he continuously returned to Bravo. He drove south on U.S. Highway 59 to Highway 77, which took him to McAllen. There he crossed the International Bridge and drove the additional thirty-five miles to Bravo. His American-born wife and two children came to know Bravo very well.

Although he worked for the same company all his life, he refused to learn English and never became an American citizen. There were schools in Bravo when Goyo was a child, but he only attended class for about three years. He did not learn to read and write. He could barely write his name. Yet, at the time I met him in 1971, he was still overhauling the engines of cars and could fix any lawn mower that was brought to him. He always saved all the money he could, and there was a rumor in town that he and his wife were very rich. He always found ways to make extra money by fixing small machines or doing all the repairs on his house and cars himself. At the age of eighty he was over six feet tall, bald, with a large nose and little eyes that often had a mischievous look. He always wore a gray fedora when he went to town.

The story of his marriage always intrigued me. I was even more curious about his choice of a wife after I began to hear stories of General Bravo and *los bárbaros del norte* (the barbarians of the north). Adelina Pena was 5' 10". She had very pale skin and naturally red hair. As a young girl she had studied at a Presbyterian boarding school. Her parents were from Mexico, and her father was born in Monterrey. Her father owned a store in Bay City, Texas, which provided Adelina some privilege. When she was about eight, her father left the family. Some years later, her mother remarried. By that time the family was living in New Gulf. The stepfather ordered Adelina, who was already eighteen and had completed high school, to earn her keep. He wanted her to find a job as a live-in domestic servant. By this time, Goyo was already living in New Gulf. He had never spoken to Adelina personally, although he learned of her situation through other people in town. He had a friend write a letter for him to her in which he told her that he understood what was happening to her and realized that he was no match for her. He professed that he wanted to marry her to help her avoid becoming someone's maid.

In this way Don Gregorio Tijerina married a woman who fit the description of a *norteña*. She was tall and fair. She had red hair like a number of women in Nuevo León. She was cultured. She knew both English and Spanish. She also almost went mad during the first twenty years of their marriage because he was always drinking or gambling. Something happened to him in the early 1950s that made him go through a major transformation. He stopped going out to bars. He began to help with the children, washed bottles, and changed diapers. Adelina never really understood what happened to him.

The one thing that never changed was his loyalty to his parents. He told me once that his father, Agustín, never had to work again after Goyo migrated to the United States. Goyo always considered himself to be from General Bravo. He was never really from Texas, at least in his mind.

Genealogy

Six years after Don Gregorio died, I met a distant relative of his. The man's name was Licienciado Ernesto Tijerina. Through Licenciado Er-

nesto, I found out that every Tijerina in northern Mexico is probably related to all the other Tijerinas. Ernesto is the regional director of the
sindicato de maestros (teachers' labor union) in Nuevo León. He told me
that the Tijerinas were a family of *norteños* that settled originally in three
areas of Nuevo León. Ernesto Tijerina wrote a book on the genealogy
of the Tijerinas titled *Familia Tijerina* (1996). Twelve years before, a prominent Mexican American businesswoman in Houston, Rosie Zamora Cope
(originally from the Rio Grande Valley), told me her version of the Tijerinas' genealogy. She is descended from the Tijerinas and said the
founders were three Italian brothers who were tailors and settled in
northern Mexico. Ernesto Tijerina told me that the Tijerina family was
founded through a union between a Spanish soldier and an African slave
in the eighteenth century, although this possibility is not mentioned in
his book.

Although I have not been able to substantiate this account with historical records, I was told that around the time of the Second World War,
a Tijerina who became governor of Nuevo León instituted a form of rule
that resembled a feudal kingdom in which people without power were
in constant danger of attack from the "authorities." Thirty years after this
Tijerina was governor, I married a Tijerina. I am asked by people from
Nuevo León if I married one of the *matones* (killers) from Bravo. Of
course he is not a *matón,* yet the name evokes the myth that the Tijerinas are known as wild men.

This association is not an indictment of the Tijerina family. However,
it appears that the myth of the hero, antihero, and wild man mirrors the
character of the *norteño* man. This *norteño* wild man is complex. He is so
courageous that he kills himself to show his bravery. He comes from the
barren land, *la frontera.* He has few laws; he kills easily. People in Nuevo
León tell me that the cemeteries of China and General Bravo are full of
men who killed each other because of minor disagreements. It was here,
in this territory, with little water and limited civilization (in the words of
José Vasconcelos) that man lost his humanity. Is the *norteño* the wild man
Hayden White writes of in his essay "The Forms of Wildness" (1978)?
White writes of the wild man without a soul who has lost his salvation.
Yet the paradox is that the wild man perhaps carries someone else's "pro-
jection of repressed desires." Is the *norteño* carrying the desire of other
Mexicans?

In *Los mexicanos del norte,* Hernán Solís Garza describes *los matones of
Bravo; Los habitantes de Bravo han tenido en su discurso histórico . . . desde un*

An abandoned bar in General Bravo with the name Cervecería Tijerina painted on the front. 1997.

Photograph by the author.

Cemetery in China, Nuevo León. This is one of the cemeteries that is said to be full of men from China and General Bravo who killed each other in the war between the two cities. 1997.

Photograph by the author.

principio . . . una escala de valores en cuya cima estaba el ser hombre bravo, de acción, de armas tomar, tener palabra, decirla y sostenerla. No importaba la forma en que demonstraba la valentía. (1971: 104) (The inhabitants of Bravo had from the beginning, in their historical discourse, a scale of values that included the brave man, of action, who took arms, had his word, gave it, and held it. It did not matter in what way he demonstrated his valor)

La Muchacha Robada

The Girl Who was Kidnapped

The history and circulation of narratives often creates a maze that leads to surprising locations. Links are made in the most unlikely places.

Thanksgiving Day 1996

I was sitting at the table of the Villagómez family in Rosenberg, Texas, thirty miles southwest of Houston. This family immigrated from Nuevo León in the early 1950s. Coti, the twenty-year-old granddaughter of Don Hector Villagómez, brought a friend with her that day. Having visited on important holidays for over twenty years, I was there by custom, as if their son Hector, who had been my best friend, was still alive. Nadia Ayala, the girl accompanying Coti, became very interested in the conversation at the table. We were talking about my upcoming trip to Nuevo León. I had just begun a graduate program in anthropology and could not wait to decide on my field site. Because of my association with the Tijerinas from Bravo and the Villagómezes from General Terán, I considered studying these two municipalities.

Nadia told me that her parents were from General Bravo. They had immigrated to Texas shortly before she was born. We all talked about the stories from Bravo, which told of a Hatfield-McCoy type war between Bravo and the neighboring town, China. The "war," which supposedly had erupted over an elopement of two lovers from the towns, was said to be the cause of the many killings that filled the cemeteries of the two cities.

Becoming very excited, Nadia said, "My parents live in Houston, but they maintain a house in Bravo. Would you like me to ask them if you can stay there? There is no one living in the house, and it is fully furnished." Nadia said that the famous "war" between the two cities was indeed over a young man from Bravo who eloped with a girl from China. Nadia's grandfather was the person who gave the couple refuge when they eloped.

Hernán Solís tells of this "war" between China and Bravo. General Bravo was originally a part of China, a city about ten kilometers away.[1] Solís says there were problems from the beginning. In Mexico, many municipalities incorporate smaller villages as part of their jurisdiction. Bravo was initially incorporated into the municipality of China. Solís says the problem arose because the men from Bravo wanted to be independent of the authority of China's leaders. He describes this confrontation in a lyrical, almost poetic manner. The description of the "problem" between China and General Bravo has the semblance of a quarrel between a parent and child or between two lovers.

Hace poco más de cien años, China, Nuevo León, significó, en el microcosmos de General Bravo el objeto dominante, el padre impositivo, -que no permitía por ningún motivo que el hijo creciera. Sucedió lo que tenía que suceder, así se escribe la historia. Un día el cordón umbilical que tenía tránsito en un solo sentido -ya que China, Nuevo León, era la engordaba, tenso de tanto estirón se reventó, y ambos pueblos se quedaron con las puntas del mismo: la distancia se alargó. En el presente persiste tal situación, y nadie quiere mostrar su ombligo. (1971: 104) (A little more than a hundred years ago, China, Nuevo León signified for General Bravo the dominant object, the negative father, who did not for any reason let the child grow. The resulting consequences had to occur, as history is written. The umbilical cord that connected the two into one became so tense that it broke in two. China was the large city, and in the separation each place was left with one end of the umbilical cord. In time, the distance became even greater. Things have remained the same and neither city wants to show its umbilical cord.)

Stories of smuggling contraband, including cotton, during the American civil war are documented in numerous texts written about Nuevo León. Solís writes of how a different "law" arose in relation to the Texas-Mexican border. Violent confrontation between the Texas Rangers and *norteños* who had crossed into Texas led to the semblance of guerilla warfare. Solís explains, "*En aquellos tiempos, el ser contrabandista no se tomaba como un acto delictuoso, sino por el contrario, se valuaba como un desenpeño de respeto y hasta honorable; mucho más si en alguna de las incursiones uno o dos rinches habían quedado mal parados. Como semejante sucedía con el pistolero.*"

(ibid. 104) (In those times, to transport contraband was not taken as a criminal act, on the contrary, it was valued because it exhibited respect and was even considered honorable, even more so if during one of the incursions one or two Texas Rangers were killed. The same occurred with the gunslinger)

Hayden White writes of the predicament of the wild man, who in many ways appears similar to Solís's *norteño*. He is the antihero. He could be the man who kills the Texas Ranger, the man who is not detained by the border or the Union's blockade. He gains honor by breaking the rules of the "more civilized" American man.

He is a gunslinger and can as easily shoot his neighbor as he can kill a County Sheriff from South Texas. The antihero is eulogized, as was the red-haired Catarino Garza, who eluded Texas Rangers, sheriffs, and local posses all along the Texas border in the early part of the twentieth century. Garza organized insurrection activity against the United States and Mexico, served time in prison, and also published a newspaper in Eagle Pass, Texas, that was distributed throughout South Texas and northern Mexico (Garza Guajardo 1989). The creation of the antihero may be the result of a form of domination. Foucault illustrates in *Discipline and Punish* what could be the sheer extent of his widely advertised crimes "against the law, against the rich, the powerful, the magistrates, the constabulary or the watch. . . . The proclamation of these crimes blew up to epic proportions the tiny struggle that passed unperceived in everyday life" (1977: 67). In time, however, the role of antihero became the image of the *norteño,* who found himself transformed into a hero by the role of antihero. This role of the antihero became the discourse that represented the *norteño* among other Mexicans. While the success of Nuevo León's industry has somewhat eroded the image of the antihero, the narratives remain. Foucault writes of this consequence: "The same group that cheers for the antihero, later becomes the 'bastardized race,' which is alien to society, whose 'vices' are obstacles to 'the good'" (ibid. 276). This description of the "bastardized race" focuses on Western society in general, yet has a strong resonance with the "barbaric *norteño.*"

The *norteño* becomes forever the wild man. New narratives cannot totally erase these old stories. The north, which is a permeable region heavily influenced by fluctuation in migration and culture, is often devalued and ridiculed. The *norteño* is the country bumpkin, his music is viewed as a less sophisticated version of American country music, and his nature is seen as violent. He/she is not seen as an individual but as the representation of this culturally disjointed (from the perspective of the "more civilized" Mexican) area. The stereotype concerns not being *educado*. The image is of being a *bruto, a brute. The description of the landscape parallels the character of its people. Visiting the towns of northern Mexico, I see sage brush, desert, and not much else. The *plazas* (town squares) of China and General Bravo are simple and sparsely populated. Few people walk around. There are few people to be found in the first place. Most *norteños* from the small towns surrounding Monterrey have left for the United States. Most of the remaining men are elderly. I am told by some people in the north that many of the local men are involved in transporting illegal drugs, for it is nearly impossible to find productive work in the area. Graduate students acquainted with the area say it is not safe to do fieldwork in these towns; when the ethnographer begins to know too much, it becomes dangerous.

Forms of Wildness

The narrative describing the wild *norteño* continues to circulate. It is the story Nadia told me on Thanksgiving in 1996, at the home of the Villagómezes, three hundred and fifty miles from General Bravo. Solís writes of the story in *El mexicano del norte* (1971). There are three fathers, three sons, and one daughter. I list the names because it is difficult to distinguish between the generations:

> I. Father—Sóstenes Cantú Leal, El Sorgatón (the stubborn one).
> Son—Sóstenes Cantú, El Sorguito (the little stubborn one).
>
> II. Father—José Tijerina Leal, El Pico de Oro (the beak of gold).
> Son—José Tijerina, El Piquito de Oro (the little beak of gold).
>
> III. Father—Juan Cavazos Salinas, Grandote (the large one).
> Son—Juan Cavazos, El Chico (the small one). Daughter—Lupita Cavazos.

Three fifteen-year-old boys were together sharing a bottle of *mezcal,* the first time they were to get drunk. Their names were Sóstenes Cantú, Juan Cavazos, and José Tijerina; El Sorguito, El Chico and El Piquito de Oro. El Chico asks El Sorguito, "What would you like more than anything else right now?" El Sorguito answers, "A gun." El Piquito de Oro asks, "What else?" "A horse." El Chico responds by telling El Sorguito, "You are so stupid, better to have a woman for yourself, all night." El Sorguito stands up with difficulty and begins walking towards the house of El Chico to look for El Chico's sister Lupita. He says, "With a gun and a horse, a woman is easy to find" (ibid. 106–107).

Solís continues:

Esa madrugada, el primer canto del gallo hizo segunda a los ruidos de un caballo que salia al galope del pueblo, eral el caballo de "Piquito de Oro." El jinete era "El Sorguito" y llevaba la pistola de Juan Chico, y en ancas iba la Lupita con toda su cabeza llena de buenos pensamientos. (ibid.) (At dawn, after the first cock-crow you could hear a noise made by a galloping horse that was leaving town. It was Piquito de Oro's horse. The rider was El Sorguito who carried Juan Chico's pistol. On Sorguito's lap was Lupita whose head was full of good thoughts)

Sometime later, El Sorgatón was sent a message via El Pico de Oro. Juan Cavazos Salinas, El Grandote, was offended because the son of El Sorgatón had eloped with El Grandote's daughter. On the 24th of June at six in the evening, Sóstenes Cantú de la Garza met with Juan Cavazos Salinas in a bar named Los Compadres. Sóstenes was the only one to leave the place alive. He staggered a few blocks, went into the church on the plaza, and collapsed at the altar.

José Tijerina Leal spoke at the funeral of his *compadres,* Juan Cavazos Salinas and Sóstenes Cantú de la Garza. Solís quotes the speech as if he had a copy of the exact words:

Señores: esta tarde las gotas de lluvia confunden con mis lagrimas, ya que me toca despedir a dos mis compadres mas queridos . . . El amor y el honor tienen caminos rectos, pero el deshonor es una vereda torcida, pueden ustedes jurar que mi compadre Juan Cavazos Salinas no conocio esa vereda. (ibid. 108) (Gentlemen: this afternoon I have confused the drops of rain with my tears, now that I have been chosen to say goodbye to my most intimate compadres . . . Love and honor both have a forthright path. Dishonor is a road that has been distorted. You can attest that my compadre Juan Cavazos Salinas did not know the road of distortion)

After José Tijerina Leal said these words he felt a shiver. Solís does not tell us anymore about the funeral; however, he provides us with the lyrics

of a *corrido* that was heard for some time after the killings. The song told
of how all three boys were eventually gunned down as the "war" continued between *los compadres*. This "war" was one of the reasons behind
the story of how the cemeteries of China and General Bravo were filled
with men who had killed each other to save their honor.

As a postscript to the story of how Lupita was robbed from her home,
I mention a brief conversation from January 1998. The location was in
the mountains near Laguna de Sanchez, a remote area on the border with
Coahuila. I was with Horacio Alvarado Ortiz and his film crew. As they
were preparing to film a segment, José Cárdenas, the cameraman, began
talking about the Tijerinas from Bravo and how they were known as *matones* (killers). Alvarado quickly told Cárdenas that there might be someone present that could be offended, since my children are Tijerinas.
Rather than be bothered, I found it very interesting that the story of the
matones would again surface in 1998 on a mountain 300 kilometers from
General Bravo.

Barbarie Adentro

The Interior Barbarian

*En este Río Grande mientras almorzaba en la fonda, escuché las conversa-
ciones, examiné los tipos. Me sentía extraño entre esa gente de pantalón pe-
gado a la pierna, lazadores y vaqueros que no hablaban sino de peleas de
gallos, apuestas y coleadores.* (Vasconcelos 1937: 355) (While I had
breakfast here in the Rio Grande, I heard conversations and examined the local men accompanying me. I felt strange among these
people, with their pants tight on their legs and cowboys who only
spoke of cock fights, gambling, and tail wagging)

All of Mexico listens to José Vasconcelos. The philosopher, who was
minister of education in the 1920s and author of the Mexican concept of
mestizaje, is the poetic voice of the nation, *la patria.*[2] What he told the
people of Mexico only emphasized what has been thought all along: The
north is a contaminated area; the *norteño* has a contaminated culture. The
Sierra Madre mountains have isolated *el norteño* and have kept him in a
regressed and medieval space. This isolation and narrative of depravity
placed the people of Nuevo León in a complicated, ambivalent mantle
of history that designated the *norteño* as Other.

In a narrative that continuously circulates in Nuevo León, Vasconcelos, who died in 1959, is quoted as saying that there is no culture or civilization in the north. This statement has been cited in various historical texts about Nuevo León and was often mentioned in conversation during the three years I traveled to the region. Alvarado writes of this in his book on the history of Monterrey:

> *En tono de insulto José Vasconcelos expresó que donde comienza la carne asada, termina la cultura, dando a entender, que por lo tanto somos unos bárbaros, pero sin lugar a dudas los bárbaros del norte. Son entre los mexicanos unos de los mejores.* (Alvarado 1995: 65) (In the tone of insult, José Vasconcelos expressed where *carne asada* [Mexican barbecue] begins, culture ends, making one understand that for this we are barbarians, without a doubt, the barbarians of the north. We are among the best of the Mexicans)

While the process of legitimizing history in Nuevo León has eliminated narratives of what were described as "impure" populations (Indians and Jews), the continuous textualization of the barbaric *norteño* has clung to what *nuevoleneses* see as their identity. Although Vasconcelos decreed the north's lack of civility early in the twentieth century, the discourse has not abated. The geographic positioning of Nuevo León is so close to the United States that it may not be seen as retaining the civility of other Mexican states. This location, combined with a harsh and inhospitable climate, has not created an inviting image of the north.

The antithesis of the wild man from Bravo is the corporate executive from Monterrey. In the global economy of the early twenty-first century, the capital of Nuevo León is now considered the most technologically advanced and most important site of commerce in all of Latin America (Snodgrass 1998; Kahn 1999). The highly cultured, urbane capitalist is so distant from General Bravo, the description of *bárbaro* (barbarian) seems like a displacement or misnomer. Yet the term *bárbaro* remains; it is the indention of a trace that history has chosen to reify and embed in what is described as *norteño* identity.

In the 1990s, the Universidad Autónoma de Nuevo León published a series titled *Orgullosamente bárbaros* (*Proudly Barbaric*). This series of books covers a range of topics from history to politics. In Houston, Texas, a radio station known as La Nueva Zeta (The New Z), which focuses on what is called Tejano music, a blend of Mexican and Texas sounds, has begun announcing a byline to describe its new format: *Salvajemente mex-icano,* which literally means "savagely a Mexican." This is most probably in response to the fluid movement of people and practices between northern Mexico and Texas. From academia to popular culture, the word *bárbaro* has entered *norteño* language as a signifier that is now asso-ciated with a space, not necessarily with an event, a people, or a practice.

Tan Lejos de Dios

So Far From God

There is a folk saying that is often repeated orally and in published texts describing the relationship between the United States and Mexico. In *El mexicano del norte,* Solís Garza begins his chapter *"El conflicto del 'hombre frontera'"* ("The Conflict of the Man Living at the Border") with *"Pobre de México, tan lejos de Dios y tan cerca de los Estados Unidos"* (1970: 73) ("Poor Mexico, so far from God, so close to the United States"). God has not favored Mexico as it has the United States, yet the two countries are joined together by the Rio Grande, also known as El Río Bravo, a river that can be crossed by boat in fifteen seconds. Solís believes that much of the friction surrounding General Bravo (and other municipali-ties in the north) emanates from the city's proximity to the United States. Even with bad roads, a car can reach the international border in one hour from Bravo.

Solís implies that the attitude of Mexico as Other permeates any rela-tion between the two countries. He believes that the United States sees Mexico as one of its "provinces;" the men of the north have to serve two masters, the United States and Mexico. Solís proposes that the *norteño* lives with a suitcase in his hand, ready to metamorphose at any moment as needed. He goes as far as saying that the student at the Tecnológico, the most prestigious university in Nuevo León, is more similar to the student at the University of Texas at Austin than to the student at the na-tional university in Mexico City. The *regiomontano* has a national identity that is caught at the "fringe" of Mexican identity and the "fringe" of American identity. There is much inner tension emanating from having to serve the two sovereigns, besides himself and his interior conscience (ibid.). This ambiguity creates a blurring of the boundaries of fealty and identity. It also creates an undetermined amount of delirium. As I will continue to explore, the delimitation of boundaries (in the actual world and in the imaginary) between Mexico and the United States, the First World and the Third World, casts a permanent flavor of asymmetry and ambiguity to relations between the two countries and their people.

CHAPTER II

Before and After History:
Los Chichimeca y Carvajal

Los Salvajes del Norte

This barbarism has its own function . . . (de Certeau 1992: 146)

Los Indios no vivieron para contarlo, o bien, si lo contaron, ni ellos ni la historia pudieron hacer que trascendiera. . . . los pocos que quedaban en el territorio de Nuevo León fueron sacrificados y extinguidos en el curso del siglo XIX (Nuncio 1997: 19). (The Indians did not live to tell, or better, if they told, neither they nor history could keep them from extinction . . . the few that were left in the territory of Nuevo León were sacrificed and extinguished in the course of the nineteenth century)

Extinction

In the Scriptural Economy of Nuevo León, the stories of the Chichimeca and of Carvajal take precedence in the descriptive origins of Nuevo León. While later they are diminished and banished, the descriptions of disgust, disapproval, and catastrophe have intensified over time. Seventeenth-century historian Alonso de León's accounts of the incorrigible *indios* are stated and re-stated in scores of history books. The Chichimeca, who had no gods, were branded the worst of barbarians. Simultaneously, the demise of the first governor of Nuevo León is narrated as the tragedy that it was in order to make Carvajal's death a symbol for the extinction of another group of people who lived in the north, the

Nuevo León's Coat of Arms. Note the only representations
of indigenous history are the spears on the side.

Sephardic Jews that Carvajal brought with him when he sailed from
Seville.

As in the rest of New Spain, at the time of the Conquest, indigenous
people were living in what was first called El Nuevo Reino de León. According to early historian Juan Bautista Chapa, at the time the city of
Monterrey was founded, there were approximately 250 distinct tribes.[1]
The Spanish came to call them the Chichimecas. They were strikingly
different from the tribes in the south. The northern Chichimecas' independence, agility, and mobility kept them from becoming automatically

subjugated as had the rest of New Spain's indigenous people. Even in the new millennium, they are still called *los indios bárbaros* (the barbaric Indians).

There is a curious connection between the barbarous *nuevoleneses* and the barbarous Indians from northern Mexico. The common narrative in the north is that there was little "mixture" between the two groups. Yet there is a mixture in the description of savagery that is alluded to in this "story" by *braveño* (person from General Bravo) Olivério Tijerina. Hernán Solís Garza places the story of this event at the end of his introduction to *El mexicano del norte:*

> *Los aztecas . . . tuvieron que pasar desafortunadamente por el norte de México, en sus desiertos sufrieron grandes problemas, no por un grupo de mendigos, salvajes, mal hablados, pendencieros, que se divertían tirando piedras y picando las nalgas de lo que caminaban adelante . . . Llegó a tal grado el conflicto que el tlatoani desesperado y para poner de una vez por todas remedio a la terrible situación, decretó, "Todos ustedes desgraciados, bárbaros, por burlistas y descontentos, irreverentes y rebeldes, se quedarán como castigo en estos lugares, a ver que hacen en estos montes pelones." No bien se quedaron solos cuando empezaron a pelear: todos querían ser tlatoanis.* (1971: 21) (The Aztecs unfortunately had to pass through the north of Mexico. They suffered great problems in the northern desert. This was not for hunger or thirst, nor for cold or heat. It was because of a group of savages, troublemakers, who were vulgar and provoked conflict, enjoying themselves by throwing rocks and poking the buttocks of those who walked in front of them. The conflict became so extreme that the Tlatoanis could no longer tolerate this behavior. To remedy this terrible situation, he decreed, "All of you disgraceful barbarians, for mimicking and being discontented, irreverent and rebellious, as your punishment you will stay in this place and see what you are going to do in these bald mountains." At the moment the troublemakers were left alone, they began to fight among themselves. Everyone wanted to be the leader, the Tlatoanis)

While Olivério Tijerina is telling a story about the Aztecs, he is perhaps also presenting an alternative story of origin in which the *norteño* was originally an Indian.[2] The *norteño's* "barbaric" behavior led to his isolation in those "bald mountains" of the north. In the story, the leader of the tribe wonders out loud as he is leaving the insolent *norteños:* What is this barbaric and incorrigible group going to do in such a desolate place? The answer is just outside of Olivério Tijerina's story. The narrator knows that the question of what they will do is located in the eventual success of the barbarian's industry. These wild men who were left in the mountains of the north organized themselves and became the richest men in Latin America. Tijerina's story provides a link between the barbarous past and the barbarous present. He takes the reader to the seventeenth century in El Nuevo Reino de León, when the narrative boundary between the Spanish settlers and the "barbarous" Indians was clearly identified. Yet, in telling the story in the first place, he is alluding to the "barbaric origins" of his own people.

There is a story told by Alonso de León that describes the "godless barbarians." The theme of barbarity and wildness continues through the establishment of the first Spanish settlements, the naming of Luis de Carvajal de la Cueva as first governor, Carvajal's death, and the barbaric elimination of his family who accompanied him to New Spain.

The Beginning of Time

Alonso de León, the most noted early historian of Nuevo León, wrote in 1643 the story of an *indio* by the name of Martinillo, whom he met in Cerralvo. In a narrative which delineates the dichotomy between the Spaniard and the Indian—those with God and those without God—Martinillo comes to tell León about an apparition:

> Behind the forest near El Río Salinas, there is an *ojo de agua* (a spring) which always flows evenly. There is vegetation at the bank of its pool . . . Near the spring is a large rock. The old men say their ancestors told them that sometimes a handsome young man would come and converse for a long time, telling them of "good things." When the handsome man did not appear, another man, who was very ugly, painted like an *indio,* told them not to believe the handsome man, that he was a liar. When the handsome man returned, and heard what was said about him, he was sad, and left feeling he had accomplished very little. When the handsome man saw that no one would follow him, he left, but there remained a stamp of his

feet in that large rock near the spring, on which he stood, and to this day it remains. (León 1961)

In his text, León asks himself if there could be some man (or angel) in El Nuevo Reino who, with God's will, could give light to the truth and leave the vestige of his message inscribed in stone. When he finds Martinillo, he begins a march, hoping to reach *el ojo de agua* and the rock that holds the imprint of what appeared to be Christ. Unfortunately, before they reached their destination, Martinillo fell ill and died. León is not wholly disappointed. Instead, he is pleased because Martinillo, being an *indio,* was with God. The miracle of the rock is for León a way of giving light to God's truth. As he mentions the travels of Cabeza de Vaca and the numerous miracles that occurred on that journey, he does not hesitate to say that in Florida even the dead were brought back to life. León seems to imply that the miraculous transcends the limited sight of the barbaric and that it might take a divine intervention to convince the Other of the existence of God. What is telling, however, is that in León's respectful description of the miracle, God is found, and Martinillo, *el indio,* dies.

The death of the indigenous is told throughout New Spain. Todorov writes that from the time of the Conquest until 1600, the population of Mexico diminished from twenty-five million to one million (1984: 133). In addition to their elimination in numbers, the indigenous people were "officially" erased with two edicts, in 1571 and 1577, which prohibited the religious community from collecting, studying, and transmitting the history of indigenous people. The second edict required approval from the Council of the Indies and the Spanish Academy of History. Whatever text could escape this censor required the author to take precautions by dedicating his work to the monarch or another highly notable person (Florescano 1994).

The history of this de-Indianization has been given the term *mestizaje,* an often used description for the current Mexican population, which blends the Spanish and the indigenous. Bonfil uses another word to describe this erasure—"ethnocide" (1996). Florescano describes this "ethnocide" in *Memory, Myth and Time in Mexico:*

> The military conquest of the indigenous peoples was followed immediately by the annihilation of their historical memory. . . . From leading actors in their historical environment, they turned into understudies . . . in which the Indians appeared as phantoms who

lived and died without their actions seeming to have an effect on the historical reality of their time. . . . the Indian was not a living subject of history. (1994: 68)

Florescano attempts to rescue "the collective imagination that . . . composes its own memory of the occurrences, creates a hierarchy of importance of these events for the collectivity, brings them up to date, and proposes them as social paradigms for living the present" (ibid. 228). It signals a trend in the late twentieth century and indicates a new trajectory for Mexican historians and social scientists to make "an effort to open new forms of comprehension . . . [for] reconstructing and spreading the memory of past events" (229). An accompaniment to Florescano's work is Guillermo Bonfil's *México Profundo*. Bonfil describes a profundity in Mexican culture that crystallized during the 1988 presidential campaign. The image that surfaced was "a kind of transcendental Indian character that survives, practically unblemished" from Mexico's new superstructure of capitalism (Lomnitz 1992: 249).

Abraham Nuncio, who writes for Mexico City's *La Jornada,* but lives in Nuevo León, follows this trajectory in *Visión de Monterrey.* He has undertaken to resurrect the indigenous from erasure in *nuevolenese* society. He believes that those in power have used regional legends and folklore to relegate the indigenous to being "objects of phobia and prey of that which makes history forget" (1997: 25).[3] Nuncio argues that social fragility and ethnocide joined together in forcing an exclusion of the symbols, rituals, and monuments of the indigenous population. Not even the rituals of death survived, as they did in southern Mexico, because of what he terms an "apartheid" that the "whites" extended from the world of the living to the world of the dead (ibid. 25–26).[4]

The process of *indigenismo* (Indianization) began with the Mexican Revolution, a *mestizo* peasant revolution. The more recent push towards *indigenismo* has assisted the Mexican nation-state in working towards a free market that caters more closely to the national community. The image of *indigenismo* has been used as a model of nationality (Lomnitz 1992).[5] The nation-state presents itself as having an illustrious indigenous past. The pyramids near Mexico City and in Yucatán have hundreds of thousands of visitors per year. The National Museum of Anthropology in Mexico City is overflowing with pre-conquest artifacts. The authorized ideology of Mexico privileges the history of the Aztecs. The image of the beautiful Aztec princess dying in the arms of the Aztec prince is on calendars

everywhere. These bronzed people with their brilliant feather head-
dresses are the representatives of the Mexican nation not only in Mexico itself but also in those places of the greatest Mexican migration.
Anywhere there are people of Mexican descent there are also representations of the Virgin of Guadalupe. There cannot be a more prolific
icon of this ideology than this *mestiza* Virgin. She appeared to an indigenous man in 1562 and within a century became the patroness of
Mexico. Despite accusations of having been a ruse invented by the
church to seduce the Indians into conversion, her importance has proliferated. In Mexico, devotion to the Virgin of Guadalupe is significantly
more pronounced than devotion to Jesus Christ. Nuncio reminds us that
one indigenous practice, which is performed by the *matachines,* who are
dancers dressed in quasi-indigenous costume, has remained in service to
the Virgin of Guadalupe. *Matachines* are groups of *"danzantes infatigables
que remuelen el ritmo de unos antepasados paganos comunicados mítica y misti-
camente con sus dioses o con la naturaleza a través de la danza"* (1997: 26).
(dancers, who perform for hours without rest, while dancing to the
rhythm of pagan ancestors who were communicating mystically with
their gods and with nature through the dance)[6]

Guadalupe indeed is nationally important, as is indicated by presidential candidate Vicente Fox's decision to parade the standard of the Virgin
of Guadalupe during his campaign rallies in July 1999. Although highly
criticized for his decision, which was compared to his public relations
gambits when he was a Coca-Cola executive, the use of the *mestiza* Virgin was undoubtedly thought to be an effective way to secure the votes
of Mexico's "brown masses."

While the intent of academicians in pursuit of *indigenismo* is unclear,
Vicente Fox's decision to pair with the Virgin of Guadalupe indicates his
understanding of the significance of *mestizaje* in Mexico. The charges of
ethnocide and the description of the Indian as being a phantom and soul
who has lost his memory are accurate. An entire civilization was lost,
having left only traces of material remnants and pieces of cultural practices. What has remained, however, is "color." Most of Mexico's population has retained the color of *indigenismo.* As seen in newspaper photographs of the different regions of the Mexican nation, this *mestizo*
population decidedly continues to appear indigenous, with dark skin and
short stature.[7] While less than five percent of the pre-conquest population survived the first hundred years, those who remained were prolific
in creating a multitude of descendants, as Mexican demographics attest.

Matachines dancing in honor of the Virgin Mary at the Sanctuario de la Medalla Milagrosa in San Francisco, Villa de Santiago, Nuevo León. 1998.
Photograph by the author.

In addition, the most significant political and military confrontation in this decade has been between the Mexican government and the *indios* of the state of Chiapas.

While still being significantly ambivalent, this revaluation of indigenous culture in Mexico has made the highly developed civilizations of the pre-conquest Aztecs and Mayas a focus of national pride. The words of Cortés's men that describe Tenochtitlán as a fantastic, sparkling city, cleaner than the cities of Europe, are often repeated in praise of the world of the Mexica. Mayan achievements in astronomy and mathematics, including the development of the concept of zero, have been agreeably used to indicate the outstanding nature of pre-conquest technical achievements. The description of the regal and gracious Montezuma and his court tell of a highly developed civilization. The pantheon of gods and carefully coded rituals signal a well-developed belief system. The proliferation of human sacrifice was all that marred the image of a futuristic people living in the sixteenth century.

Although this image of Mexico before the conquest emanates from the southern region of the country, not all of modern Mexico possesses a history or landscape that is suited to this representation. Moving north-

A painting of the Virgin of Guadalupe with the
Mexican flag draped across the bottom of the image.
Taken in the church Nuestra Señora de la Soledad in
General Terán, Nuevo León. 1998.

Photograph by the author.

ward, past the colonial city of San Luis Potosí, the landscape begins to
change.

Spatial Myths

In Nuevo León, landscape and history create the myth of a space. In-
dentations in the land form a texture in the personality of that space.
What is seen by the eye is folded into the narratives that tell the story of
this place. The physical characteristics of El Nuevo Reino substantiated
and intensified these stories. Dryness, desolation, and extreme tempera-

tures made it seemingly uninhabitable. The inhospitable nature of the land forced other myths to appear, offering another type of advantage, resource, or warning. Stories began to circulate that described the Spanish who came to live there as extreme in their character. The violence and barbarity initially attributed to the Chichimeca blurred into that of the colonizer. The evil land contained evil people.

The landscape is evil. The winters are harsh and extreme, as are the summers. There is rarely an in-between period. The adaptable Chichimecas moved as needed to find resources of water and food. The Spanish established mines in El Nuevo Reino in the mid-sixteenth century. Needing food supplies for the mining communities, they attempted to mold sections of land for agriculture, an almost impossible task. Although there were water sources, the winters were at times as harsh as those in the northern United States. The summer's heat was barely tolerable. It was a dry, mountainous area with brush and cactus. It was not a welcome space. During the initial phase of the conquest, the wild men, the Chichimecas, were the only ones who could thrive.

As the Spanish arrived in the north, it seemed as if the landscape took the form of a god, creating trials to see if the warrior (Chichimeca or Spaniard) could prove his prowess. He was a wild god, estranged from the more poetic landscape of southern Mexico. He did not provide a pleasant sight, except when the distance of the Sierra Madre came into view. The landscape exacted violence. It took three tries to establish the city of Monterrey. The entire Nuevo Reino de León had to be completely re-colonized in 1596 after losing nearly all its Spanish settlers. Within 300 years the Chichimecas were totally eliminated. Although remnants of the Chichimeca blood remain in the skin color of a few *norteños,* their culture has been erased; people in the north have no conscious memory of having been *indios.* In this space of death the *indio bárbaro* of the north disappeared.

Locating the Wild Man in the Arid North

The Chichimeca—Sixteenth Century

. . . the appreciation of landscape. . . . must be the focus of a historical, political, and (yes) aesthetic alertness to the violence and evil written on the land, projected there by the gazing eye. (Mitchell 1994: 29)

Wildness. . . . is indiscriminately [a] . . . place; that is to say, it is not only the what of a sin, but the where as well. . . . the place of the curse (the desert, the dead, the wasteland) is also described as a wilderness. (White 1978: 158)

The English translation óf Chichimeca is "wild dog." The indigenous people thus named lived in numerous tribes'in the area between El Río Bravo (the Rio Grande Rivel, which now separates Texas from Mexico) and an area slightly north of San Luis Potosí. It is said/ that the Mexicas, who later became the Aztecs, were from the land of the Chichimeca, far to the north of Tenochtitlán. Over several centuries the Mexicas were able to control the surrounding tribes and began to move farther and farther south.

The Chichimeca who remained in the north were nomads, hunters, and gatherers. The limited information available on their practices indicates that their lives were such as many North American Indians. They lived in small bands and were highly adaptable to the geographic environment. They were totally different from the Mexica of the south and the Maya of Yucatán. They built no pyramids or temples. They did not have a large pantheon of deities. The only remaining traces of their material culture are petroglyphs in northwestern Nuevo León.

According to accounts from the early Spanish settlers,

Los hombres andaban desnudos y algunos usaban suelas de cuero de animales que cazaban y se las ataban a los pies con unas correas, a esto le llamaban cacles para defenderse de las espinas, los cabellos lo traían hacia atrás atados con unas correas o los traían suelto les llegaba hasta las piernas, la cara se la pintaban cada nación o grupos como les gustaba siempre rayas horizontales o verticales, ondeadas y algunos se peleaban la coronilla. (Alvarado 1995: 20) (The men went about nude and some used leather soles from animals they had hunted and would put them on their feet with straps. These were called *cacles* and were used to protect them from the stickers, their hair was tied back with string or it was loose and went down to their legs. Their faces were painted according to their tribe or group and were always horizontal or vertical stripes, curves. Some would shave the crown of their head)

This description was published in a book by local television personality Horacio Alvarado Ortiz. It was a popular book that was heavily distributed throughout Monterrey in celebration of the 400 years since the founding of the city. While not an academic historian, Alvarado is considered a local "expert" and his knowledge is taken as "the word" by a significant percentage of *nuevoleneses*. More formal histories corroborate the information given by Alvarado Ortiz (León 1972; de Hoyo 1973; Roel 1963). The Indians have been described as *bárbaros* (barbarous) from the time of the conquest until the late twentieth century.

Alonso de León described the indigenous:

> *Es gente cruel, feroz, naturalmente vengativos y guardan mucho tiempo el enojo. De buenas estaturas, muy ligeros, que andan y corren como un caballo. . . . Inclinados a hurtar. Es gente mentirosa, vana y enemiga de todo lo criado. . . . viven libres, en ociosidad; raíz de todos los males en que están sepultado.* (León 1961: 20) (They are cruel people, ferocious, naturally vengeful, who stay angry for a long period of time. They are of good height, and very thin, they walk and run like a horse. . . . They are inclined to steal. They are people who lie, they are vain and are enemies of all that is taught by civilized society. . . . they live freely lazily; the root of all the evil in which they are buried)

Hayden White explains the gradual demythologization of concepts like "wildness," "savagery," and "barbarism" as due to the extension of knowledge into those parts of the world which, though known about (but not actually known), had originally served as the physical stages onto which the "civilized" imagination could project its fantasies and anxieties (1978: 153).

In 1649, fifty-one years after the establishment of El Nuevo Reino de León, Alonso de León wrote of the Chichimecas' cruelty and thievery. Is the subtext of his work a structure to support the Inquisition's view of the ideal citizen and Christian? His *Discurso primero,* which focuses on the Chichimecas, begins with a chapter entitled "*Cómo el hombre es inclinado a buscar a Dios*" ("How Man is Inclined to Search for God"). In his description of *los indios,* León cites Marco Tulio: "[N]*o puede haber en el mundo ningún hombre racional que . . . no tenga conocimiento de Dios . . .* (there cannot be in the world a rational man who does not know God) (León 1961: 8). León tells the reader that, in the entire world, it is only the Chichimeca that do not have gods. He describes them as beasts. They eat friends and they eat enemies. A dead enemy is eaten raw. However, when a friend dies, they make a fiesta. They make *barbacoa* and grind the bones and mix the powder with peyote. An *india* from Tamaulipe la Vieja told León that when a friend died, the women of the group would eat the meat, but the men would not. Both men and women, however, drink the concoction made of ground bone.

According to León, when the company of Captain Bernado Garcia de Sepúlveda was traveling through El Nuevo Reino, they found a container of *mezquitamal,* a drink mixed with burned, ground-up human bones. The *indios* in the company were very happy to find the *mezquitamal,* which they drank along with the Spanish soldiers. The Spanish discovered the contents of the drink when they found some bones that were not completely ground. But the Captain tried to keep the men from vomiting by telling them the bones were of a deer (León 1961). Here León emphasizes the dichotomy between Spaniard and Indian by indicating the Indians' joy at finding the *mezquitamal* and happily ingesting the drink, while Spanish soldiers would have needed to purge themselves of what they drank if the Captain had not lied to them about its contents. Thus in León's story, the wild man ingests what the Spaniard finds disgusting.

In his treatise on the Wild Man, Hayden White writes, "[I]t appears quite difficult to distinguish between a moral condition, a relationship, and a place . . . in all those instances in the Bible where words that might be translated as 'wild' or 'wilderness' appear" (White 1978: 159). It is at this juncture that the physical wilderness and the moral wildness are conflated. The Chichimeca, whom de León describes as not having gods, are also cannibals. They were considered even less human than the *indios* of the south who had a pantheon of gods. In this context, the definition of Chichimeca as dogs, as the furthest from God, and as cannibals comes together in the usual strategic trajectory of colonization in which the colonized becomes the subaltern and the subaltern becomes a ghost or a monster. They are the wild men who are less than men, living in the untamable wilderness.

There were significant differences between the Chichimeca and other tribes to the south. Actually, according to what Cristóbal López explained to me, the Chichimeca did have a system of deities, but it was not as complex as that of the Mexica and the Maya. Since they did not develop any urban areas, there remain limited traces of their civilization.

The War

Indeed, the entire history of the state revolves around the "Indian War." The moments of national turmoil, such as the War of Independence with

Spain, the Texas Revolution, the War with the United States (1848), the French Intervention, and finally the Mexican Revolution, seem to be only sporadic moments of distraction compared to the ongoing tension and brutality of the conflict between the "whites" and the "Indians."

Israel Cavazos Garza, El Cronista de Monterrey (Monterrey's official historian), wrote in his essay *"Las incursiones de los indios bárbaros"* that the people in Nuevo León lived in terror for centuries. As the population of the Chichimeca diminished, the Apache and Comanche moved into Mexico from the United States due to pressure from the U.S. Cavalry. Presenting the same war-like practices, the violence between the settlers and the indigenous people continued until the end of the nineteenth century (1964).

What was most important to the post-conquest settlers was that the Chichimeca were much more warlike and independent than most other tribes in Mexico. It took several centuries for the conflict to end between the Spanish and the Indians in the north. This length of time in itself is a paradox, since the highly developed Aztecs in the south lost their Empire to Cortés in a matter of days.

According to limited textual accounts, the Chichimeca reacted much more fiercely because of mistreatment by the settlers. There was active use of Indian slavery until the nineteenth century. Eugenio de Hoyo reports the incidence of an Indian massacre that was very similar to the Americans' Wounded Knee (1985). Yet, in comparison to the mistreatment by the colonizers in southern Mexico, there was not such a significant difference. Todorov describes continuous incidents of savagery and murder on the part of the conquistadors (1984).

By 1640 the "Indian Wars" resumed, although in the beginning they consisted of isolated Indian assaults on small groups of Spanish or native leaders. These attacks were responded to immediately by the "Europeans" who ordered the "punishment" not only of those responsible for the attacks but also of their wives and children. In this way, he believes, these isolated attacks and counter-attacks that did not appear to be as significant as isolated incidents grew into a long, bloody, and barbaric war (Cossio 1925).

One of the earliest written accounts of violence between the Spaniards and the Chichimeca is located in the memoirs of Luis Carvajal el Mozo, the nephew of the first governor of El Nuevo Reino de León. The year was 1589. The governor was in Mexico City meeting with the Viceroy. The younger Carvajal had stayed behind in the settlement of San Gregorio de Almazen (later to be known as Monclova, Coahuila).

Supplies were running low. Carvajal wanted to leave, but Capitán Linares, the alcalde of the village, urged him to stay because of significant concern over the threat of an attack by the Indians. Considering some of Luis el Mozo's adventures (he at one time got lost in the wilderness and a group of settlers had to go find him), he probably was not considered much of a protection except that he was one more able-bodied soldier that could help Linares in case of Indian attack. Regardless of the situation, Luis el Mozo was anxious to leave San Gregorio. Within a few days Carvajal received word that his sisters were getting married in Mexico City. This excuse provided enough impetus for him to find a way to get out of San Gregorio. He gave Linares an ingot of silver, which the alcalde could use to trade for supplies. Several weeks later it was reported that the Indians did attack San Gregorio and entered the house of Linares, who was disemboweled and killed.

According to Eugenio de Hoyo, part of the conflict stemmed from the early practice of slavery. In *La Historia de Nuevo León* (1972), Hoyo reports that Governor Luis de Carvajal y de la Cueva was actively involved in trading the indigenous as slaves, which was one of several reasons that Carvajal was removed from office in 1589. Most of El Nuevo Reino was "de-populated" after Carvajal's demise because of conflict with the Chichimecas. For much of the colonial period, the Spanish settlers would "kidnap" Indians and use them for labor for several months. Then they would deposit them in another settlement, only to recapture them when their services were again needed (Hoyo 1985).

Although there were periods of tranquility, the violence would erupt again without notice in some part of Nuevo León (Cossio 1925). The use of the term *barbarous* was at the time reserved only for the Indians. However, from textual descriptions, the Spaniards' responses were equally "barbarous." The distinction between the perpetrator and his "kin" was not acknowledged; entire families were killed when the Spaniards attacked the Indians. Oftentimes in the desperation of the moment, the Spaniards would hang whomever they could find, only to find the persons "guilty" at a later date and then hang them as well (Cossio 1925).

Going Underground

It was in relation to the Indian Wars that I was first told of the underground tunnels in Monterrey. The most significant is the tunnel between

El Obispado, a three-hundred-year-old church on the west side of down-town Monterrey, and the Cathedral, which is in the center of the city. Ofelia Sepúlveda and Horacio Alvarado Ortiz both told me that the tunnel was used by the settlers as shelter during Indian raids. Alvarado actually filmed the tunnel and found it to be so large a horse-drawn wagon could easily travel from El Obispado to the Cathedral. Ofelia Sepúlveda said that people would travel through the tunnel to reach the Cathedral in order to attend mass. The people would enter the Cathedral from an underground stairway and would remain protected inside. The giant doors of the Cathedral were built to withstand an Indian attack.

Celso Garza Guajardo, the late director of the educational center, La Ex-hacienda de San Pedro, told me in 1997 that there were also under-ground tunnels under the seventeenth-century hacienda, which is located about twenty kilometers north of Monterrey. The tunnels protected the water supply from Indian attack. When the Indians were approaching, the residents of the hacienda descended and locked the exit above them, leaving them safely inside, with their water supply accessible to them. In the recently restored hacienda, there is an underground opening that at first glance appears to be a water well. It is covered with Plexiglass. The steps that go down into the original tunnel come into view when the visitor approaches the opening. What lies beyond the Plexiglass resembles the history of the Indian Wars. The narratives are slightly visible, yet they are impossible to access.

Family Stories

Stories I gathered from my family, who left the area of Nuevo León well over a century ago, tell of the threat of "Indian attack." There were kid-nappings and killings. One side of the family was adversely affected during three different generations. There has never been any "talk" of in-digenous practices. The only material "leftover" is a *molcajete* (mortar and pestle) that every household in the family still owns. Other references to Indians occurred when one of the following stories was retold:

> Sebastian Hernández was kidnapped by Indians when he was eight years old. It was somewhere around 1870. He lived near the town of Candela, which at the time was still part of Nuevo León. Ac-

cording to family stories, while with the Indians he was responsible for the horses. This duty gave him the opportunity to escape. One evening he fed them and stayed nearby waiting for complete darkness. Then he began to run. He ran at night, and at dawn he dug a hole and hid inside until night came again. After running for three days, he found his family. This was after three years of captivity. Years later, his wife, María de la Luz Esquivel, wanted all her sons to be born in Candela, even though they were already living in Texas. She always said that the men from Candela were "real men."

There is a faint trace of a story about a woman that was kidnapped by Indians just outside of Laredo sometime in the nineteenth century. There is no name. All that is said was that she was never seen again.

Jesús Paredes was born on the Mexican-Texas border around the time of the Texas Revolution. He lived in a village named Uribeño, which was near the city of Laredo. In 1863 Jesús joined the U.S. Confederacy with his brother Francisco. They were both honorably discharged in 1864. Sometime between 1865 and 1869 Jesús was shot and killed by Indians in San Agustín Plaza in downtown Laredo. It was a Comanche raid, the last one to attack Laredo.

Cavazos Garza writes of the constant tension:

Viven los pueblos en zozobra perpetua. No hay seguridad de los bienes ni de la vida. . . . Los giros comerciales y del campo están paralizados. De nada vale a Nuevo León a que la Comisión Pesquisidora ya alude en 1873. . . . Con el botín de guerra el salvaje lleva también a los cautivos . . . Los niños son llevados a lugares remotos . . . Hay niños o jóvenes que han permanecido cautivos tres, seis, diez y hasta diecisiete años. (1964: 349– 350) (The communities live in constant anguish. There is no security for life or goods. Commerce and ranching are paralyzed. Nuevo León is worth nothing, according to a statement made in 1873 by the Comisión Pesquisidora. The savage takes his loot and his captives. The children are taken to remote areas. There are children and adolescents who have been kept as captives three, six, ten, even seventeen years)

Los Morenos

The Dark Ones

In the stories from my family, and many others I heard while in Nuevo León, I did not hear about how the families of Indians and settlers mixed together. The national character of the *mestizo* did not enter these narratives. The separation between the two groups was marked very clearly. The "darker" people were from the south: indigenous looking women who sold goods at street corners (or begged) were known as "Marías." Among the middle-class families I knew in Monterrey, this was mentioned virtually whenever we went anywhere in the car together and passed a "María" trying to sell or beg.

There remains an additional story that was told by another side of my family. It had also had a tragic theme that has actually haunted me for quite some time:

Hilario Hernández, a "Teco" Indian, kidnapped the criolla Ysidra Alvarez from a convent in San Luis Potosí. Some family members say he was the gardener at the convent; others say he was the coachman. He took her to Coahuila. The marriage records at the Cathedral in Saltillo, Coahuila, state that in 1870, Hilario Hernández married Ysidra Alvarez.[8] They had three children. It is said that she died around 1888, and that he may have killed her. He was not arrested for her murder.

The story of Hilario Hernández and Ysidra Alvarez has been more vivid than the other stories because about forty-five years after Ysidra died, my paternal grandmother actually lived in the same house with Hilario for several years. In 1922 she married Hilario's grandson Lauro. She told me that Hilario was of very small stature, and that he often did not speak Spanish, but instead, spoke an indigenous dialect.

Lauro's father, Lazaro Hernández, was a gifted musician in Monclova and Saltillo. People called Lazaro *el indio* because he was dark-skinned. For three successive generations, the Hernándezes continued to be dark. It is only in my generation, after several marriages with "light-skinned" spouses, that Hilario's genes have allowed the creation of "white" children who would not be called *indios*.

In Vasconcelos's idea of *mestizaje,* the ideology of Mexico is immersed in the idealization of the indigenous, the dark brown color and the triumphant stories of the Aztecs and their spectacular cities. The Scriptural Economy of this message lauds the indigenous. Yet the discourse promoted by Vasconcelos has produced a cast of hypocrisy. What has become a slogan for the Mexican nation-state has in reality been a false narrative. Lomnitz Adler writes in *Exits From the Labyrinth*: "Mexico is a society where Indian ancestry has been proudly acknowledged. On the other side, it is a society that clearly values whiteness as both a status symbol and as an aesthetic" (1992: 280). He agrees that the Mexican Revolution assisted in the development of the prototypical "Mexican" giving respect and honor to the indigenous and the *mestizo*. He also reminds his reader that in the Colonial, post-Independence and post-Revolutionary periods of Mexican history, "[W]hites have been at the top of the economic and status ladder, and Indians, blacks and *mestizos* have been undervalued and discriminated against" (1992: 280−281). Lomnitz-Adler places a bit of humor and irony in his text as he tells the reader of how Mexican President Porfirio Díaz (himself an Indian from Oaxaca) would put powder on his skin in order to appear "lighter" (1999).

Disappearance

While the original history of the savage Indian still exists in history texts, he no longer exists in the present, at least according to the narratives in Nuevo León. There is evidence of outright genocide on the part of the state. Cavazos Garza writes of an edict given by Governor Vidaurri in the late nineteenth century that ordered poison to be distributed to local ranchers. The poison was placed in streams used for water by the Indians (1969). There is also a symbolic narrative of the "misbehaved Indian" who was expelled from the "group" and the "discourse."

Sara Aguilar Belden describes how a "white" couple "lovingly" adopted an Indian child and then "had to" expel him from their family. Their names were Don Manuel and Doña Soledad Feijoo. The author describes Doña Soledad: *"[E]ra blanquísima, y sus cabellos . . . de rubio . . . parecían de oro"* (Aguilar 1970: 47−48) (her skin was extremely white, and her hair was blonde and looked like gold). While the Feijoos were in Ixmiquilpan, they adopted an Indian child and named him Montezuma. They did not have their own children and treated the boy as if he were their own. After he became a grown man, he arrived one day in a state of intoxication and told his parents many vulgarities; for example, he said they were not really his parents and were just common Spaniards. Don Manuel took "the Indian" by the arm and kicked him into the middle of the street. Aguilar finishes the story by saying: "*Jamás volvieron a ver al indio aquel*" (ibid.) ("They never saw that Indian again.").

For suggested reasons of "misbehavior" or even the more covert issues of "regional purity," the narrative was transformed from the never-ending conflict between the "whites" and Nuevo León's indigenous to Indians that never existed. In numerous conversations I have had with *nuevoleneses* and in a number of texts, several people observe that the people from the north were "white." When I asked Alvarado why there was such little "leftover" culture from the Chichimecas, Alvarado told me that this was not because of genocide, but because there were not that many Indians to begin with.

This "disappearance" is not without its consequences. Olverio Tijerina's story of how the Aztecs left behind the Chichimecas in the north tells of the marginality of this narrative. One might say that the fate of the Chichimeca is akin to what de Certeau argues about the story that "slips away": "The cannibal is a figure on the fringe who leaves the premises, and in doing so jolts the entire topographical order of language" (1986: 70). It is the Chichimeca who have left the premises of the normalized indigenous world in Mexico. The Chichimeca were left behind because of their barbarism. They become the Other in Mexico's indigenous world. Their expulsion from the world of the Aztecs indeed "jolts" the order of language. Lacking the qualities of the Aztecs, they are relegated to an invisible history in a nation that proudly displays its indigenous heritage.

Descriptions of the indigenous of the north include the words *nomadic, savage, barbaric,* and *cannibalistic.* De Certeau finds these words in Montaigne who tells the reader in his essay "On Cannibals" that "what is near masks a foreignness." Continuing his study of the essay, de Certeau writes, "Nomadism is not an attribute of the . . . Cannibal: it is their very definition" (1986: 70). The author has a need to dissociate, to make the savage disappear, as the Chichimeca disappeared. The transformation occurs simultaneously in the status of the term *barbarian.* It has become an adjective describing the *nuevolenese.* The indigenous barbarian is gone. In a paradoxical way, the *nuevolenese* has remained to become the barbarian who created a *cultura de casta criolla* (Nuncio 1997: 24) (caste of creole culture), a culture that has embellished the fantasy of the pure blood line, which of course is Spanish, not Indian or *mestizo*.[9]

El Nuevo Reino de León

The Colonists—Sixteenth Century

El antiguo villorrio de nombre grandilocuente ha llegado a ser la metrópoli que no fue y a dar a luz un reino que nunca antes existió (Nuncio 1997: 15). (The ancient hamlet with the grandiloquent name has become the metropolis that was not and gave birth to a kingdom that never before existed.)

Governando como Virrey de los reinos de la Nueva España, D. Martín Enríquez de Almanza; . . . viendo los muchos daños que hacían los indios fronterizos a la provincia de la Huasteca; dio orden al capitán Luis de Carabajal de la Cueva . . . el año de mil y quinientos y setenta y seis, para que con una compañía hiciese entrada en la tierra de guerra, castigase y apaciguase las naciones alteradas. (León 1961: 43) (Governing as Viceroy of the Kingdoms of New Spain, Don Martín Enríquez de Almanza, observing the massive destruction incurred by the Indians in the province of La Huasteca, ordered Captain Luis de Carvajal de la Cueva . . . in the year 1576 to form a company to enter the territory of war, to punish and pacify the hostile nations)

The historical intersection between Spain and the Chichimeca officially began when the Spanish Viceroy, Martín de Almanza, requested Luis de Carvajal y de la Cueva to settle the northern area of the frontier and "pacify" the Indians. Almanza requested Carvajal to "enter the territory of war." The conflict was declared before El Nuevo Reino de León existed. As a result, Carvajal was presented to the Spanish Court with the request for territory in what at that time was known as "La Huasteca." The year was 1586. At the time, Felipe II was in desperate need of money. Spain had placed itself in a stranglehold. A century before, many of the Jews, known as Spain's intellectual and professional class, were expelled. The nation had isolated itself from other European nations and the revenues from its new territories had declined. Upon ascending to the Crown in 1556, Felipe II inherited a debt of twenty million ducats.

There was an unfinished war with France. In 1568, misshapen military decisions led to the beginning of the Eighty Years War with the Netherlands. Felipe II received significant monies from well-financed *conversos* (Caro Baroja 1961) who paid for "favors." These favors included titles of nobility, territory, and *limpieza de sangre* certificates allowing *conversos* to enter New Spain. Income also included the erratic but often lucrative silver mines in the Americas. Felipe II continued to maintain that these revenues would re-stabilize Spain.

At the same time, Carvajal enjoyed significant success in two voyages to the Americas and was designated a hero after capturing a famous English pirate. Hoyo reports that Carvajal received a large inheritance from his father and was involved in the slave trade. His marriage to Guiomar Rivera also provided generous financial backing for his exploits. Hoyo writes that for the sum of two million ducats the king gave Carvajal unprecedented authority over a region that came to be known as *el cuadro trágico de Carvajal* (the tragic square of Carvajal). According to Robles, the territory ceded to the governor encompassed 702,244 square kilometers, equal to one third of the present Mexican nation (1938).

There were other fantastic accommodations given by the king. The families accompanying Carvajal to the Americas were not required to submit certificates of *limpieza de sangre,* which was the law at the time. Governor Carvajal was also authorized to name his own successor and, most importantly, El Nuevo Reino was to be *"independiente por completo del virreinato de la Nuevo España"* (Hoyo 1972: 79) (completely independent of New Spain). Mexican historians have written profusely on the ability of Carvajal and his followers to travel to the Americas without certificates of *limpieza de sangre* (Hoyo 1972; Roel 1977.) Yet, as Caro Baroja and Castro (among others) repeatedly mention, many things could be bought. Hoyo writes of a remark made by the monarch; when asked why he made such concessions to Carvajal, Felipe II responded, *"[P]ero la necesidad es mayor que los escrúpulos de conciencia"* (Hoyo 1972: 78–79) (however, necessity is more important than the scruples of one's conscience). Even so, Robles writes that Carvajal's concessions were *"hasta casi increíble en el marco de aquellos tiempos de intransigencia feroz, y sobre todo tratandose de un monarca tan fanatico como Felipe II"* (1938: 100) (incredible considering those times of ferocious change, and above all, coming from such a fanatic monarchy as that of Felipe II).

The establishment of El Nuevo Reino began with a fantastic narrative. Carvajal, a *converso,* was designated first governor of a territory that was almost three quarters of a million square kilometers. The territory was called a "kingdom" (*reino*). Carvajal maintained the right of succession; his heir would be the next governor. A *converso* receiving such a favor (whether he bought the favor or not) was a significant rarity in a time where hundreds of *conversos* were burning at the stake.

The factors behind the establishment of this independent kingdom were pragmatic. La Huasteca was an isolated territory with a resistant native population; was far from New Spain's center of power in Mexico City; and could be served by a Spanish hero who had significant financial backing during a time when many of his compatriots were infiltrating the power structure of the Spanish monarchy. All of these developments occurred while El Santo Oficio, the Holy Inquisition, continued to detain, interrogate, torture, and execute scores of Portuguese *conversos*. The separation of two continents and the isolation of the northern territories made the presence of the Inquisition a remote possibility in El Nuevo Reino de León.

The Sacrifice

Villa de Almaden (Monclova, Coahuila)
1589

A murmurous scream exacted by torture, which must create fear without creating a scandal, legitimizes the system without toppling it. (de Certeau 1986: 41)
. . . history . . . reiterates . . . the myths built upon a murder of an originary death and fashions out of language the forever-remnant trace of a beginning that is as impossible to recover as to forget. (de Certeau 1988: 47)

Felipe II's concessions to Luis Carvajal y de la Cueva created an inevitable disaster for Carvajal and for El Nuevo Reino. The territory extended into the boundaries of other Viceroys, including La Nueva Vizcaya and Nueva Galicia. The excuse of the crown's ignorance regarding geography is also noted. Believing that "his" territory extended two hundred leagues in each direction, Carvajal continued extending his jurisdiction to the limit of his "concession." When he arrived in Santiago del Saltillo, he took over administration of the city and seems to have won over the combative founder of Saltillo, Alberto del Canto. Carvajal's demise began shortly afterwards. According to León (1961), there were other disputes besides those of the territorial boundaries. Charges were made by a certain friar against Carvajal in 1583 concerning mistreatment of the Indians (Hoyo 1972). According to the stipulations of Carvajal's contract with the Spanish monarchy, the governor had several responsibilities: discovering new territory and creating new settlements, introducing livestock to the area, constructing a fort, establishing seaports, and opening new roads. According to Hoyo, Carvajal met none of these requirements (1972).

As mentioned previously, a number of texts report enslavement of Indians as one of the charges leveled against Carvajal. Although it was a fairly common activity for the time period, historians have repeatedly mentioned this issue as a problem for Carvajal. It was known that Carvajal was raised by his uncle, a slave trader living in the Cape Verde Islands. Hoyo relates the Governor's later problems to having been raised in such an "immoral" environment (1975). Another narrative regarding "Carvajal's downfall" is referenced in several historical texts. It concerns his niece, Doña Isabel Rodríguez de Andrada. Isabel lived with Carvajal's wife, Guiomar, for several months before Isabel left for New Spain. During this period, Guiomar made Isabel promise that the girl would do her best to bring the governor back "to the law of Moses." Two years later, after the family learned that Guiomar died, Isabel attempted to fulfill her promise. She tried to tell Carvajal of the dangers of "not believing." He responded violently and struck Isabel. There were witnesses. The statutes of *limpieza de sangre* required every Spanish citizen to report any "Judaizing" when becoming aware of such a transgression, which Carvajal did not do. Ultimately, Carvajal was sentenced on charges of not reporting the incident.

Textual accounts report that the Viceroy made public the governor's genealogy. A petition was presented to the Holy Office on April 13, 1589. The following day a judge left with a company of soldiers with orders to apprehend Carvajal. Diego de Montemayor, Carvajal's Captain, led the soldiers to Carvajal, who was at San Gregorio de Almadén (later known as Monclova, Coahuila). Carvajal was imprisoned and brought before the Holy Office in Mexico City. He was sentenced for harboring Jews. Ordered to leave New Spain, he died before he began his sentence. León writes, "*En la prisión, de pesadumbre murio*" (1961: 55) ("In prison, he died because of the weight of his sadness").[10]

Carvajal's family was arrested in Mexico City. They were tortured and confessed to practicing "the law of Moses." They were sentenced to three years of imprisonment and forced to wear the garment called a *san-benito,* indicating a Jew in repentance. In 1595, the Inquisition renewed its accusations against the family. All but two of his relatives were condemned, including the governor's heir, Luis de Carvajal, el Mozo. They were burned at the stake in Mexico City on December 8, 1596.

Remaking El Nuevo Reino

We must inquire into what effects this confession [during torture] has, what it enables the initiate to do, and what benefit an institution derives from such an enucleation (de Certeau 1986: 42).

The question at hand concerns either the *utopia* which, since the Reformation . . . has enacted the will to remake (rotten) institutions using fictions of "purity". . . . the institution is the putrescence that must be reformed by recourse to more originary innocence, freedom, and purity. (de Certeau 1986: 45)

The Inquisition's torture of the Carvajal family has become a major Mexican legend. It has been described in scores of texts, including the famous *Libro rojo* (1989), which was authored by the director of the Mexican National Archives, Vicente Riva Palacios (1989). At a regional level, Santiago Roel's popular school textbook on the history of Nuevo León describes Carvajal's mother as "betraying" her family while being tortured on the rack (1977). There are numerous painted images of the Carvajals being tortured, including that of Carvajal's sister standing naked before the judges of the Inquisition. For the duration of four centuries, Mexico's Scriptural Economy has allowed these disturbing images to circulate without censure.

Four months before the Carvajal family was executed by the Inquisition, Diego Montemayor, Carvajal's former capitán, established the city of Monterrey. Those accompanying him were members of Carvajal's original group who had fled to Saltillo after the governor's death. Others accompanied Gaspar Castaño de Sosa on a renegade expedition to New Mexico. This effort ended in failure with the execution of Castaño de Sosa.

There is no written text describing how the demise of the Carvajals affected the re-formation of El Nuevo Reino. There is no mention of this tragic history in the "Official Decree." Montemayor signed the *cé-*

dula (Decree), establishing the city, Nuestra Senora de Monterrey, on the same spot where Santa Lucía had been designated by Alberto del Canto (most probably) in 1577 and again by Carvajal in 1581 or 1582. The decree, signed on September 20, 1596 reads as follows:

> . . . *se espera descubrir y Poblar, y en fé y testimonio de verdad lo otorgué y fundé en el Valle de Extremadura Ojos de Santa Lucía Jurisdicción del Nuevo Reyno de León en veinte días del Mes de Septiembre de mil y quinientos noventa y seis . . .*
>
> . . . *El dicho Señor Gobernador y Capitán Diego de Montemayor Dixo: que para el siento y Congregación de los vecinos y Pobladores . . . señaló primeramente sitio y solar para la Iglesia mayor que es una cuadra de la Plaza hacia la parte de Norte Este, y se hade intitular é intitula de la Limpia Concepción y de la Anunciación de Nuestra Señora.*

(. . . it is expected that there will be discovery and settlement and in faith and testimony of the truth is consented and founded in the Valley of Estremadura Eyes of Santa Lucía, Jurisdiction of the New Kingdom of León on the twentieth of the month of September of 1596 . . .)

. . . The person of the Governor and Captain Diego de Montemayor stated: "that for the placement and congregation of the neighbors and settlers . . . indicated first a place and land for the main church which is one block from the Plaza, on the northwest side, and it should be named and titled from the Pure Conception and the Annunciation of Our Mother."

Santa Lucía

QUE BONITOS OJOS TIENES—
WHAT BEAUTIFUL EYES YOU HAVE

. . . *podemos imaginarlas tal y como las pintó Francisco de Zurbarán en el siglo XVII. Sus jóvenes mujeres, vestidas de manera espléndida, ostentan todas los símbolos de su tortura. La leyenda nos dice que Santa Lucía fue sacrificada en Siracusa cuando su pretendiente rechazado la denunció como cristiana. Acto seguido, un soldado romano le clavó la espada en la garganta. Se ve a la santa llevando sus ojos en un plato.* (Fuentes, 1992: 48)[11] (. . . we can imagine how Francisco de Zurbarán painted these women in the seventeenth century. His young women, dressed splendidly, exhibiting all the symbols of their torture. The legend tells us that Santa Lucía was sacrificed in Syracuse when her rejected suitor denounced her as a Christian. In the next moment, a Roman soldier stabbed her in the throat. She is seen carrying her eyes on a plate)

Laredo, Texas
1932

Julia Nieto Hernández often told a story to her children about Santa Lucía. There was no blood or violence in this story as in the one described by Fuentes. A soldier is walking by Santa Lucía, he notices her eyes and tells her "What beautiful eyes you have." In a wish to please him, she takes out her eyes and offers them to the soldier on a platter. At the same moment a new pair of eyes appear on her face.

The image described by Hernández is similar to the one painted by Zurbarán. There is no violence in this image, only an offering, a gift, and regeneration.

The term Ojos de Santa Lucía was not original to the founding of Monterrey. Santa Lucía is said to have been a Christian Virgin from the city of Syracuse in the fourth century A.D. In rejecting a "pagan" suitor, she gashed out her eyes with a dagger. She is one of several "Virgin Saints" that were popular in Sevilla at the time of the settlement of El Nuevo Reino.[12] The imagery produced by Los Ojos de Santa Lucía is startling. Images of this saint often portray her with eyes pierced by daggers and blood dripping down her cheeks. In other presentations, her eyes are on a plate or chalice or pierced at the end of a stock. Art historian Joanna Hecht explains that the saint is blind in many of Santa Lucía's images.

According to Hecht, the cult of Santa Lucía was not prominent in Mexico, although my conversations with *norteños* and Mexican Texans has proved to the contrary. For whatever reason, the name was on the mind of the Portuguese who established El Nuevo Reino. Even after the name was officially changed to Nuestra Señora de Monterrey, the name Santa Lucía was used in official correspondence. As late as 1601, documents from the office of the Viceroy use the name Santa Lucía in referring to the city of Monterrey.[13] The word *ojo* (eye) relates to the origin of the water source. *Ojo de agua* means "the spring" or "where the water comes from." "Santa Lucía" was a name given to the area by Alberto del Canto, in the "first" founding of Monterrey. The choice of this particular saint has some significance. In the present day, there is a popular folk legend told among many people from Mexico (and perhaps other regions of Latin America) regarding Santa Lucía. Santa Lucía is invoked when a treasured object is lost. She provides assistance in finding the lost object.

The city's choice of a patron saint who gives away her eyes betrays a desire for a "lost" history that the city may not really want to remember. This choice of Santa Lucía bears out de Certeau's thesis that history is, at times, decidedly distanced from the moment of practice (1986). Questions remain: Who does Santa Lucía represent? What do the extra set of eyes symbolize for El Nuevo Reino de León? Does her ability to locate "lost objects" designate her as a most appropriate patron for a city that chooses to lose its history, yet at sporadic moments decidedly retrieves traces of the past?

Residual History

In a conversation I had about Governor Luis Carvajal y de la Cueva, Michael Taussig, a professor of anthropology at Columbia University, said he thought that Carvajal was perhaps the only governor in New Spain who was tried by the Inquisition. (October 14, 1999, New York City)[14]

Analogy and Succession: the link between one organic structure and another can no longer, in fact, be the identity of one or several elements, but must be the identity of the relation between the elements . . . and of the functions they perform . . . (Foucault 1970: 218)

. . . the two cardinal principles of this religion (1) the notion that at the beginning, things took on their character because of marvelous events that took place in the once-for-all, and (2) living men must memorialize what happened then and somehow keeps on happening. (Taussig 1999: 177)[15]

The narrative of the death of Luis de Carvajal y de la Cueva has not been repressed, at least not in written texts. Every history of Nuevo León has a generous section on his demise. What is curious, however, is that the only statue of Carvajal is on the edge of downtown on the way to Saltillo. There is no major street named after him. Instead, the name of Diego Montemayor, the second governor of El Nuevo Reino, is all over Monterrey. There are many people in northern Mexico and in Texas that are named Montemayor. There are very few Carvajals, which is not necessarily because there were few Carvajal males to carry on the family name. In his essay on the early history of Nuevo León, Vito Alessio Robles speculates that the remaining Carvajals changed their names to avoid further problems with the Inquisition (1938). This theory was corroborated in a more recent book by Irma Salinas Rocha, in which the author writes of "certain" families in Nuevo León who changed their names in order to avoid being identified as Jewish (1970).

Carvajal's demise and Montemayor's triumph are clearly described in the popular history books as "true" factual history. Residual history lies between the narratives. It lies in the moment, as Salinas Rocha states, "[F]amilies changed their names," leaving history grasping at what the author would say next, but ultimately finding a space of nothing because Salinas Rocha says no more. She does not give names and places, only the trace of an event.

In *The Writing of History,* Michel de Certeau provides assistance to this space of nothing. Using his work, the story of Carvajal can be seen as something other than how it has been represented by *nuevolenese* historians. De Certeau proposes that writing "is illusory only insofar as, not realizing what it is doing, one takes its secret to be what it puts into language, and not what it subtracts from it" (1988: 87). History tells us of how the Spanish settled Nuevo León, yet we do not know what has been subtracted. Narratives of the Carvajals' torture surely affected Montemayor's people as they reestablished El Nuevo Reino. Perhaps the choice of Santa Lucía as a name is about what may have been occulted. A close reading of Monterrey's *cédula* provides a few indications of how the prevailing Scriptural Economy influenced Montemayor and his followers. The choice of date for the "official founding" is strikingly close to that of Rosh Hashanah. The word *limpia concepción* (pure conception) is a telling phrase for a community whose leader (and his family) were destroyed for being Jews, which means not having *limpieza de sangre* (purity of blood). Nuevo León moves forward by what is officially told in texts and *cedulas* (governmental proclamations). History book after history book on Nuevo León is full of *cédulas* gleaned out of the state archives, as if there has been a continuous need to present the "official" documents which give the official story.

Carvajal was subtracted from the history of the region and Montemayor was granted the position of founding father. Ironically, while Carvajal was the only governor in New Spain to be tried and sentenced by the Inquisition, history has saluted the man who led the Inquisition's jailors to Carvajal. De Certeau's idea of writing equating an inversion of practice can be molded within the selective narratives that represent the beginnings of the new kingdom of León.

PART TWO

LANDSCAPE AND NARRATIVE

While there cannot be an assumption that landscape creates the narrative of a place, *nuevoleneses* often say that their people were created by the land. In his sardonic story, Olivério Tijerina alludes to this belief when he tells how the Indians were ordered to stay in those "bald mountains." Tijerina questions what the Indians will do in such a desolate place now that they have been left behind.

According to popular narrative, it is the desolation that has created the industrious *norteño*. People work harder in a region that is "bald" and dry. Resources do not come easily to anyone in this place. Yet some people, such as former museum curator Amado Barrera, believe that it was actually the *norteño* that ruined the once fertile land by poor land management and sheep grazing. Others say that the tremendous water usage in Monterrey dried the remainder of the state. This argument was made about the barren land around Mina in northwest Nuevo León.

CHAPTER III

Televisa: Finding Alvarado

> . . . counteracting the crisis of legitimacy of the news was the cre-
> ation of an "authority figure," . . . The reintroduction of orality
> and gesture, the appearance of personal proximity, gave the re-
> porter the aura of an "electronic storyteller." (Carpignano et al.
> 1993: 103)

> The storytellers are "making something of" what is happening to
> them as a people, and so maintaining the place for the young people
> to come back to. (Stewart 1988: 239)

Encuentros

Encountering the fieldwork site can at moments stir passions and excitement that are not often paralleled in other phases of one's life. Feelings
of idealism and expectation can cloud one's depth of field. When I em-
barked on my fieldwork, I was not the typical young student in my
twenties encountering a native tribe that was her polar opposite. I was
returning to a place that was part of my past experience. My memories
of having been "there" were refracted through the eyes of a child. I was
twelve years old the first time I saw the Sierra Madre and visited with my
cousin on Ruperto Martínez Ote. in downtown Monterrey. However,
the numerous trips I made between the ages of twelve and twenty-one
provided me little preparation for what I was to find two decades later.

In January 1997, I visited Monterrey with the specific purpose of eval-
uating Nuevo León as a possible field site for my research. I made the
trip with a childhood friend, Heriberto Villagómez, who had relatives in

Heriberto Villagómez at El Januco. Taken when he accompanied me on my first field-site visit to Nuevo León. El Januco is an exclusive area of weekend homes for Monterrey's elite. His cousin Antonia González owns a home there. January 1997.

Photograph by the author.

Monterrey. Within a few days I was meeting with Horacio Alvarado Ortiz, a famous television personality from Nuevo León, discussing myths and traditions from northern Mexico.

Alvarado is an elite of the upper middle class of Monterrey, Nuevo León. When I first met him in 1997, he was seventy-four years of age. He inaugurated television in northern Mexico. He appeared on the first live broadcast that was made in the city. For seventeen years, he has been producing the television program *Reportajes de Alvarado,* a documentary program aired on Sunday afternoons on the Univision network. In *Reportajes,* Alvarado narrates the myth and history of Nuevo León.

He speaks with affluence and confidence. Yet while I interview him, he is helpful and provides suggestions. I am suspicious. I wonder about his narcissism. I remember unpleasant memories of working with persons in the media. I question his motives regarding the portrayal of the lower classes in Nuevo León. Yet, despite this doubt, Alvarado and I continue to engage in dialogue. This chapter attempts to portray this "cultural producer" from the perspective of his "distant relative."[1]

First Encounter

In January 1997, I find myself sitting in Alvarado's office, surrounded by old photographic cameras, movie cameras, crystals, and pyramids. The room has a high ceiling with ornate decoration. Carved in the Mexican tradition, his desk is massive. The antique bookshelf behind him once belonged to the locally famous Dr. Gonzalitos. The bookshelf holds a portrait, perhaps painted in the late nineteenth century. At first I thought he was a blue-eyed man; I later realized he has brown eyes. In seeing the painting I silently wonder if the painting is of Alvarado's father. I imagine a mythical story of this man being Alvarado's ancestor, a proper and prosperous man. After all, Alvarado eventually tells me that his father was once a military doctor who later practiced medicine in the rural area of Los Garcia. Months later I finally asked about the identity of the man in the painting. Alvarado told me that he is Dr. Gonzalitos, who lived in the last half of the nineteenth century. He was the previous owner of Alvarado's office furniture. A community near Monterrey is named after him; so is a local hospital.

Perhaps the reality of Dr. Gonzalitos not being Alvarado's father is ir-

Horacio Alvarado Ortiz sitting in his office in front of a portrait of Dr. Gonzalitos. 1997.

Photograph by the author.

relevant. Whether a genealogical ancestor or a powerful male precursor, the doctor is an antecedent of Alvarado. He appears to be a *criollo* or light-skinned *mestizo*. He is of the upper class. He is of the old world. His presence, together with the furniture from Gonzalitos's original office, are like companions to Alvarado's program. His image and his objects are the past. His portrait is present to oversee all the work of the program and to listen to conversation regarding topics, locations, attitudes, and possibilities. Alvarado contains the past within himself and his surroundings.

Inside this environment, Alvarado himself is massive, tall, and imposing. I felt like a child during my first conversation with him. Taking on the role of the pedagogue, he carefully described his work and his project, telling me a few, and only a few, bits of information about the exotic history of his region. He stresses to me his health and strength and his mission. He believes that his purpose is to search for the forgotten history and document the story for his compatriots to see and remember. He says that he wants people to know the truth. His television program, which is broadcast weekly through his native state of Nuevo León, trips over the Texas border, and gives viewers a taste of Alvarado's (and Televisa's) version of *frontera* history.[2]

My encounter with Alvarado evolved like an adventure story. I made an initial trip to northern Mexico in search of a field site that would provide information regarding the myth and folklore of the region. My initial intent was to find a semblance of the narratives I had heard from my paternal grandmother and her family in Laredo, Texas. Perhaps it was my nostalgic attempt to retrieve the comfort and location of those early visits to Laredo, where the exotic stories helped give me a sense of belonging and union with my border relatives. These memories included remembrances of wagons pulled by horses (in the 1950s); vendors selling cantaloupes; an outhouse in my maternal grandmother's backyard; my great-aunt dancing the Charleston on Christmas Eve; gladiolas on the cutting table in my great-grandmother's kitchen, which served as a workshop for the family flower shop; and, most importantly, the stories of ghosts and witches that were told in my Tía Chata's bedroom. Chata was an invalid. We would gather around her bed and listen to stories about the myth and folklore of the border region. Each trip to Laredo was like going back in time to a cocoon of identity or a book of narratives that on each journey told me more about who I am. My storyteller was Tía Chata; she would lie in her bed (she had been a blue baby whose heart was not properly formed) and weave stories about La Llorona and other ghosts that accompanied the family in their long history in Laredo. They were immediate, intimate stories. There was an aura to the circumstance, as Benjamin would say. The aura revolved around Tía Chata and my numerous cousins who crowded around the small bed in that small bedroom. There was a sense of magic, a nostalgic importance in her stories.

This experience led me into what seemed like a fairy tale of *mexicanos,* of my family as *mexicanos,* and into my own memory as a listener. As Benjamin argues in "The Storyteller" (1968), stories enter the memory of the listener and are integrated into her experience. As it was, it firmly implanted itself into my little-girl memory and became part of my own history. As a grown woman I chose to retrieve those storytelling memories and begin an attempt to understand the meaning and purpose of Tía Chata's stories, which, in essence, comprised the myth and folklore of *la frontera.*

Upon arriving in Nuevo León I searched out the small towns surrounding Monterrey. I went to various towns by the names of Linares, General Terán, China, and General Bravo. Without realizing it, I was searching for another Tía Chata. I knew that I could not find her in this short trip; eventually, though, when I did my fieldwork, I would have the time to establish a solid relationship with another Tía Chata somewhere in northern Mexico who would tell me stories in the evening and remind me of her family and the ghosts that accompanied them in their history of Nuevo León. It was as if I was searching for a pre-modern narrator: someone unable to move, lying in bed, focused solely on telling a tale of woe or tragedy, and wanting nothing else but to fill my need for a sense of history and identity. Consciously I was focusing on finding the history and identity of any other *mexicano* who had ties to south Texas, who might have had a Tía Chata who told stories in her small bedroom. My sense of the change in the structure of the *mexicano's* symbolic order influenced me to seek out the old so that it would not be lost. This quasi-rural way of living, which was enmeshed in tradition, oral folklore, and superstition, seemed to be disappearing. It felt like my initial journey to Nuevo León was an attempt to retrieve a narrative that had retreated into Mexico, away from south Texas and the rush of American technology that was quickly being embedded in every narrative and personal interaction.

It was Doña Olivia Oviedo, who owned the *molino* in General Terán, who first told me of Alvarado.[3] Without the help of a husband, Doña

Olivia had a thriving business for several decades in Terán. Her grand-daughter, my student at the University of Houston, took the role of mediator and arranged my visit. When I arrived at her home, she was prepared with a map and a short history of General Terán. She told me how she started her business, how her husband died, and how she raised her children before they all immigrated to the United States. She told me of Alvarado: "Well, there is this television program, everyone watches it on Televisa. It tells of all the stories and myths and histories of this area. The producer's name is Alvarado. He knows all about Nuevo León. You should watch the program."

Later at the dinner table at the González home, where I am staying in Monterrey, I am again reminded of Alvarado. The Gonzálezes live on the side of a mountain, El Cerro de la Silla, an area exclusive to upper-middle-class families. This particular house is made mostly of glass. They tell me, "Yes, you need to see this program with Alvarado. He tells of strange happenings and stories of how Nuevo León was founded. You would learn so much from seeing this."

The next day, my friend, Yolanda González, learns that Alvarado's son is a friend of her cousin. Ultimately, Yolanda finds Alvarado and schedules an appointment. We go together to see him. He is a gracious man. He is glad to speak to us. Introducing myself, I show him the letter from Rice University. He tells me that there is much rich history in Nuevo León. Do I know about the mystic rites of certain Indian tribes outside of Monterrey? Do I know of the violence between the men of China and General Bravo? Do I know that most of northern Mexico's families were structured as matriarchies?

This strong test of masculinity is represented in a legend Alvarado has filmed, entitled *"Los Dos Hermanos/* The Two Brothers."

Two brothers are always competing with each other, since childhood. As young men they are excellent horsemen who see themselves as courageous and powerful. They decide to test their bravery and prepare to jump, riding their horses into a ravine. Because of their determination, they both jump the ravine and are killed instantly.

As the story is told on the program, there is no analysis. The intense desire of the *norteño* to be courageous and powerful leads to his own extermination. In *Reportajes,* the *norteño* wild man is complex. He is so courageous that he kills himself to show his bravery. He comes from the barren land, *la frontera.* He has few laws; he kills easily. It was here, in this territory, with little water and limited civilization (in the words of Vas-

Yolanda González in Alvarado's office. 1998.

Photograph by the author.

concelos) that man lost his humanity. Is the *norteño* carrying the desire for other *mexicanos?* Is he expressing his wildness for men like Alvarado, who in their upper-middle-class worlds remind us how civilized they are?

As mentioned previously, Hayden White writes of the predicament of the wild man who represents repressed humanity, which has evolved because more civilized men take their needed security and peace at the expense of the man who becomes the anti-hero. Does Alvarado represent those who took the wild man's humanity?

Alvarado is the civilized man. In his office he has hundreds of books, including those of Vasconcelos. Alvarado is Benjamin's *s*toryteller personified. He becomes the monumental figure, shrinking the visitor to child-like posture. He is the superhuman hero that Bettelheim writes of in his conception of myth (1977). Alvarado is larger than life; he has constructed his office as would be expected. Evidence of his interest in film, photography, and mysticism lie about and come into the view of his visitor, who remains awed by his presence. Alvarado has an aura unto himself. He is a character, an actor, and the actual hero. He characterizes the part of the educated *norteño,* who knows the myths and has been chosen (by himself and/or the local hegemonic structure) to tell the myths and the fairy tales. The disjuncture with Benjamin comes in the filming of the story itself. The character who is Alvarado is then lost; he is an image projected onto the television screen; he has lost his vestige of humanity. He is now a myth of another sort—a ghostly apparition that is telling a concretized story. Projected through the film, he becomes immortal and takes on the mythological characteristics of Bettelheim's hero and sage.

Professor Celso Garza Guajardo, a historian at the Universidad Autónoma de Nuevo León until his death in January 2000, wrote a biography of Alvarado in which he describes Alvarado's role in the production of Nuevo León's images. During an interview with Alvarado he pays homage to the hero: ". . . your news reports have much value, because they are virtual documentaries of our culture and our history. . . . You gather the cultural way of life, a past in time and space with the people present, similar to a live inheritance that we make our own . . ." (Garza Guajardo 1993: 43).

Here Alvarado's power and influence enter the lives of the people of Nuevo León. Doña Olivia, who owns the *molino,* tells me, "You should see Alvarado's program." Doña Olivia takes her own history and narrative, a story of myth and fantasy of her town, General Terán, and gives it second importance to what Alvarado's filming has to say. It is clear that Alvarado affects how people see the concept of myth and folklore in Nuevo León. Perhaps Alvarado and Televisa are using myth as a tool for influence. Theodor Adorno, as he writes in "Odysseus or Myth and Enlightenment" (1968), believes that epic and myth have in common domination and exploitation. These are drastic terms that would appear dramatic against the study of a television program that appears innocuously on Sunday afternoons. Yet a studied analysis of *Reportajes* may yet support, at least in part, Adorno's theory.

After a summer of daily conversations, I begin to see Alvarado less as the idealized hero and more as a complex personage who contains local history. He is a hero to some, a painful reminder to others, and useless to those steeped in the capitalism of Monterrey, the industrial city.

It is August 6, the feast day of the Cristo de Tlaxcala in Bustamante, about 100 kilometers from Monterrey. We are sitting in a *panadería* (bakery) next to the main plaza. The camera crew has run after the procession with the Cristo. I make a decision to stay with Alvarado. I am tired and hot. I need to sit down. In the past weeks, he and I have taken these opportunities to talk of different issues concerning his culture and mine.

The Señoritas Rocha are sitting next to me in the bakery. It is María Rocha's birthday. They see Alvarado, but do not speak to him. I speak to them. They say that the program is very beautiful, recalls the past for them, and makes them feel good. He is the hero to them who brings relief and nurturance.

It is this sense of nostalgia that brings him into the role of hero. I discuss this idea with Professor Garza Guajardo. Asking him about the function of nostalgia, I propose that it is not thought of favorably in the postmodern era of anthropology. He replies that nostalgia is about feeling and sentiment. Garza Guajardo perceives nostalgia not as a romanticized return to the impossible past, but a return to previous relationships that harbor the history and community of the region before the change. He sees much of popular culture centering on loss, the loss of persons who immigrate to Texas with all their possessions packed in their pick-up trucks or the loss felt inside those who stayed behind. This *herida* (wound) is soothed by Alvarado's program. He documents that which is valued by the remaining few—Garza Guajardo among them. Garza Guajardo intensely explains the importance of sentiment. As he speaks, he accentuates his comments with his fist pounding the top of his desk (he does not break anything). He does not speak directly of the division between the *norteño* and the *mexicano* who has immigrated to the United States. He says there is really no border; the culture is the same. I disagree but do not tell him that the division is evident every day in every conversation I have in Nuevo León.

Yet, in spite of this division, my collaboration with Alvarado continues. We disagree on many things, but the dialogic relationship proceeds in the office, in the offices of Alvarado's colleagues, in the van on the way to film, and in the plazas waiting for the camera crew. We talk, disagree, and tell each other our perspectives. We continue despite differences.

As we speak, I see him less and less as a hero. He tells me that intelligent women in Mexico need to be silent about their knowledge. This leaves me bristled. I continue to ask him why this should be so. Why has he seen things this way? Why is he this way? This keeps me from idealizing him. He presents himself as who he is, an upper-middle-class man born in the early part of the twentieth century, educated, and accustomed to functioning with the perspective of this history. Within this perspective, he has explored his culture and society and found variances and nuances. He is accustomed to deference from most people he encounters.

The analogy of *Reportajes* with that of an epic is possible if the program is seen as a weekly installment of the story of the "hero." This hero may be Alvarado or not. Regardless of the personification, he is the representation of the *norteño* who established Nuevo León and values the region's myths and traditions. The saga that continues *cada ocho días* (every eight days) is a continuing story that gives the *norteño* viewer a small piece of information at each juncture.[4] It is long, as long as the program has aired—years, decades, as long as Alvarado continues to live and work. A concerted effort by Alvarado and those who support him commercially, the saga produces a narrative that provides capital for their efforts as well as a symbolic advantage in how it affects the attitudes and self-perception of the *norteño*.

If *Reportajes* is indeed the epic narrative that creates the culture of the state in Nuevo León, then Alvarado is Odysseus and his technicians are the oarsmen who have wax in their ears. Adorno writes that Odysseus is akin to the "prototype of the bourgeois individual" (1972: 43), a protagonist who is compelled to wander. Such is Alvarado, mythically wandering throughout the foothills and mountains of Nuevo León while searching for the "true" story. What is subsequently aired on the program provides a framework for how Nuevo León "should" be. Alvarado's presence in radio and television since their inception in northern Mexico provides him the credibility needed for this task. His influence is significant, at least with the older generation of television viewers in Nuevo León.

Perhaps Alvarado speaks the truth to me and says purely what he envisions as his agenda. This need for truth has significant power in itself. Alvarado is wandering, yet tied to the mast, unable to be swayed by the song of the sirens. Metaphorically, Alvarado is tied to the mast not by ropes but by his own conviction. He forces himself not to be swayed by the sirens, whom he sees as false influences, untruths, and misrepresentations. His technicians have wax in their ears. They work efficiently and carry out his orders with no outward resistance. He dominates them by denying them the rational basis for their labor. They only know their craft, which is making film, producing interesting images, and making sure the sound is adequate. It is Alvarado who has achieved "rational labor." He is aware not only of the technicality of producing such a film but also of the reason for his quest. In his work he produces *tekné*, technology as labor with reason. Alvarado labors to produce *Reportajes* and reasons that he is improving the life of the *norteño* by providing truth amidst falsehoods.

Close in proximity to the small towns is Monterrey, which is approximately 200 kilometers south of the Texas border. It is an industrial city that rivals many larger American cities. Numerous international corporations have offices in Monterrey, which is a place clogged with people and with pollution. The urban culture of Monterrey is in stark contrast to the surrounding towns. Yet the insecurity of the *norteño* plagues the citizens of Monterrey. Alvarado works and resides in Monterrey. In this haven of technology, Alvarado creates his television production, returning every week to film in the rural areas as he searches for the truth and past of his region. Adorno (1972), in his dark assessment of the search for the primitive, ascribes "alleged genuineness" to those who are making what they claim to be an "honest search." This particular search is for the purpose of self-advertisement. If the dark side of Alvarado is to be found, it could be as described pessimistically by Adorno: the self-advertisement of Alvarado himself, who makes money and maintains status in a capitalistic system that rewards those who reap from what is seen as primitive.

If Alvarado is searching for reality, many questions can be raised. Is the reality according to his definition, or that of Televisa? Is the reality according to the specifics of what his informants provide during his filming? Not doubting his sincerity regarding this issue, is it even possible to seek out a tangible, concrete real that will tell the true story of the mytho-history of Nuevo León? He constantly reminds me that he seeks the truth. He may be most cautious of what he terms as would-be "charlatans." He gives me strong warnings anytime he thinks I am consorting with someone who may be misrepresenting herself. He reacts this way, for instance, when we discuss the *curandera* María de Jesús Cepeda of La Petaca. "She just takes people's money," he tells me. He says he is against dishonesty, false influence, and those who would seduce the local people into believing something that is untrue.

The *ratio* in Alvarado's labor is that of the hero; his ideology is that of the man who will save the myth from falsehood and extinction. There is a paradox in the view of the hero and the myth. Adorno (1972) contends that it is the concept of rational labor, labor with a purpose or reason, that pushes the epic in its story, yet rational labor is what destroys myth. It is as if two dialectical positions face each other in the very nature of Alvarado's production. He presents myth and history in his program. He searches the small towns and foothills for unusual stories and disappearing myths. He seeks to document these narratives in his weekly program aired throughout the region. Yet, in reifying the myth by filming the narrative, he is affecting its natural circulation. His particular perspective on the myth as transmitted in the program has a certain influence, whether Alvarado's, Televisa's, or that of the program's commercial sponsor. His understanding of his "mission" destroys the myth; the myth is no longer mythological. Myth dictates how men and women should live their lives. It is now Alvarado and his sponsors that dictate how *norteño* men and women should live their lives. The myth they reify in the program becomes the book of wisdom for viewers, telling viewers who they are and where they come from. No longer simply the myth of Nuevo León, the myth now has been developed and circulated by Alvarado and Televisa.

The question remains. Is Alvarado using *Reportajes* as a vehicle for self-preservation and success; is he sincerely seeking a clear resolution to the myth of the raucous, ill-bred *norteño;* or is he working his agenda through the embedded Scriptural Economy of Nuevo León? By using the technology of this program, is he attempting to rescue the tarnished image of the *norteño?* Or is he reifying, without his conscious realization, the *norteño/as'* subaltern position within Mexican society by focusing on explanations of their myths and tradition?

Restoring Order

What society seeks through production, and overproduction, is the restoration of the real which escapes it. (Baudrillard 1988: 180)

In the daily, lived conflict between what is and what might have been if people had not lived the lives they were forced to live or chose to live, there is a double vision of two lives (caught and free, *used to* and *anymore,* the city and home) differentiated by a lived experience of loss and the dream of redemption. (Stewart 1996: 50).

There is something about Nuevo León that reminds me of Appalachia. As I travel around the countryside with Alvarado, I see few broken down trucks, but I do see the emptiness and strong contrast to the energy, movement, and affluence that is situated in Monterrey. Many of the residents of Monterrey once lived in the small towns in Nuevo León. The González family who live on the Cerro lived in General Terán. The jeweler who designed the Virgin of Guadalupe pendant I wear is from Linares; his wife, who drives a new Cadillac, is from Cadereyta Jiménez, thirty kilometers north of Monterrey. These people *dwell* in Monterrey, but their *alter* is still in the *pueblitos*. There is a companion image to their memory of the place and time they lived in before. As Kathleen Stewart writes, this memory contains "a nostalgia of being inescapably haunted by the images they dwell in. A responsibility to remember what happens, especially those things that 'try' to erase someone" (1988: 235). Among the many reasons Alvarado's program has continued for seventeen years is that it assists the *norteño* in meeting that "responsibility to remember," helping to *rescatar* (rescue) that person or culture that is slowly being erased.

Disappearance of culture propels the search for the nostalgic return to a previous moment. It is not necessarily specific to the *norteño* or persons such as Alvarado. However, the area of northern Mexico has been particularly affected by drastic environmental and cultural shifts. The Texas-Mexican border is extremely permeable. Most of the people of the small towns have moved to Monterrey or to Houston. Many families build houses in the towns and return periodically to visit. However, most of the year the houses remain crisply new, empty, and waiting to be inhabited. Other families, like Doña Olivia's, await holidays for the children to return. There has been a significant demographic shift, a diaspora of sorts. People are left alone or with part of themselves belonging to the culture on the other side of the Río Bravo.

There is ambivalence about the shame of having emerged from this thatched-roof community; yet there remains the memory of a type of Eden. The quiet of the streets and the silence of bathing in that separate room can fill a person's memory. It is not surprising that nostalgia would easily influence the *norteño* into idealizing the traditional and mythic past of his towns. Even in Monterrey, urban and urbane as it may be, most inhabitants come from these little towns that only a few years before were isolated spaces of Wild West and adobe homes.

The desire to return to the previous order may or may not be in the conscious awareness of Alvarado's purpose. Yet, even without a determined pursuit of this "state of grace," there may also be an interest on his part (or that of his sponsors) to seek nostalgic return. The order that was prominent before the rush of technology and meandering diaspora was profoundly patriarchal and reminiscent of an ancient caste system.

The Señoritas Rocha sitting in the bakery in Bustamante tell me that viewing the program is like taking an aspirin. If there is some type of wound causing pain, the program heals the wound. The music is soothing. José Cárdenas, the cameraman, films images that are later turned into soft, soothing objects that move slowly through the frame, almost suggesting a meditative state. Alvarado himself reminds me that the purpose of the program is to make everyone important, not just the elites of Nuevo León. What is immediately observable is this initial attempt at localizing and valuing everyone. The Rocha sisters attest to the program's popularity. They ask me, "Is that Horacio Alvarado? We want to meet him but he appears to be too busy." I introduce the sisters to Alvarado; they exchange a few words, but nothing more. They continue to speak to me about the program, how it affects them, and how they watch it every Sunday. It makes them feel good, they say.

Alvarado captures the sense of "evocation" described by Stephen Tyler's proposal regarding ethnography in the postmodern era (1986). Tyler's concept of evocation concerns the production of a feeling, a sense of the nostalgic, and a sensation of experience that cannot be reduced to one source. In this type of "evocation" the ethnographer attempts, albeit imperfectly, to re-create the sense of occurrence in the narrative. Alvarado's informal ethnography is non-academic; it is about popular culture and reaches the masses. Yet the program is an investigation into the culture and customs of Nuevo León. It follows a linear model, describing one occurrence after another, reactions to and consequences of the *norteño's* life. Sentiment, as Celso Garza Guajardo tells me, means the person has a connection to humanity. Without that, Garza Guajardo states, people are lost. With this sentimentality, the nostalgic is retrieved. There is a nostalgia for a metaphorical, maternal *nuevolenese,* which produces a warm nurturance that emanates from the place of origin. This is markedly relevant with respect to the predominance of diaspora as part of the *norteño* culture. In one edition of *Reportajes,* Alvarado calmly mentions that eighty percent of a community's male population has left for the United States. One could say these men left the mother/city, abandoning it because of its own inability to provide nurturance/work/income.

The sense of nostalgia is present in those who remained behind such as Garza Guajardo and Alvarado. It is also in those who have left such as my own ancestors. The nostalgia of those remaining may be for that more complete community before the abandonment. The nostalgia of the exiles is for that complete family before they abandoned their mother/region.

The viewers are seeking in Alvarado's work a sense of completeness in which no one has left and no one has been left. They seek a portrait of a complete family/culture. Alvarado promotes this search in seeking music from the nineteenth century for the program. Songs that describe pastoral scenes begin the program and thereby evoke, again, a sense of return in what appears to be a less complex and more sustainable life. Although in the north this type of language is generally located only in poetry and song, romantic and idealistic lyrics are accepted and revered.

Susan Stewart describes such nostalgia in her book *On Longing* (1993). In her study of nostalgia, she quotes Englishman Joseph Hunter from the preface of *Antiquarian Notices of Lupset, the Heath, Sharlston, and Ackton, in the County of York* (1851).

There are two sorts of countries that divide the face of the globe, new countries and old . . . I conceive it to be one of the advantages which the fortune of my birth reserved for me, that I was born in an old country . . . where . . . I find some object connected with a heart moving tale. . . .

Stewart observes, "[I]n works such as Hunter's, the antique is linked to the childhood of the nation, to the pastoral, and to the origin of narrative" (1996: 142). It is as if Hunter and Alvarado have shared conversations. I read these lines and think of the images, sounds, and gentle voices on *Reportajes*. I question myself regarding the importance of the program to the childhood of Nuevo León, the pastoral of the rural areas and the origin of the *norteños* narrative.

Alvarado, a man from the "old country" (the old Nuevo León, spending summers as a boy with his physician father in the pastoral community of Los García), has combined the need for the maternal with his own strong paternal presence. He provides soothing, motherly images and sounds and presents himself and his son Eduardo as the paternal figures explaining and protecting the region's emotional valuables. This is reminiscent of what Bill Nichols describes in *Blurred Boundaries*. He analyzes the film documentary *Dear America,* which concerns the Vietnam War, as setting "out to find voices that might heal the breach in masculinity that war has ripped asunder" (1994: 140).

Nuevo León's history of war is lengthy. The history of the city of Monterrey often begins with the great emotional trauma resulting from Mexico's loss of so much of its northern territory. This history describes the sense of loss and pain the *norteño* has experienced. The northern region, especially due to the American occupation from 1847–1849, embedded a greater hostility and ambivalence towards the "*americano*." Later came the French Occupation, the Mexican Revolution of the early twentieth century, the violent rivalries between municipalities that methodically eradicated most of the men, and lastly, the lack of industry (outside of Monterrey), which allows immigration to the United States to pull young men away from home. Alvarado lists these events for me. There is no sadness in his voice; it is a clear explanation for the matriarchy. Yet the masculine representation in the program that is rescuing Nuevo León is reminiscent of Kathleen Stewart's description of Appalachia:

> Forms of cultural agency emerge out of powerful lyric images of a world got down so that when the young people are sent off to the city with the words 'there ain't nothin' here for 'm . . .' they are sent off with the weight of the place behind them. Then the others follow their 'progress'—the drifting back and forth are not so much assimilationist as they are revivalistic. (Stewart 1996: 48)

This sense of agency is in response to those losses Alvarado presents on the program. People who have left Nuevo León tell me that the children of the *norteño* leave Mexico with heavy hearts. There is no other way. They are ambivalent. They yearn for what they might gain, yet realize their final betrayal in leaving. For those who stay behind, the progress of those who left is followed closely with yearning and envy. In early August on the feast of the Cristo de Tlaxcala, Alvarado and I stand on a street corner off of the main square of the town of Bustamante. He sees a black pick-up truck with Texas license plates; "*pasaporteados,*" he tells me.[5] His tone indicates that he has some ambivalence about seeing the Texas plates. These people have left and returned for what? For the fiesta? To show the new vehicle to their family? To flaunt their new material wealth? I sense from his tone that he sees them as traitors who have abandoned Nuevo León. Yet, despite this ambivalence, Alvarado and other *norteños* continue to follow the "progress" of these migrants.

Alvarado is conscious of the *pasaporteados'* own sense of loss and at times attempts to seduce them into wanting to return. He does this with "lyrical" scenes, music, and the constant presence of nostalgia. He is attempting to regain these "lost men for Nuevo León" who are described by Hernán Solís in *El mexicano del norte.*

Alvarado interviews men on the program who left the *frontera* to work in the United States. These men worked four or five decades and then returned to live in their original communities. Wearing cowboy hats, they sit in the plazas on park benches. He makes a point of filming them. Perhaps as an enticement to return? Or is it another way to display the eternal desire to *return?*

Alvarado's son Eduardo narrates the programs, describes the legends, and tells the viewers stories about the communities. His masculine presence, at least on film, shows a strong solidarity with his father. It provides a solution to the problem of the lost men. I recall Alvarado telling me at our first meeting of the matriarchy in northern Mexico. I ask, why a matriarchy? He responds, "[T]hrough war and immigration the women have often had to stay behind to run the farms and ranches. They have become strong women who controlled their sons very well." After speaking with Alvarado and other *norteños,* I concluded that the sense of honor instilled in the *norteño* is even more intense when it came to his mother, for whom he had to prove he was a man of honor, especially in the absence of his father. Ernesto Tijerina tells me the story of a mother in China. "Her son was accosted by a man. She was present and saw the entire incident. Thus her son tells his assailant, 'I am sorry, but I now have to kill you because my mother saw you attempt to humiliate me.' " In a paradoxical way, the mother has replaced the father for the *despadrados* (those without fathers, as Solís Garza describes). Tijerina is describing what he sees as the need to present an unquestionable masculinity to the mother. This type of compensation would be logical in a situation where, according to Alvarado, Tijerina, and Solís, the men have all left.

The matriarchy Alvarado describes does not involve the actual freedom of women. Men still continue to control the land and wealth. Sexual mores remain traditional. While women have continued to control the feelings and sentiments of their families, however, what has changed in Nuevo León in regard to gender is that women also have to be physically adept at maintaining the land and livestock. Ultimately they were still required to adhere to local standards of morality, yet the myth remains that they had control of life in rural Nuevo León.

This predominance of the matriarchy, combined with the barren quality of the land and region, has demanded the paternal presence of Alvarado and his son. These two men, appearing in the soft, maternal program that provides emotional support and nurturance to a wasteland of small towns, productively counters the feeling of loss and abandonment Nuevo León experiences due to the loss of its masculine population. Alvarado is the best male representative that the media could provide in assisting the correction of this loss.[6]

Everyone I ask in Monterrey who is over 30 years of age tells me the same thing: Alvarado was one of the most important men in the city. He was on television constantly. This response makes me reflect on how prominent he actually was; since his image was consistently broadcast into every home with a television, perhaps in a sense he was more powerful than the Alcalde of Monterrey. As Garza Guajardo describes Alvarado's work, it does appear that he was/is a hero. In this role as hero he attempts to rescue Nuevo León. The word *rescue* (*rescatar*) is expressed repeatedly in the interviews I have with Alvarado and with Garza Guajardo. They tell me that it is culture that is being rescued—old traditions, interesting stories, inexplicable events, developmental history of the region. Yet beyond this formidable production may possibly be a different type of *rescatar* (rescue). It may be, as Nichols writes, an attempt to heal the breach in masculinity in Nuevo León, which has been decimated by immigration. Perhaps Alvarado is attempting to rescue the rural culture from *matriarcado* (matriarchy). What better approach than Alvarado and his son Eduardo. It is a "restoration of the real," as Baudrillard describes, restoring the masculine order and overshadowing the matriarchal presence with the strong father and son. On a less visible scale, Alvarado's second son, Horacio Alvarado Ginesi, edits the program. The masculine presence dominates, whether visible or not.

The Technical and the Spontaneous

I am the only woman in the van. Every Thursday we meet at 8:30 A.M. to leave for a day of filming. The crew consists of Alvarado; his son Eduardo; José Cárdenas, the cameraman; Teodoro, Alvarado's valet; and a camera assistant, usually a contract worker called *el conejo* (the rabbit) by the crew (for reasons about which I'm not clear, perhaps because there are very many *conejos*). After several weeks, Alvarado tells me, "[I]t's gone really well, considering you are the only woman." Eventually I find that José Cárdenas likes to film young girls. The crew is always on the lookout for pretty girls, which they film as sequences between interviews and narratives of *leyendas*.

José, Teodoro tells me, is the best cameraman at the station. José likes

"The Simpsons" and has a teenage daughter. He speaks English and, on one trip, read one of my books, Michael Taussig's *Shamanism, Colonialism and the Wild Man*. I ask José about his work on the program. He tells me, "I watched the program for years before I had a chance to do the camera work. I like the style and jumped at the opportunity to work with Alvarado."

Sometimes I think José is reckless. Oftentimes the crew drives around the small towns with the side door to the van open as José hangs on to the side of the van with his video camera. Other times he sits with me in the back (where there are no seat belts), the door remaining open. I ask José, "Don't you think this is dangerous?" He replies, "Not really, as long as we are in town and not on a highway we are OK." At that moment we are traveling at a speed of about seventy kilometers per hour.

While the crew filmed the town's plaza, someone told them that Espinazo was divided in half. Part of the town is in the state of Nuevo León, and the other part is in the state of Coahuila. Neither of the Alvarados had known this fact before. So we drive off to find just where the place was divided. At the juncture, a man in a pick-up truck approaches us. Another man quickly joins us. They are both wearing cowboy hats. As it turns out, both are local judges of each municipality. In conversation, Eduardo is informed that the judge from Coahuila is also a musician. We are then led to his home, a run-down adobe room. On his bed is a beautiful red accordion. He was given the accordion as payment for his composition of a *corrido*. Eduardo asks the man to sing the *corrido*. The judge then sits on his fence made of *leña*, sings, and plays the guitar. His performance of the *corrido* he composed was recorded and appeared on Alvarado's program in July 1997. Afterwards, Eduardo tells me that one has to look for things, ask questions, and always keep searching.

As I witness the filming, Alvarado rests nearby. Eduardo conducts the interview. José is busy with the camera. I decide to photograph the singing judge and am faced with an interesting dilemma. The setting is picturesque, the fence of *leña*, the two room house of adobe, old plates and hubcaps strewn around. The photographs I take of the singing judge will be stereotyped versions of Mexico's Other. Predictably, when Eduardo sees the resultant photographs, he is concerned that the people at Rice University will see "that" side of Mexico. He assures me (although of course I already know) that all of Mexico is not so decrepit. Conscious of this conflict, I photograph the judge while José films the sequence. In

Alvarado's crew filming the judge from Espinazo, Nuevo León. Walking towards the camera is Alvarado's son, Eduardo Alvarado Genesi. 1997.
Photograph by the author.

these photographs the mood is changed, altered, the nostalgic view of
this man singing with his guitar and cowboy hat, is indented with the
presence of the cameraman, no longer this idyllic yet Other type of
image. The camera is simultaneously an intruder and also a signal of post-
modernity. The resultant still photographs appear less clichéd and nostalgic, but also portray an aspect of "staging." Does having the cameraman in the frame affect the perceived authenticity of the image? Does
this combination of images create a counterfeit copy of the singing
judge's narrative?

Is it possible that the program does copy/document/reify the story of
the singing judge? It brings the singer to artificial life and sets him in
miniature in the homes of the viewers watching on Sunday afternoons.
The rustic scene with which Eduardo is concerned is copied, broadcast,
archived, and viewed again by others. The adobe house, the desert-like
surroundings, and the singer's cowboy hat evoke a feeling of the past,
while the camera brings the image to the present.

Again, the word *rescatar* (rescue) comes to my mind. The rescuing of
this singer and his culture express the desire of Alvarado and his viewer

to return to the *before,* which includes the mystic and supernatural. In the desire to return to this real sense of history and place, Alvarado has created seductive copies of Nuevo León's original stories. These are significantly different from the stories told by the woman who owned the *molino* in General Terán.

Magic, iMagination, and iMage

The film with its ability to explore the optical unconscious, to come close and enlarge, to frame and to montage, creates in this juxtaposition a suffusion of mimetic magic . . . Small wonder that years later Rouch, on the basis of thirty years work in Africa, would talk of his film-making as comparable to the sorcerer's hunt for spirit doubles. (Taussig 1993: 242)[7]

Teodoro says it cannot be talked about—magic, that is. He says that people only discuss their beliefs in private. The search for the exotic in academia is now discouraged, yet public interest in magic, esoterics, and the like has intensified. On the Spanish language networks aired in Latin America and the United States, Walter Mercado, a self-proclaimed astrologer and seer, is immensely popular, appearing almost daily in his own program and as a visitor to other programs. Bookstores in Monterrey have huge esoteric sections that contain more books than any other topic. Classes in New Age doctrine are common throughout the city. There are several active sects of the Rosicrucians, the Gnostics, and a cult known as Oromu.

People don't tell each other publicly, Teodoro says, that they believe in magic. Yet the belief is intensely ingrained in the culture, whether it is a public or private matter.

I view previously broadcast programs of *Reportajes* and see repeated images of ghosts that intervene for the living, statues that move to other locations, and people who are mysteriously punished for wrongdoing. The stories are public folklore, not a genuinely personal narrative that has actually happened to anyone connected to the program or who is interviewed. They are about the unexplained past.

In seeing the stories on film, I wonder if they are shown because of audience appeal or if they truly are representative of what is of major concern to the *norteño.* Searching for the answer to this question is problematic; if the desire for the unexplained is so important to the *norteño,* does that not make him/her a person with strong involvement in superstition, an *Other,* in western terms?

In early 1997, as I drove through the *frontera* with Yolanda González who lives in the glass house, we talked constantly of unusual occurrences and strange apparitions. These were not isolated incidents. Later, as I am preparing for the writing of this section, I find a passage that reminds me of that day. Taussig quotes Alejo Carpentier on magical realism in Haiti:

> . . . finding myself in daily contact with what we could call the marvelously real . . . found at every step in the lives of those who inscribed dates in the history of the Continent and left names still borne by it . . . America is far from having exhausted its wealth of mythologies. (Carpentier 1974: 12–14)

The interface between hearing the stories of Yolanda González and seeing *leyendas* presented by Alvarado is reminiscent of what Taussig calls "nonsynchronous contradiction," which "comes to life where qualitative changes in a society's mode of production animate images of the past in hope of a better future" (1993: 166).[8] Alvarado produces magical images of the past, perhaps hoping that the future will bring resolution to the disjointed story of the *norteño.* I remain intrigued and perhaps a bit confused. At one level, Alvarado's search for a better future suggests his nostalgic past was lacking in something. The conversations of Garza Guajardo, Alvarado, and Solís explain the composition of "a better future." It is a future where the history (as they present it) of the region is maintained as important. Their repeated use of the word *rescatar* is evidence of this position. It is also where old traditions are still maintained and honored. The continuous filming (and airing) of "old" or "lost" traditions serve as a constant reinforcement against "loss." Nuevo León with a "better future" is a place where those who have left return and stay. Garza Guajardo was emphatic about this when he pounded his desk with his fist as I asked him questions about the people of the north. Solís Garza is a psychiatrist who is concerned with the mental health of *nuevoleneses.* His interest in abandonment is clinical, yet his description of the "lost fathers" is accurate. Numerous families that I spoke with told me of their men leaving for Texas. This included Yolanda González's father, and uncle, and most of the Vásquezes in Potrero. Whether they leave illegally or immigrate to study in the United States, the movement north is constant. The phone call I received from Ana Sáenz one night at 11:00 P.M. in which she asked if she could come to live with me in Houston in order to study English is further evidence of this movement. It is not only the "better future" that consists of subsequent generations that leave their children behind creating more generations of *despadrados.* It is also the children who leave the parents behind, as in the case of Ana Sáenz or Olivia Oviedo.

Alvarado works with the *norteño* personality who believes in myth and magic. He realizes that there is an intense need to revitalize and circulate the myth of magical realism. For the *norteño* it is not a trite, New Age story. It is an inherent aspect of his/her history. During the colonial period, as today, the church actively discouraged esoteric practices. Yet the settlers not only found the use of magic in the indigenous population but also brought their own beliefs in the occult from Spain. As in other historical narratives, local historians focus on indigenous magic, yet there is ample textual evidence of these types of practices on the Iberian peninsula (Carola Baroja 1996). From my conversations with persons from northern and southern Mexico, I found that interest in the occult is similarly intense in both regions. The polemic between the two regions lies in the "descriptors" of each other's beliefs in magic. People from the north say that the southerners are most interested in magic due to a larger indigenous population. People from the south say that the northerners are more superstitious due to their lack of sophistication.

The need for secrecy is a complication. It is not a story that is told openly and readily in public. There is a sense of propriety associated with the theme. People discuss their ideas and interest regarding the myths in private conversations that occur in small bedrooms among friends and family. Beyond the sphere of the private there is little communication regarding personal views towards myth and superstition. Among individuals who are economically affluent there is a greater need for secrecy. There is a dual expectation regarding the occult. Private interest and involvement is acceptable as long as it does not become public. Thus Alvarado denied learning of magic from his own family, publicly saying his current involvement is only with *Reiki,* a Tibetan form of curing. He does not deal with *curanderas* or *brujas.* However, it is possible to imagine that Alvarado is aware of the public's desire for communication about this hidden subject. His open discussion and representation of the mythic aspect of the *norteño* is welcomed. It is a public display that does not threaten the personal. It also breaks the chain of communication between the individual *norteño* who discusses his/her ideas regarding magical realism with an intimate relation. The television production itself creates a rhizome, to use Deleuze's term, that spins off and away from the natural chain of discussion among *norteños*. Alvarado's television stories create spirals that change form and direction. What is made tangible in one sequence of *Reportajes* may evolve into numerous side stories, all related to Alvarado's original narrative, but inherently different.

Some years ago, Alvarado filmed a program about a bird man who lived on the side of the Cerro de la Silla. People, including one of my University of Houston students who was spending the summer in Monterrey at the time, tell me that Alvarado had the entire city in hysterics for fear that the bird man would suddenly appear.

There is another story related to a pair of statues in Alvarado's office. The statues are about 18 inches high. One is of St. Francis, and the other appears to be of the Virgin. They seem to be made of concrete and are rather worn. I observed them for the entire summer and did not realize that they belonged to a legend that I had found in Alvarado's notes:

> There was a man who had a beautiful daughter. She wanted to marry a young man, but the father was against the marriage. Because of this the father did not let her leave the house. He had two statues made, which were put at the door of her house. He said that the statues would not allow her outside. She soon died of a broken heart. Later, at her grave, the statues mysteriously appeared outside her tomb, continuing to stand guard as her father requested.

I wonder how the statues came to Alvarado's office. He tells me he bought them from someone in the town where the legend occurred. I wonder if they might have been stolen. A few days after I learn of their origin, they become just more artifacts that he has displayed. The constant reminder of the story which faces me while I see the statues every day becomes so quotidian that the story is also less dramatic, less intense, with each passing day.

It is as if the idea of magic and the irrational becomes "everyday." It becomes part of the quotidian language, the mundane thought. Of course the movement of the statues to the grave site of the girl in the legend was indeed mysterious. Being with them constantly, however, I find they begin to lose their aura. Their appearance is not so unusual or surprising. Their presence in Alvarado's office becomes part of my daily routine.

Half of the *mercado* (public market) in Monterrey is now *yerberías* (herb stores). It was not this way twenty-five years ago. These stores sell amulets, candles, potions, statues of saints, and prayer cards of folk saints. There is a new intensity and openness about these beliefs that had already been so prominent in the region. As in the United States, many people I have spoken with say that the surge in interest is related to the fear of the new millennium. Latin American novels written in the mode of magical realism have indeed represented what some *norteños* see as an integral part of their life. The belief in spirits, Divine Providence, magic, and myth appeared most important as I lived among Alvarado and other *norteños*. While it often appears that women are the most interested in these practices, I found in my meetings with several *curanderas* and *curanderos* that both men and women used their services in almost equal number. It would not be appropriate to say that this interest in the occult is an important aspect of the Mexican national character. What can be said in the form of a generalization, however, is that these issues are not part of the discourse of governmental and official culture at the national and international levels. They are, though, a part of everyday culture that transcends all economic levels.

I ask Alvarado if he knows of these things from his family. He said he does not, but he has seen so many things in his career in television that he developed an interest in the esoteric. Indeed, for a time, there was a pyramid in the logo of his program. He even explained the use of pendulums to his viewers, saying that they could be used as tools for divination by observing the direction of their swing. While I am in Monterrey he gives me daily classes on esoteric thought. However, he constantly states that he is not teaching me *brujería* (witchcraft). Instead, he is giving me lessons of what he has learned regarding Eastern ideas of healing and energy. He does not describe himself as a *curandero* (healer). Yet his television program has a strong emphasis on the supernatural, the non-rational. Eduardo tells me that what is not logical is central to the program. Everyone prefers this content—the viewers as well as Eduardo and José.

On several occasions, Alvarado asked me to watch a video of a *leyenda* or to talk to him about a particular subject. One *leyenda* that he specifically wanted me to view was *La leyenda del espejo* (*The Legend of the Mirror*), which is a story that took place during the Mexican Revolution in the town of Marín:

A woman is at her mirror combing her hair. The reflection, however, does not show her face; instead, it presents an image of her husband lying mortally wounded. The woman panics. She runs to the church to tell the *sacerdote* (priest). He tells her that she is wrong; there has been no news of an ambush. By the next day she learns that her husband was killed by federales while he was transporting arms to the rebels. The location she saw in the mirror was indeed the spot where her husband had been killed.

This legend is specifically important to Alvarado. He asks me to see it in the editing room. A colleague of his played the part of the aggrieved widow. She dressed in period costume and proceeded to re-enact the story of the woman's discovery. I can only guess why Alvarado senses the importance of this vignette. Perhaps he is confident of his choice in filming such a story and is proud of how he collected the various persons and objects necessary for what he perceives to be an accurate representation.

Beyond these elements, there may be another way of understanding the story of the mirror. There is a symbolism in the woman seeing the vision. This *norteña* woman, with the special gift, the *don,* sees her husband's image in an otherwise everyday household object. Perhaps she symbolizes that *norteña* woman who has the power to see beyond the ordinary, knowing of special occurrences and important losses before the average mortal man would be aware of them. The story also gives an indication of how the church is seen in the north. The woman runs to the priest, who negates her ability to see.

This story may be a link to the turbulent nature of the *norteño* belief in mysticism. Alvarado's valet, Teodoro, tells me, "There is a strong belief in the supernatural." Repeated encounters that I have with persons from Monterrey are in accord with Teodoro's statement. There is strong belief in the idea of spirits, visions, and black and white magic. It is known that this knowledge can alter a person's life in love, work, and health.

The *leyenda* of the mirror is perhaps an attempt to locate this knowledge in a space that does not devalue or make vulnerable the *norteño*. It acknowledges women's superior abilities in this regard, showing their concern for family, yet does not totally locate the *norteño* in the space of the uncivilized or barbaric.

Alvarado tells me that he does not deal with magic. Yet he is a healer; he is trained in the healing technique of Reiki. He does not cure others, only himself. He says he is not skilled enough to work on another person. As he explains the issues of energy and the strength of one's thoughts, he continues to emphasize that he does not work with magic. I tell him that it does not matter to me, because I take issues of magic seriously. He continues to say that most Mexican *curanderos* are charlatans, reminding me again of our first conversation, eight months before, in which he told me of the *curandera* María de Jesús Cepeda in the *ejido* of La Petaca.

Alvarado does not speak of spirits directly. However, the issue of spirits is accentuated in the *leyenda;* indeed it was the spirit of the murdered man that provoked the scene in the mirror. Alvarado does not involve himself with spirits, but the television program does.

I ask myself how this issue of magic, spirits, and energies enters into the study of *Reportajes.* I recall how I began my search for a fieldwork site. I was interested in seeking out a community that is known for its healers/*curanderas.* Because of many persons actively guiding me to Alvarado, I shifted from individual *curanderas* to a program that in certain ways "manipulates spirits." It is similar to my searching for another individual storyteller. I was looking for a personification of my Tía Chata and found a television program. In my search for a *curandero,* I actually found one, yet he is a post-modern *curandero* who says he does not practice magic but deals in energies, pendulums, and healing. It was fitting that I find Alvarado; it suits the time, the very late twentieth century. He is a global healer, integrating eastern thought with Western esoteric practice. He also removes himself from any indigenous interpretations such as those of *curanderas* and *brujas.*

Despite his distancing from this magic through its representation in his program, he also perpetuates it. He transforms the teachings of the *curanderas* and puts these musings on film that are broadcast *"cada ocho días,"* as he said once on a program. The *leyenda* of the mirror becomes part of the epic of magic, nostalgia, and someone's history. The *curandera/o* becomes Alvarado, who injects much of his esoteric knowledge into his filming in his stories of spirits, ghosts, and tragedy.

The program constantly reminds the viewer of "spirits." It recalls the past, reenacts stories and incidents, pushes nostalgia into our vision. Although Alvarado is the producer of the program and appears in every sequence, he can also disassociate himself from his own filming. It is perhaps because this filming is a copy of mythic representations. It is a material thing, separate from the person of Alvarado himself; it stands independent of Alvarado as creator. Although he is active within the images himself, he is also separate. The program is filmed, edited, and disseminated through Nuevo León and now throughout Mexico and parts of the United States. It travels without him. Each viewer sees these representations from his/her own reflections and draws his/her own conclusions.

The program takes the spirit of the *leyenda* in the mirror and presents it to viewers who may be affected by its representation of the *norteña*. The viewer may reminisce about stories heard at home (similar to my experience), become further convinced of the mysticism and primitive quality of *mexicano* thought, or may see the program as an exotic way to hold the viewer's attention. Regardless of the interpretation, the *leyenda* will be interpreted, and it will be remembered.

Authenticity

Espinazo is a very dry town located at the western edge of Nuevo León. In late June we arrive and see a large sign announcing the place and its significance. Espinazo is where the folk saint El Niño Fidencio lived.

Alvarado tells me that the city government of Espinazo charges people to enter the municipality during the feast days of August and October. The near deserted town swells to the thousands. People come from all over northern Mexico and south Texas. He tells me that it is mostly "Chicanos" (Mexican Americans) that believe in this folk saint and he points to a shrine that was built from the donations of a grateful follower from the Texas border. As the crew walks through the city, we meet a "Chicano" from Amarillo, Texas. He is living in Espinazo paying a *manda,* thanksgiving, to El Niño Fidencio for granting a request. The man speaks English and asks us what we are doing there.

We walk toward the main plaza and see a pond that has concrete borders. Alvarado tells me that El Niño Fidencio heals people in the water. We walk into the shrine and are confronted by a woman in her 50s or 60s. She is dressed in a thin cotton house dress. She asks Alvarado if he has asked permission to film inside the shrine. He tells her he does not need permission. She is outraged and tells him that all the other television stations ask permission. He also becomes angry and tells her that the "whole group of Fidencistas are a bunch of charlatans, taking money from innocent people who are seeking assistance."

Alvarado tells me that several Germans discovered Fidencio and organized a following for him, making great quantities of money for themselves. I hear this aspect of the story yet see the numerous mementos of healing and history. Yes, Fidencio was androgynous. I see his "dresses" encased in glass along the side of the shrine. I see the "tumors" that were taken from his followers who were ill. I see photographs of those who believed he helped them.

Alvarado knows that many things have happened in the seventy-year history of Fidencio's presence. He also knows that many people have found support and assistance. Among the small group at the shrine, Alvarado tells the woman that he believes people have been robbed and maligned. Yet, once he is filming, what he says is different. He presents total respect and acknowledgment of the phenomenon of Fidencio. The woman is calmed by Eduardo. We leave the shrine after making peace with Fidencio's followers whom Alvarado had confronted earlier.

Perhaps there is truth in both stories. There was a German. There was probably much money to be made, at least from the religious tokens that are sold outside of the shrine. For that matter, Televisa is making money from this filming. Everyone benefits. Fidencio gives something to his followers, the followers give to the Fidencistas (those who practice his teachings), and those who watch the television program buy the products that are advertised during the commercial breaks. There is a circularity to this commodification of El Niño Fidencio. Even I benefit—I gather material, record the conversations, take photographs, and write an essay regarding this encounter.

The filming of the program allows Fidencio to remain sacred. His mystical narrative is left intact. Alvarado was able to state his perceptions to those at the shrine, yet the program's content does not question Fidencio's authenticity. It does not matter that Alvarado argues with the shrine's caretakers. It does not matter if he believes that people in Espinazo stole money from visiting "Chicanos." These encounters do not appear in the film. Instead, Fidencio's myth is presented in a form that will perpetuate its power. That is Alvarado's task—not the representation of his own reality but the reality he believes needs to be represented.

Representation

Alvarado says that he is seeking to save the culture, the history. He tells me of how he was filming near the town of Zua Zua, north of Monterrey, when he found the ruins of an hacienda in a pasture. By investigation he found that La Hacienda de San Pedro, which is from the early seventeenth century, is the oldest structure from the time of colonization. Through the efforts of Alvarado, the hacienda was restored and made into an educational center. The stories and legends of the rural areas surrounding Nuevo León are like San Pedro, falling into ruins amid pastures. Alvarado tells me of the differences between high and low culture. There is little high culture in Nuevo León outside downtown Monterrey or the richer suburbs. I am reminded of Mexican intellectual José Vasconcelos's negative comments about *carne asada* (barbecue). Varying interpretations generally center on the lack of sophistication in the food of the *norteño: carne asada* is cooked on an outside grill or pit and is thus a referent to a more primitive or pre-civilized way of life. Such interpretations make me wonder about what Alvarado does not say. Is restoring La Hacienda de San Pedro in Nuevo León a restoration of the colonial order and therefore a way to bring culture back to *la frontera?* Will this rescue or redeem the *norteño* from final condemnation as a brute and a *matón?*

As I told Garza Guajardo, this notion of rescue/redemption is problematic in the "eyes" of current social theory because of redemption's intricate relationship with nostalgia and romance. Yet Garza Guajardo defends the notion, telling me that nostalgia and romance are inherently connected to feeling and human desire. There is an aspect of this declamation that may be noteworthy. It is the American way that denounces romanticism and nostalgia; they are seen as emotional, unrealistic, cliché, and child-like. These perspectives are placed in the subjective realm of the desire to have what is impossible. They are counter to the First World valuation of reason and logic in which emotions and desire are judged secondary to progressive enhancement of a capitalistic economy.

However, the culture of the *norteño* finds romance and nostalgia as a basic characteristic that should not be devalued or eliminated. They are to be enjoyed. Perhaps this form of low culture is Alvarado's ambivalent way of separating himself from the masses who view his program. Yet this ambivalence is intense. As intently as he separates himself from the masses, when he talks to me of *educación, cultura y presencia,* he also seeks and enjoys the adventure and connection to the Other. Through his program, he becomes both subject and object. As an upper-middle-class, white son of a doctor, he is the subject who is not to be mistaken for the devalued Other. He is also the object, the person being filmed, for although he is tall and fair, he is still a *norteño* who comes from a time when romance and rural tradition were valued. He is also from Mexico, a Third World country. It is not my task to judge the value of his work, for an attempt at placing value on his program would be as if I were to assess a language I do not know. For although I am a "distant relative," as my father was born a *norteño*, I do not know the intricacies and meanings of each sign and movement made by Alvarado and his program.

Finally, what he tells me is that he wants to save something—the culture, the history, the importance of certain people. Perhaps this leaves the destructive, older order in place. He may have a plan, a *ratio*, a method to his work. Yet at the same time, the thousands of people who see the program every Sunday also voted for the new order, the Partido Acción Nacional (PAN, the new political party that has recently taken over government in Nuevo León). Alvarado's attempt to rescue/redeem culture and history continues to happen as something else disappears with the Partido Revolucionario Institucional (PRI, the old political machine). Alvarado was allied with the PRI. He had been promised unlimited funding for his program and other projects should the PRI candidate win the election. Instead, the PAN won and Alvarado is now forced to find other ways of surviving. This seems assured as long as he is alive, for Nuevo León sees him as the narrator/hero who tells the legends more completely than the individual storyteller remaining in General Terán, Zua Zua, or Marín.

CHAPTER IV

Spaces In-between

It was November 1997. I returned to Monterrey after an absence of two months. The work with Alvarado was continuing. However, it seemed necessary to study how the history and narratives were told by people outside the realm of the media. Alvarado had been a most excellent guide. I learned the topography of northern Nuevo León. He taught me well. I learned of the social intricacies among colleagues and business and political acquaintances. I learned of what Alvarado wanted the people in Nuevo León to see. The pastoral history that continued to live in many ways in the rural areas and in the memories of *regiomontanos* who lived in Monterrey was accentuated by Alvarado's project. It was a knowledge I acquired about a certain level of representation, public knowledge, and cultural production. I did not know what was false. I was not sure Alvarado would tell me.

I continued to take note of practices regarding institutional religion and folk religion. It had seemed to me that because divine images appeared so central to so much of everyday life in Nuevo León (as in most of Latin America), a key to understanding the region was to study the concept of God, the Virgin Mary, the church, and all the peripheral aspects of believing. What I had found thus far was that folk religion was deeply conflated with and was perhaps more significant than church belief. There is more devotion practiced in family homes than in parish churches. A pantheon of saints is available for most every need and occasion.[1]

One of the most striking experiences I had was with a group of Dominican nuns whom I met in Mina, Nuevo León. From our conversations, I learned a great deal about how people saw the clergy and about the remnants of what the nuns called "the persecution," which occurred in two periods of Mexican history (during the French Intervention 1860–1865 and the Mexican Revolution 1910–1920).

Although this moment in my fieldwork could easily be seen as an unnecessary digression, I still believe that my work with the nuns in Mina was necessary to my project. The complex issues of authority, control, national and regional identity, and the ambivalent relationship between the church and "the people" became more palpable as I made my trips to the monastery. These issues were evident from my first visit, when I found the nuns living in poverty, to recent events regarding the completed construction of a lavish monastery and the nuns' comfortable lifestyle (with a cellular phone) in the deserts of Mina. The nuns, who were from southern Mexico, told me how they saw *norteños*. They described the official position of the church and its missionary challenge in the north. The position of this particular group of nuns in Nuevo León was indicative of how money, gender, and obedience factored into the world of the *nuevoleneses*. When I first met them, their poverty indicated their lowly position and lack of support within the Mexican church hierarchy. After several years of struggling, the support they received from private sources became significant. Their relationship to this support was questioned and their ultimate success was criticized, yet they completed their mission. Their monastery was built. The first and most important phase of their work was accomplished. The monastery is a symbol of "the lack" of orthodox spirituality in the north. While the conversations with the nuns never directly dealt with the lost histories of the indigenous and the unsubstantiated narratives of *nuevoleneses*' Jewish origin, the nuns represented the presence of the official word, the formal authority of the church in the most traditional way. Although talk of *gente bárbara* (barbaric people) only appeared occasionally in our conversations, the entire existence of the convent belied the barbaric nature of the environment, the desert-like area of Mina, Nuevo León.

Filming the Convent

I made a brief trip during the Thanksgiving break. It was cold in Nuevo León at that time. I arrived in time to accompany Alvarado and the crew to their next filming. We were to visit a convent in Mina, which was an hour's drive northwest of Monterrey.

Alvarado explained to me that he had been told that a group of nuns were establishing a convent and were building a monastery in Mina. They needed donations and he thought it would be an interesting sequence in his television program. The day of filming was not very different from many others. We left at about 9:00 A.M. The group consisted of Alvarado, José Cárdenas, Teodoro, the *conejo,* and myself. The landscape was not appealing. We went through the neighborhoods of General Escobedo. The city is divided between numerous industrial complexes and subdivisions for the working poor. We passed a market that was a series of makeshift shanties lining both sides of the highway. Plants, pots, statues, and food were sold at this market. The same items were sold at other markets near Monterrey, but at the market of Escobedo, as people called it, the prices were much lower because of the location. We drove past a series of factories that had the most terribly rancid smell I had ever experienced. They were processing plants for the production of dog food. At one point we also passed a motel that seemed to be in the middle of nowhere.[2]

About half an hour after we passed the roadside motel, we arrived in Mina. It had sloping hills on the right side of the highway. Everything was extremely dry. It had no trace of affluence, at least from what I saw when we arrived. As we entered into town, we slowed down to look for a blue sign that said *Monasterio* (Monastery). There did not appear to be a road, only a driveway that was not paved. We turned to the right and proceeded over a path that would have normally required a sports utility vehicle. There were deep ruts in the road, large rocks, and overgrown brush on the sides. After a couple of minutes we approached a three-story building under construction. It was towards the left. We went into another "driveway" that did not look like a driveway and drove to a small ramshackle house. The nuns seemed as if they were expecting us. I knew, though, they were not, because Alvarado never liked to let people know he was coming. He said it made people too nervous.

We entered the house through a screen door. On the left wall was a mural painted with life-size images of St. Joseph and the Virgin Mary. There was an older nun sitting next to the wall, wearing a traditional habit of a white robe and black headdress. She appeared to be about sixty. There were six other nuns present. As we walked in, a touch of nostalgia pulled at me. As a child, I had attended a Catholic school staffed by Dominican nuns. Seeing the nuns from Mina in their pre-Vatican II traditional "habits" was like returning to the past.

The architect who designed the monastery was also present. We all sat in a large room that held several kitchen tables placed together. The architect explained to Alvarado the construction of the monastery. It was very large and would contain numerous single rooms so that people from other areas could come and pray without distraction.

Although they told us they were a cloistered order, they said they could have contact with people while the monastery was still being built. With this encouragement, I began a conversation with several of them and learned that the youngest one (in the all-white habit of the novitiate) was only seventeen. She was from the village of Espinazo.[3] I photographed the young woman and another nun who said she was originally from Guadalajara and that her name had been González. The conversation with Alvarado was expectedly superficial. He captured on film how they had arrived, their purpose, and their hopes.

The Mother Superior told us that the Archbishop had requested that the group establish a convent in northern Mexico because the "north" needed more direction from the church. The families, who had been isolated in the mountain villages, had developed practices that were openly contrary to the teachings of the church. There had been stories circulating for many years about the "depravity" in some of the villages in the mountains. One of the nuns told us that "all sorts of things happen there." Actually I had also heard about "strange things" from other people in Nuevo León. There were stories circulating about magic, witchcraft, incest, and bestiality. At least one story of this type was actually substantiated by historian Cristóbal López.[4] Religious doctrine was not incorporated into the life of the people as it was in other regions of Mexico. The nuns, in a sense, had come as missionaries, hoping to convert the people of Mina to a more traditional Catholicism.

The nuns said they had no income. Everything was from donations. They did not say they had financial backing from the church. However, they would pray for people who requested prayers. Many people offered money for these prayers, as a donation for the miracle they expected to happen after the nuns prayed for them. They made church vestments for priests and small religious articles, which they sold along with inexpensive plastic rosaries. They sold religious articles for about ten pesos each. They would cut a picture of St. Jude and cover it with a plastic oval and seal the back with glue. The oval was edged in lace. I bought one for my mother, and now, two years later, she still has it next to her bed.

Their poverty was striking. They gave us a tour of the convent, which was seemingly a house that had been put together room by room; the

Young novice from Espinazo outside the convent of
the Dominican nuns in Mina, Nuevo León. 1997.
Photograph by the author.

floors were uneven, and there were drafts everywhere. Interior walls had
not been finished, and the house had no heat.

Missed Representations

Two hours later we found ourselves sitting at a table that seated fourteen.
It was no longer the mismatched kitchen tables of the convent. We were
in a dining room of what appeared to be a museum. Four servants moved
briskly, bringing us so many different dishes we knew we could not eat

everything. The silverware was elegant, and there were crystal goblets at the table. I was uncomfortable and cannot imagine what Teodoro was thinking at the time, since he grew up in a ranch in southern Mexico where there was no running water or other similar conveniences. Our hostess was Ernestina Lozano, the director of the Museo de Antropología Bernabé de las Casas in Mina.

Earlier in the afternoon, as we were walking through the property next door to the convent, Lozano drove up in her new Chevrolet Suburban with two young women accompanying her. She described to Alvarado a vegetable garden tended by local residents. There was an empty swimming pool on the property. It was rather large and had shower rooms and a type of patio that was also no longer used. She then had us follow her to downtown Mina, which was about three kilometers away. We were led into the Museum. It had a number of skeletons of prehistoric animals, a few indigenous artifacts, and a room dedicated solely to El Niño Fidencio. Upon leaving the museum, we were given directions to a location a few blocks away. We were led to what appeared to be a bakery full of women who were standing by a large table working with bread dough. They were all wearing identical hats and aprons. Ernestina told Alvarado that she had created an organization that produced bread and provided those involved with a small income.

We were then invited to dinner in the place that appeared to be a museum but was actually a house belonging to Lozano and her husband. The house was so elegant and extravagantly decorated with scores of antiques that José, Teodoro, and I thought that maybe Lozano actually did not reside in the place. The director and her husband, who looked about ninety years old and was in a wheelchair, entertained us. Alvarado did most of the talking. We were served *cabrito* (baby goat), which I could not eat.

It all felt rather odd to me. On the many trips I had taken with Alvarado and the film crew, we had never been treated so lavishly. I was uncomfortable with the servants standing by our table to wait for our requests. Ironically, after the meal, Teodoro and I found that there was no clean bathroom for us to use. Before we began our trip home, the crew and I had to go one by one into an abandoned bathroom at the back of the house with no toilet paper, soap, or towels. While most of us were dealing with our adventure with the bathroom, Alvarado was having a discussion with the museum director about his allocation of film time for her museum and civic project. Lozano had complained to him that he had spent too much time with the nuns and not enough time with her. The conversation became tense as Lozano became angry with Alvarado for his "slighting" of her projects. Two weeks later, I learned that her husband died only a few days after our visit.

The Convent Next to the Hill Where the Witches Danced

My initial conversation with the nuns was so interesting that I made several subsequent visits. I first returned with Yolanda González. I had been staying with her family during my trips to Monterrey. They were the family that lived on El Cerro de la Silla. Yolanda and I visited for a few minutes, having arrived at the wrong time. The nuns had posted the times they could have visitors, but since they had no telephone, I was not able to verify the schedule. They greeted us warmly. We talked mostly with Sor Carina (the Mother Superior) and another nun, Sor Martha, about general things. The conversation drifted to how they would pray for people and for the prayers they were paid money.

A few days later, I returned with my cousin Citlalli and her friend Emma.[5] Both professional women, they seemed to view the nuns with disdain. Emma is an expert at embroidery; in fact, she has started her own small company that produces embroidered articles. The two women thought that the work by the nuns was poorly done. All the way back they compared them to a group of nuns in Monterrey who also sell embroidered goods. To Citlalli and Emma, the nuns in Mina were no match when compared to the outgoing and assertive nuns in Monterrey.

Perhaps what seemed to surprise me most was the attitude that people from Nuevo León had toward the nuns. I returned to Monterrey from each of my visits full of excitement, having enjoyed our conversations and learned about "cloistered" life. When I would tell someone about the nuns, I would get responses like "You know, nuns come from wealthy families, they have never known poverty," or "the church has a great deal of money, the nuns don't need anything from us."

There was a significant difference in the responses I heard from people in Texas, including relatives of the same *nuevoleneses* who had voiced their dislike for the clergy. People in Texas were very interested in the convent, the proposed monastery, and how the nuns prayed for people. When I would return to Texas, people would give me food and household supplies for the nuns. They also sent small amounts of money, asking the nuns to pray for them. When I discussed these different reactions with the nuns, they told me it was related to *la persecución* (the persecution).[6]

It was then that I remembered my father telling me many years before that priests were not allowed to use their clerical collars in Mexico. His best friend, a Basilian priest named Jack Broussard, had lived in Mexico City for a number of years. Every time my father and I talked about his friend, Father Jack, he reminded me that Jack could not openly be a priest in Mexican society. This experience, and a memory of seeing a "hidden" convent in Puebla in southern Mexico in 1972, brought to mind that there had been some type of radical exclusion of church society in the recent past. As I spent more time in Nuevo León, I found a significant distance between the church and the people, which partly had to do with *la persecución* and partly with a centuries-old resistance to church control.

The comments about "wealthy" nuns related to the assumption that the church has a considerable amount of money and that the clergy live lavishly among the poor.[7] Although there were moments when local churches were filled, more often than not, most people did not go to mass.[8] In addition, the number of Protestant groups is growing so rapidly that the church is worried. I did not ask Sor Carina and Sor Marta, but I now wonder if the placement of their monastery was also an effort to combat the presence of these "new sects," as the Protestant congregations were often called.[9]

Although this local ambivalence finally determined my distancing from the Dominican nuns in Mina, I continued to remain in close contact with them for several months. While in Houston, I would write to them. As soon as I arrived in Monterrey, I would go see them. Part of my impetus in getting to know them was nostalgia for my childhood, though this motive was not my only one. I sensed that the nuns knew something. I did not know exactly what it was. It was about the workings of the church, the role of women in the Mexican world, the role of the spiritual in the minds of the clergy. By talking to them as much as possible, I hoped that I would come away with a sense of some of these issues.

On one occasion in January 1998, I brought my wool blanket and spent the night. It was about -2° Celsius and the convent had no heaters. Having argued with my cousin in Monterrey before I left the city, I drove to Mina in the dark; not surprisingly, I got lost on the way somewhere in the suburb of General Escobedo. Somehow in the dark and cold I finally made my way to Mina. The nuns were singing in their chapel when I arrived. I walked in and knelt at a bench and one of them gave me a hymnal. I was so stressed from the argument with my cousin and from getting lost that I began crying. They continued to sing, gave me Kleenex, and did not say anything to me. After prayers we had a dinner of corn tortillas and beans. They had a small bit of chicken, just enough for each one to have about half a portion. We spoke briefly about what they were doing, their aspirations, and their problems living in Mina. During this and other visits we discussed their initial intent to settle near Monterrey. Their motherhouse was in Morelia in southern Mexico. During the visits I made to the convent, I had ongoing conversations with Sor Marta, a nun who looked to be in her late forties. She was very engaging. Once she told me that she knew she was not pretty; however, that was not the reason she did not marry. During another of my visits, she also told me a frightening story of how she and another sister went to the city to solicit donations. A woman who befriended them gave them a room. They were sleeping in two small beds and during the night the other nun became frightened and asked Sor Marta to sleep with her. A short while later, in the middle of the night, Sor Marta's bed opened up from below. There was a mechanical device under the floor that moved the bed, creating a large space that forced the person asleep to fall into the basement. The two women rapidly ran out of the house into the dark. The next morning they were told the place was a house of prostitution. As Sor Marta told me the story, she began to cry.

My conversations with Sor Marta continued. We used to talk of going on walks when there would be time. There was a foothill next to the convent. We never were able to walk up the hill, because every time I visited, the nuns were extremely busy with their daily tasks. The walk up the hill became a symbol of our friendship. Later, when I no longer returned to the convent, Sor Marta wrote to me and said she hoped I would return so we could finally go on our walk.

In one of the last conversations I had with Sor Marta, she told me a story of a group of women who used to gather across the hill, on nights of the full moon. They were said to be witches. According to local people, they would cry and howl in the night. Since the nuns arrived from southern Mexico, the other women no longer meet across the hill when there is a full moon. Perhaps they have moved to another site. Perhaps they disbanded.

The image of the witches stayed with me for some time. It was a conflation of imaginaries, since both groups of women sang simultaneously; the witches sang at the full moon, and the nuns sang their ancient chants at dawn and at dusk. When *norteños* talk of folklore, there is often speculation whether a witch practices white magic or black magic. Sor Marta could not tell me more about the witches except that they howled in the night. There is no way of telling if the women singing on the hill work for evil or work for good. What appeared most salient, however, was that both groups of women used the power of the spiritual in a strategic way.

The last time I saw Sor Marta I was returning to Monterrey after an absence of four months. I was anxious to see her. I had taken the women all sorts of food and kitchen supplies. I even took them envelopes and paper. They teased me about the envelopes, saying that I had brought that gift because I wanted them to write to me. I had decided to stop on my way from Laredo to Monterrey. I missed the turn off the highway and took twice as long driving through the desolate roads. I arrived exhausted and frustrated. The temperature was over 40° Celsius (over 100° Fahrenheit). They had one fan in the dining room. The air from the fan was so hot it stung my face. Although they still lived in dire conditions, the construction on the monastery had progressed. Most striking, however, was the cellular phone they had. They told me a small group of professional women from Monterrey had been giving them supplies and later gave them the phone. I was glad to see them and was expecting to return within a few days.

However, everything changed once I arrived in Monterrey. As soon as I could, I went to see Alvarado. By this time, I had been working with him for over a year. I told him I had stopped on the way into Monterrey to see *las monjas* (the nuns). He firmly told me not to see them again. During our association, he often treated me as if he were my father, ordering me not to see certain people. He told me these associations would not be in my best interest. I was not able to tell if he was being sincere in this regard, or just wanted me to continue to spend as much time at his office as I did the first summer I was in Monterrey. Yet he had an interesting reason for his caution. He said *las monjas* had called him requesting a donation. They told him he could deposit the money in a bank account they had in Monterrey. While he had several decades of history working with a local priest who provided free meals to the poor, he had never been asked for money in this manner. Also, he said, they were not providing anything "tangible" for the community. They did not provide education or religious training to the local people of Mina. They were only concerned about the monastery, which Alvarado believed would ultimately be used by the elite of Nuevo León. Several months later he told me the nuns were buying a statue of Christ for the monastery that cost over 50,000 pesos.

With this information, I was not sure whether I should return to Mina. During my last visit, Sor Carina, the Mother Superior, made two requests. One was to pass an American car from Texas to Mexico. Someone had donated the car; only an American who claimed to own the car could cross the car into Mexico. In effect, they were asking me to do something illegal. The second request was for Sor Marta and another nun to return to Houston with me. They needed to solicit money for a raffle they were having. They needed continued donations for the construction of the monastery and thought they could be more successful in Texas.

The combination of these requests and Alvarado's warning made me hesitant. I asked the family I was staying with and they were just as bewildered. I did not return to Mina that month. Yet I was haunted by Sor Marta and the others. I missed them and felt guilty for not going to see them but felt compelled to stay away. On my next trip to Texas, I began a conversation with a Border Patrol officer when I was stopped at the border. He told me he had gone to medical school in Mexico but was from Laredo, Texas. He did not have a license to practice in Texas, so he began to work with the Border Patrol. He asked me about my fieldwork and the towns that I had visited. I told him it was basically most of northern Nuevo León. He asked if I had been to Mina. He had worked there while doing his medical training. He was assigned to a public health clinic. Before I responded that I knew the town, he asked me if I knew the nuns. It was an odd coincidence, that as I was running away from Sor Marta and her cohort I should be reminded of her existence as I crossed the border.

A few weeks later, back in Houston, I received a fax at the anthropology department at Rice. One of the nun's benefactors who gave them a cell phone had sent me a fax from Monterrey. Sor Marta and Sor Carina were frantic because I had not returned. Several months later I received a letter from Sor Marta, wondering if I would return to Mina and, if I did, whether we would finally take our hike up the hill.

Within the past year I have received several letters from Mina. Sor

Carina has finished her term as mother superior. She said it was a heavy burden. Sor Marta was able to go to Dallas to see her brother. The monastery is almost finished. The last time Alvarado and I spoke about the nuns, he was still adamant that something was irregular about their project. I was never able to find out if he was right. Even though in 1999 I spent most of the year in Nuevo León, I did not return to Mina. Several times when I was about to take the forty-five minute trip, something would delay me and then I would change my mind about going there. I have never returned.

PART THREE

ETHNOGRAPHIC
IMAGINARIES

We are fishing. As ethnographers, we go into uncharted waters and attempt to retrieve something with our nets. The place we are searching may be a distant, different body of water or land. It may be a space in which our own familiarity gives us a false sense of knowledge. Before we leave for fieldwork we learn of other fishermen/ethnographers. For a time in the past they raced to find the most "unknown" spaces. There are few of these spaces remaining. Yet as we are letting our minds follow the threads of new ideas, we also find "unknown" spaces within close reach. We only need to see things in a different way.

What will happen the next time? Perhaps the ethnographer will believe he/she is collecting information about the culture and what may actually be happening will be a studied "performance" of the informant in which the ethnography becomes a representation of a subtle jousting between the questioner and the questioned. The responses may be formed according to knowledge of past ethnographic projects and how the informant chooses to encircle the ethnographer. An elaborate narrative can be formed to keep the academic inside a cocoon. If he/she is bound up in the protective shell, the informant believes he/she remains safe and removed by forming a story that will satisfy the questioner and her *patron*.[1]

CHAPTER V

A Place of Origins

The Production of History

As Foucault aptly states, if one continuously searches for the origins of something, the quest will never end. The search can continue to go further back into the preceding phases of the concept or event, with "causes" becoming increasingly minute and difficult to capture.[1] It is because of this that I will not search for an authentic discovery of Nuevo León's origins. The location of San Isidro del Potrero as a place of origins is not meant literally. There is nothing "first" about Potrero, not as an indigenous or colonial settlement. It does, however, have other distinctions. It is hard to find. People rarely talk about the place. When a visitor goes to Nuevo León, recommendations are given for visits to the caves in Los García, one hour northwest of Monterrey, or Cola de Caballo, a waterfall south of Villa de Santiago, or to Saltillo, a large city one hour west of Monterrey. Potrero is not a place a stranger would normally visit. It is not pretty; it is dry; there is not enough water. It is one of the poorest, most sparsely populated areas of the state. It is not the first place in the history of Nuevo León's people. It is a place where past and present are hidden, chaotically joined together, and hold the surreal nature of Nuevo León's history.

For Potrero and Nuevo León, and the production of their "history," it is narratives and texts that implement the discourse of origin and assist in the circulation of this produced history. It may not be possible to locate the formation of this world. Yet the desire to find an *originary* location is generated and mobilized in the writing and publication of the fantastic stories from Potrero. It is also sustained by the partially stratified movement of time in this particular village. This conglomeration of existing limitations created by the past and the sporadic markings of technology entering into the present produce a phantasmic location in which stories of what de Certeau calls *le réel* can easily situate themselves, become comfortable, and seek to represent this place that at moments feels as if it does not even exist.[2]

In an inverted sense, Potrero is actually placed as last. It is in the traces of a nearby past that contain an allusion to a place of origins. These traces have stubbornly remained inside the boundaries of Potrero, probably because of its isolation. Yet once a person moves inside that space, these traces of origins intensely seek to puncture reality. The material remnants of previous centuries stand out, as the visitor, unaccustomed to the scenery, enters what seems to be a time warp. While most of the small houses contain color television sets, and the tall metal Telmex (Teléfonos Mexicanos, the national telephone company of Mexico) antenna tower overlooks the village, there are inconsistencies. At moments these images appear as if they are hallucinations. On a Sunday afternoon, when former residents of Potrero return to visit their mothers, a nine-year-old boy drives a new Chevrolet Suburban down an unpaved street full of rocks. A young girl tells the visitor, "That boy has only been driving for three weeks."

Astride the markers of modern technology, one sees that Potrero continues to resemble those places that existed in the nineteenth century. Many of the streets are not paved. Many families live in houses that were built centuries before. The visitor walks to the outdoor restroom in the middle of the night. The moon shines brightly, but a flashlight is still needed to avoid walking into a tree or a goat. The restroom has toilet paper but no septic tank. Human waste travels down a metal sheet towards the back of the little room.

Toward the right side of the main road in the village are a number of houses that have slowly deteriorated. These brown walls have no roofs, doors, or windows. The walls are thick, some as much as a meter. Trees have grown inside these houses; so have cacti and other desert shrubs. How old are these houses? How long have they been abandoned? Many families have left. In the plaza are benches with names of families. Listed under the names are their destinations—Dallas, Corpus Christi, San Antonio.

Potrero is a metonym for the point of departure. From here, the dried place next to the mountain that sends down water, young men have left for centuries. It is in this surreal place that the mythical origins of the ethnographer have joined with the mythical origins of the interlocutor. Aquiles Sepúlveda and I convened there. With his guidance, I found myself traveling about the village and talking to relatives I never knew existed. During our long conversations, which lasted into the evenings while we sat in the back porch of *la casa de alto* (the two-story house), he told of his numerous conjectures regarding the lost and nostalgic past of Potrero and Nuevo León. A genealogy, whether imagined or real, provided part of the impetus behind our connection. We are linked together by a wedding in Villaldama. In the early part of the nineteenth century, our ancestors were probably cousins of cousins who were named Treviño.

I was told that about 150 years ago, a man named Juan Vásquez left his village of El Venado, San Luis Potosí, and traveled north over 1,000 kilometers to Villaldama, Nuevo León. He was a carpenter and made *carretas* (carts) for the mines. For several centuries there had been mines in Villaldama. It is an area that is moderately above sea level. It is very dry. It also has a long history. For at least two centuries Villaldama was known as Boca de Leónes (mouth of the lions). It was at one time the seat of the regional government. Its past importance is evident in the ruins of an unfinished cathedral in the center of the city. The building would have rivaled the Cathedral of Monterrey. The walls rose high above any other building in Villaldama. Built of solid stone, some of the walls have turned black over time. Alvarado once told me that the importance of a city paralleled the size of its church. People said that the large church in Villaldama was never completed. The church that was completed stands in the main plaza. It is quite beautiful, with a striking life-size statue of María Dolorosa looking serene with a dagger thrust into her heart. She is gazing at the congregation from the sanctuary. However, the church is much smaller than the unfinished structure in Villaldama's other plaza.

According to local talk, the people from Villaldama are said to be "white." They are tall people, fair-skinned, frequently with the surnames of Villareal or González. The term "white" in northern Mexico may mean people with blond hair and blue eyes. It may also mean those with swarthy skin and black hair. What it does not mean is anyone that looks *mestizo* (part Indian and part Spanish) or indigenous.

After Juan Vásquez arrived in Villaldama, he married a woman from a wealthy family. Her name was said to have been Teresa Treviño.[3] Among the "white" people of early Nuevo León, the name Treviño was associated with power and wealth. Capitán Joseph de Treviño is often mentioned in texts and oral narratives as a very wealthy man. He was said to have arrived in Nuevo León from Mexico City with a thousand head of cattle in the early part of the seventeenth century. He was in command of La Santa Hermandad (the Holy Brotherhood), an organization established by the Spanish monarchy for the purpose of providing law and order in outlying areas of the Spanish Empire.

During some unknown period, the Vásquez family moved to San Isidro del Potrero, eight kilometers south of Villaldama on what is now Highway 1. Juan Vásquez and his wife, María Teresa, had one son (perhaps more). The only name I know at this time is Creséncio Vásquez. At the age of forty Creséncio Vásquez married Antonia Guzmán. They had, I believe, eight children, one of which was my grandfather, Felipe Vásquez. His mother, Antonia, died of tuberculosis in 1904 (she was twenty-seven years of age). His father died in the 1920s, shortly before Felipe left for Texas. At the time it was almost impossible to survive economically in Potrero.

Another family in the village, also descended from the Treviños, were the Sepúlveda Gonzálezes. Josefa González Treviño and her husband, José Sepúlveda Gutiérrez, lived in the only two-story house in the village, *la casa de alto*. It was just across the *arroyo* (small stream) from Potrero's church and plaza. The original part of the house was said to be about four hundred years old. The second floor, which was connected to the first by a ladder, was added at the beginning of the twentieth century.

José Sepúlveda was an administrator for the mining company, Peñoles, in Villaldama, eight kilometers north of Potrero. Over time, he saved his money and, with additional investment coming from a British partner, Don José was able to accumulate over 600 hectares of land around the *ejido* (cooperative community) of Potrero. In 1936, when Mexican president Lazaro Cárdenas appropriated land from the "wealthy classes," the 600 hectares (about 1,500 acres) of Don José were confiscated. Although the family continued to own *la casa de alto* and a few other hectares in town, Don José moved his wife and thirteen children to Monterrey. The family divided their time between their colonial house one block from Monterrey's Alameda and *la casa de alto* in Potrero. While their finances diminished significantly after the loss of the land and Don José's subsequent death, they continued to live in a tranquil and civilized manner. Sixty years after Don José's death, his son Aquiles generally spent at least one week out of every month in Potrero. Although no one lived in *la casa de alto,* Aquiles had it maintained and cleaned regularly. It was still full of furniture and appliances, as if someone lived there. Aquiles had built himself a small house/studio a few blocks away.

As recently as the 1970s women from the Vásquez family were the domestic servants of the Sepúlveda family. At the end of the twentieth century, most of the Sepúlvedas looked much like their ancestors. They were "white" and somewhat taller than average height. Don José's children had come to be writers, artists, school administrators, and other types of professionals.

The Vásquezes maintained some of their ancestors' appearance. The men that I came to know were at least two and a half meters tall. They were also fair-skinned, often with curly hair. Yet, many of the women were dark and appeared indigenous. The cultured and civilized manner of the Sepúlvedas was lacking in the Vásquez family. Although one Vásquez, Don Jesús (also known as Quechú), was known to be the wealthiest man in the village, the other Vasquezes lived in houses that mostly had outside bathrooms and few conveniences.

Carretera Numero Uno

Monterrey-Colombia

The road from Monterrey to Potrero is narrow and somewhat off-balance. Several people have told me that the state government was given a large sum of money to build a modern, ample highway to Colombia, Nuevo León's only border crossing into the United States. However, the story is that the government officials kept the money and had a dangerous, rickety highway built that became known for a high incidence of fatal traffic accidents. In recent years, because of the need to provide proof of an anti-narcotics movement, the Mexican government has stationed troops on Carretera Numero Uno. Passing by numerous trucks and tanks painted in camouflage, the traveler on Carretera Numero Uno is subjected to questions about her destination and her purpose. The soldiers, those asking questions and those standing solemnly by the painted vehicles, hold loaded sub-machine guns and point them towards the driver. The presence of the soldiers and the condition of Carretera Numero Uno keep many people from driving at night.

The first time I drove from Monterrey to Potrero, I was nervous and hesitant. The condition of the road did not help. I had decided to go alone. Some of my friends had insisted on accompanying me and thought it was strange that I did not let them come along. It was July 1998. There were several issues that made me tense: I was traveling alone to an unknown place. I knew that the town was not like Monterrey or Villa de Santiago. It was much less affluent with few resources. Aquiles Sepúlveda had described it as an idyllic place where he could read and paint his watercolors. Perhaps the most important thing on my mind that day was that I was going to meet my relatives who did not even know I existed.

Aquiles's nephew, Alejandro Sepúlveda, had described the turn-off to me. On the highway, eight kilometers before Villaldama, I was to encounter the *rancho* (a group of houses) of El Alamo. This small place consisted of a *depósito,* a religious sanctuary painted white with purple trim, and a few other houses. In the middle of El Alamo was a bus stop where people sat and waited for the bus that came twice a day to take them either to Monterrey or Villaldama. Next to the bus stop was the road. There was a sign that said "Potrero." I turned left.

The road between the highway and Potrero was in much better condition. It was level and had few potholes. I saw few cars. Mountains framed the scene behind the flat brush area that lay between El Alamo and Potrero. One of the first signs that I saw as I passed the curve entering Potrero warned against drinking water that was not boiled. I thought about cholera and dysentery. I had brought my own water. Alejandro had also told me to bring snacks. "There are no cafes and restaurants in Potrero," he told me. In fact, there were no banks, no stores, no apartments, no gasoline stations. There were only a plaza, a couple of schools, and a small church that was almost always locked. There was no *preparatoria* (high school).

Aquiles Sepúlveda had directed me to the home of Don Jesús (Quechú) Vásquez. Don Quechú and Aquiles were not necessarily close friends. However, they did have frequent conversations. It was often Don Quechú who drove Aquiles, who did not drive and did not own a car, from the bus stop to Sepúlveda's studio just past *la casa de alto.*

As I drove into the village, I looked around and saw this desolate, dry place that looked very poor. It was strikingly different from almost any other place I had seen in Nuevo León. My work, *Reportajes de Alvarado,* had taken me to many of the small municipalities in the northern part of Nuevo León. Few looked as surreal as Potrero. The houses were made of stone or adobe. Many were painted white, but some were painted turquoise. The place was very dusty, yet every hundred meters or so, there appeared a small canal, so narrow that a child could jump across easily. These canals traveled throughout the village, bringing water down from the mountain behind Potrero. Alongside every little canal were greenery, trees, and flowers. Just about everything else in town was dry and brown.

I arrived at Don Quechú's house. He greeted me with an ambivalent handshake that made me think he was suspicious about who I was and why I was there. Aquiles had made several phone calls before my trip, telling Don Quechú that I was a distant relative. Quechú was not convinced. He sent me a few blocks away to talk to a woman who appeared to be in her eighties. She asked me questions about my grandfather and his family. Once she was satisfied that I was indeed the granddaughter of a Vásquez, she sent me back to Quechú. He asked for her opinion and she said that she did know of my grandfather and that he had gone to Texas some seventy-five years before. After this, Don Quechú was friendlier. His twenty-three-year-old daughter, Rosie, was living in Potrero at the time. He told Rosie to take me to meet other Vásquezes and to see the town. Rosie was tall, perhaps 5'10", with fair skin and a round face. She left home at age 14 to attend school in Monterrey. Recently graduating from college with a degree in accounting, she had not yet found a professional position. In the meantime she was staying with her parents, Don Quechú and Doña Petrita. As we later studied the family tree, it turned out that Don Quechú was actually my second cousin. His grandfather and my grandfather were brothers.

Rosie took me to meet seventy-eight-year-old Doña Elena Vásquez. Elena's father was also Felipe's brother. She remembered Felipe very well. For the first twenty-seven years after Felipe left for Texas, he continued to visit his family in Potrero regularly. His last trip was in 1951. She started crying when she realized I was Felipe's granddaughter. She said that another nephew of hers looked just like him and that recently she had been wondering what happened to all these people who had gone away.

Doña Elena's given name is Magdalena. Although everyone calls her Elena, she has reminded me on several occasions that Elena is not her real name. She is also fairly tall; perhaps at a younger age, she was at least 5'9" or 5'10". Her skin is tanned a very golden brown. Her hair is gray and curly. Her voice moves to a higher pitch as she completes her words.

When she answers the telephone, instead of saying *bueno* (which literally means "good," but in Mexico is the common way of answering the phone and is sort of like saying hello), she asks, "*¿Quién habla?*" (who is speaking?) in a loud, high-pitched voice that gets higher as she speaks.

After living in American-style comfort in Monterrey, I found life in Potrero to be a surprise. Doña Elena washed her dishes outside, using a pan of dishwater that she brought from one of the large drums near the "bathing room." There was no real running water in Potrero. For one hour, around noon every day, water rushed down long hoses from the mountain. People scrambled to catch the water in large drums. Everything was used. Dirty dishwater was used to water the plants. Bathing was done in a separate room that held soap and towels. The door was locked with a piece of twine that twirled around a nail.

Doña Elena's kitchen had an open area where she started a fire with *leña* (firewood). This was not unique in Potrero. Almost all the houses, including that of Don Quechú, had these open cooking areas. Doña Elena had a gas stove, but said that the food cooked over the open fire tasted better, especially the pinto beans. There was a sink with a faucet that did not produce running water. On the floor of the kitchen was a large earthenware jar full of water. Doña Elena said her mother gave her the jar when Elena and Jesús were married.

Stories of *le Réel*

Las Leyendas de Potrero—The Legends of Potrero

In the thirteen months between July 1998 and August 1999 that I traveled to Potrero, I came to know most of the people named Vásquez in the village. I attended festivals, took hikes up the mountain, went to church, had late-night conversations on the porch of my cousin Juanera's house, and ate many meals that Doña Elena prepared for me. I also spent long hours talking to Aquiles Sepúlveda when the occasion arose that we were both in Potrero at the same time. As time went on, the conversations with the people from the village, which began with everyone attempting to give me what they knew of the Vásquez history, ended up being stories of pragmatic issues such as work, land ownership, family, relationships, and migration. Even though the town had a significant surreal quality to it, I did not hear many stories about anything fantastic.

There did, however, already exist a body of written texts on the phantasmic world of Potrero. These were stories written by Aquiles's sister, Irma Sabina Sepúlveda. In these stories, which formed a textual image of Potero's landscape, Irma documented the most exotic and the most unusual circumstances she found in the village. Her style is simplistic. They seem like stories that are told about daily occurrences or conversations. They often display irony or end with abrupt scenes that seem almost nonsensical. They are allegories about the ideology and moral climate of the village as seen by the author, perhaps from the second-story room of *la casa de alto*. It was the room that could only be reached by a ladder. There was no stairway.

A Reason for Witchcraft

The Death of La Melga y Media

One of the most dramatic stories is "La cruz de Jacinto Rocha" ("The Cross of Jacinto Rocha"). Published in 1961 in *Agua de las verdes matas,* the story tells of a woman who sought help in resolving her daughter's marital problems.

It is late in the afternoon; a woman is crushing seeds in her *molcajete* outside the door of her house. She is alone. She sees the village taxi drive by with two women dressed in black. Normally she closes the windows when there is a car going down the street; this time she does not. A few minutes later she begins to hear familiar clicking noises outside of her house. She quickly closes all the windows and bolts the door. It is too late. The *lechuzas* (witches who transform themselves into birds) have entered her home and quickly wreak havoc upon the lone woman. As she is lying in bed trying to pray, they pick the bed up to the ceiling and abruptly let it fall. The woman is sure she was saved by crying out, "María Purísima!"

The next morning she hears her daughter screaming. A house down the street has burned to the ground; there is a strange smell in the air. The burnt house belonged to a woman named Chona Miranda. They called Chona La Melga y Media because she was so tall and thin. Chona was a witch, known to be the most powerful witch in the village. The charred skeleton of the witch is found inside, chained to her bed, along with the remains of her cat and her thirteen goats. Surely it was because of envy. The same witches that entered the first house were those who killed Chona Miranda.

The exotic description of the women/witches entering and flying about the first house and the murder of the witch and her animals seize the reader's attention. Were these stories told in Potrero? Did people actually believe them?

Beyond the descriptions of flying women, burning cadavers, and envy, Irma Sepúlveda presses upon the reader a cosmological interpretation of the fantastic and the demonic and how they are pragmatically situated in the quotidian world of Potrero. Sepúlveda accomplishes this by describing a mother's dilemma, whose daughter married a man prone to falling in love with other women. The daughter is crying day and night. Desperate, the mother seeks out the help of La Melga y Media. The solution is offered at midnight at a crossing of two roads. The witch tells the mother to go to the cemetery and retrieve the tombstone of a man who was murdered with a machete. The mother promptly obeys. The tombstone of Jacinto Rocha, a cross, is buried under the daughter's bed. The power of this object changes the fate of the married couple. The husband no longer strays from his wife.

The witch gives instructions that, after the problem is resolved, the tombstone is to be returned to the cemetery. The mother does not do so, thinking that the husband might resume his wandering ways if the tombstone is moved. When she is alone, the mother often hears a moaning from her daughter's bedroom. It is the moaning of the dead man, Jacinto Rocha, asking for his tombstone to be returned.

The mother makes decisions that counter both legitimate authority and Chona Miranda's illegitimate authority. The rules of the Catholic Church and traditional Mexican society forbid the use of witchcraft, even in desperate situations. This is an event the mother will not be able to tell her priest. As I write this I recall how a local priest, Manual González (actually a cousin of Irma Sepúlveda), told Juanera Domínguez that he knew Juanera did not believe in witchcraft. To this statement Juanera smiled and merely nodded, only later to tell me she was a *sobadora* (a spiritual healer who cures by giving massages). The use of enchantment, the movement of the tombstone from the space of the Other (the cemetery) to the interior of the home, brings a certain power that controls the husband's need for outside sexual adventures. The mother thinks it is a rule worth breaking. When she talks of Chona's death, she says that some people did not like the witch, but Chona had been most helpful in a very serious situation. The use of black magic is justified. Even so, the mother does not fear the dead man's wrath. The risk of having the son-in-law revert to his old ways is more terrifying than the terror produced by Jacinto Rocha's moans.

Sepúlveda's use of fiction removes her text from the "burden of proof." It is, as Costa Lima argues, Western society's need to document fact that leaves any text designated as fiction in the category of "non-truth" (1988). Related to de Certeau's concept of the Scriptural Economy, the powers-that-be relegate fictional non-truth to writing that is for pleasure and not to be taken seriously or as actual "history." This dilemma provided an advantage for Sepúlveda's work. Even though, as her brother Aquiles repeatedly said, the stories were based on narratives the author documented in Potrero, their identification as fiction eliminates controversy. The stories are fiction; they did not happen; they solely emanate from the author's imagination. Within this space, the stories do not require an investigation into whether Chona Miranda was murdered in Potrero sometime in the middle of the twentieth century or whether Castulo Rodela (in the story I describe next) should be charged with bigamy.

Even though considered fiction, the narratives in Sepúlveda's manuscripts and publications contain sufficient resemblance to reality that her observations were devoured by *nuevoleneses* who left their *ranchos* a generation before and sought to hear the stories they heard on the porch of their grandparents' houses at sunset. There are many aspects to this storytelling. The nostalgia implied in the dramatic seduction of the narrative perhaps belies Irma's own wish to return to the fantastic past. The use of fiction eliminates the confrontation between the power of the state and the church with regard to the heresy of sorcery. Yet the descriptions are vivid. Empathy for the main character, who experiences terror when her house is invaded by *lechuzas* and desperation over her daughter's broken heart, leaves the reader almost out of breath. The narrator's terror is so vivid that I begin to wonder if Sepúlveda herself experienced such fear; Irma's siblings, after all, said she used her own experiences as a foundation for the stories.

The author speaks of more than fear. There is need to live alongside the dead. The tombstone of Jacinto Rocha is buried under the daughter's bed. This keeps the dead man inside of the house, his moans can be heard during the night. Yet the mother defies the dead man's calls. Not only has she displaced his tombstone, but she also refuses to return it to its proper place.

The mother's stealing of the murder victim's gravestone tells of an inversion of the rules. The good mother will steal from the dead for the sake of her daughter; she will ally herself with the most powerful witch in the village; she defies the witch's authority by not completing Miranda's instructions of returning the gravestone to the cemetery; and, lastly, she is not moved by the moans of the dead man calling for the return of his gravestone.

The story indicates the inverted power of the women of Potrero. The use of esoteric practices to control their lives and relationships would be considered normative for those living on the margins of a Third World society. With the exception of the betrayed daughter, all of the women in the story show agency: the visiting witches break into the mother's house and later tie up Miranda and her animals and burn her house to the ground. The mother, who has the courage to negotiate with the witch and go to the cemetery alone in search of the gravestone, is also able to resist the *lechuzas* who invade her home. Although Miranda dies in the end, her life had been full of agency. She was the most powerful witch in the village.

The Transformation of Castulo Rodela

En primera fila se encontraban los trece apóstoles ataviados con sus túnicas amarillas y mantos cafés. Al verlo, se fueron tras de él y en fila india dieron la vuelta a la plaza, marcando el paso con los sonoros tamborazos de Checho, "La pachorra." (Sepúlveda 1963: 26) (The thirteen apostles found themselves in the first line of the parade. They wore yellow tunics and brown mantles. When they saw Castulo Rodela/San Andrés, they followed him in single file and walked around the plaza, following the rhythm of the sonorous drum of Chencho, whom everyone called La Pachorra [the slow one])

The story of Castulo Rodela from Agua de las Verdes Matas delicately combines the theme of heresy and resistance with an almost fairy tale structure. It is titled "El Pajarito Triste." The name *Rodela* stood out to me because it was a woman from Potrero, named Lola Rodela, who in 1984 first told me about my grandfather and the village where he was

Doña Magdalena Vásquez's grandsons at the ermita outside of Potrero, Nuevo León. This is the same ermita where Castulo Rodela went to pray in Irma Sepúlveda's story "El Pajarito Triste." 1998.

Photograph by the author.

born. Lola lived in Corpus Christi, Texas. My biological mother lived with her for a time before I was born. Lola said she was a cousin of Felipe Vásquez. Aquiles's words continued to sing in my mind: "Irma used real people in her stories; she did not change their names."

Castulo Rodela went through a major transformation at the age of forty-five. One evening, the neighbors saw him walk out of his dark cottage dressed in a purple tunic. Walking with firm, determined steps, Castulo went up to the *ermita,* the little sanctuary on the mountain. The next day he came down announcing that his name was now "San Andrés." After a week of going daily to the *ermita* to pray, he gathered his friends and told them that God ordered him to evangelize the village. One of the first he converted was a butcher named Abundio, who became "San Pascual." Eventually he had his thirteen apostles. The narrator describes these apostles as *flamantes* (outrageous). San Andrés chose the number thirteen because he said that God liked odd numbers.

The village was in an uproar over Castulo's evangelization of the thirteen men. The merchant who sold fabric was making money selling great quantities of yellow cloth. The seamstress put a new roof on her cottage with the money she made from sewing so many tunics and mantles.

The turning point of Sepúlveda's story is when the apostle, Don Hilarión, comes down from the mountain and discreetly whispers to San Andrés a new request from God. After this, Hilarión tells Castulo/Andrés, "*Bendito Andrés, no sufres más. La voz del Señor será obedecida.*" (Blessed Andrés, do not suffer any longer. The voice of the Lord will be obeyed.) "*¡Que así sea!*" ("It will be done!") responded Castulo/Andrés. San Andrés returns to the *ermita* on the mountain to do a night of penance. San Hilarión begins preparation for a festival. The plaza is filled with wreaths of flowers. The seamstress is busy making orange tunics with lime green belts for the wife of Castulo/Andrés and the niece of San Meliton. The butcher, San Pascual, slaughters some sheep and twenty chickens. Doña Olegaria and the wives of the apostles prepare tamales, *mole,* and *barbacoa.*

San Andrés returns from the *ermita.* He solemnly washes his face and feet. The stars begin to shine as he approaches the plaza. The thirteen apostles wait for him. As he passes, they form a line and follow him to a place where two chairs are adorned with flowers and white gauze. San Andrés stands with his wife and the niece of San Meliton at his side. At this moment he tells his wife, ". . . *esposa mia, el Señor me ordena que no vuelva a tocarte. Desde este momento eres sagrada para mí. Ve a la casa de San Roman, el casto, donde hallaras asilo, que yo debo unirme a la nueva esposa que el Señor me manda*" (. . . my wife, the Lord has ordered me not to touch you again. From this moment you are sacred to me. Go to the house of San Roman; he will give you a room. Do this because I will unite myself with a new wife that the Lord has sent me). With this, he removes the crown of flowers that had been previously placed on the head of his wife who is now crying; and he places the flowers on the head of the curvaceous niece of San Meliton. Castulo/San Andrés thus completes the mandate of the Lord.

In "El Pajarito Triste," Sepúlveda reduces the story of Jesus and the twelve apostles to a comedy of men who fabricate an authority from God which allows them to circumvent the rules of the everyday world. Placed safely inside the distant limits of Potrero (and the genre of fiction), there is no danger that the church will descend upon the villagers and excommunicate Castulo Rodela or Sepúlveda herself. Yet in this carefully constructed fairy tale, Sepúlveda levels her critique at the established order of the church, which allows men to create worlds that suit their desires. This story has a strong resonance with narratives I heard of an underground city in Monterrey that housed the mistresses and children of local priests (I discuss these narratives in later chapters on Monterrey).

Although Potrero is not an underground city, it is occulted. Situated far enough from the locus of *nuevolenese* "civilization," Potrero is hard to reach by car or bus. It does not maintain enough amenities to lure many people who do not already have familial connections to the place. The village is not a frequent topic of conversation among *regiomontanos*. It is hidden away in a dry area, just east of the Sierra Madre, where water only comes down the mountain one hour per day. The boundaries of the community are strongly enough situated in the past that they easily contain fantastic stories, either old or new, written or oral. These quotidian narratives are held in reserve until they are needed for future use.

While Rulfo has his characters come from an Other side, which he defines as death, Sepúlveda has her characters come from an Other side that is Potrero. The village in many ways represents a past life, a world that in some ways is no longer living, insulated against the transgressions of modernity. There is a boundary between Potrero and those who do not or have not lived there. There is also a boundary between those who grew up in the normal constrictions of that type of society and those who "had privilege." Ultimately these two divisions kept me from getting any closer to those who were my own "family." I was too far away, being from an "outside" that could not be conceptualized. This distance began to create what felt like a presence of danger. There was something sinister about the silence and the secrets in Potrero. Aquiles let his imagination go as far as possible and even began to say that some of the older men in the village who herded their goats up to the mountain were actually transporting narcotics. I have no way of knowing if there is any truth to this assertion. It appeared to me, however, that the danger was in the socioeconomic distance. It was too great to be bridged.

While not producing the striking distinction and asymmetry that is often shown between the traditional ethnographer and his "primitive" informants, the inherent differences in culture, education, and privilege were too many to hold together the myth of "kinship." The tenuous connection to a man who left Potrero three generations before did not sustain my relationship to the Vásquezes.

There were also other issues. The people of Potrero know that the village is light years from the world in Monterrey. They are aware that people are constantly coming into their space to "take" something: the *ingeniero* (engineer) with the *escrituras;* Luis, Aquiles's nephew, who wanted to buy *la casa de alto;* and I, the ethnographer disguised as kin. As in the other hidden histories and artifacts in Nuevo León, Potrero is itself an artifact to be "rescued." The curiosity evoked by the surreal landscape and the stories written by Irma Sepúlveda forty years before leave one hoping to touch and feel the ghosts and *lechuzas* that were said to have flown over the skies next to the mountain. In a more literal sense, it is similar to the ongoing problematic of anthropology. It is the search for the Other. It is the writing of the Other that creates the text. Tom Conley proposes in the introduction to de Certeau's *The Writing of History* that "unconscious allegorical tendencies" are "often at the basis of historiography" (Conley 1988: viii). Even as I write this ethnography, which provides an aspect of Nuevo León's history, I seek out these allegories, at moments without my conscious awareness. The allegories, stories, and narratives tell of "lost places" and "stories that seek out the Other." As I mentioned previously, Potrero is a metonym for the lost place. In many ways it reminds me of the village that Rulfo's Pedro Paramo visits in search of his father. It is dry and desolate. People know many things but don't often tell. In a surreal and mystical way, it is the land of the dead.

Clearly, Juanera Domínguez, Doña Elena Vásquez, and the others are very much alive. Yet the momentary sense of "being outside of time," outside the past but not quite in the present, places Potrero in the space of the Other. Conley locates de Certeau's thesis in this paradigm: "The writing of history can begin only when a present is divided from a past. An initial act of exclusion separates current time from past time, or the living from the dead" (1988: viii). The problem with Potrero and other "spaces" that are part of this ethnography is that the line that divides the past from the present is blurred. The boundary is permeable. Potrero is both past and present.

CHAPTER VI

The Mystic and the Fantastic

The Frenchmen

May 1999

Sitting in the cafeteria of the Museo de Historia in Monterrey, I asked blue-eyed Felipe Montes about the legend that French soldiers had settled in Nuevo León. I had heard stories from local people about the French being in Villa de Santiago, Allende, and General Bravo. Felipe told me previously that he was trying to learn everything he could about the history of Nuevo León. Thus he had enrolled in the *diplomado* on the state's history.[1] That is where we met.

He said that the story of the French was told all over Mexico. Because I had not considered the possibility of this settlement happening in other regions, I was surprised. It seemed logical that any "escaped" soldiers would head north, which at the time was one of the more isolated areas of the country. The first I heard of the French narrative was from Manuel Rodríguez. He was a college friend of mine who migrated from northern Mexico to southeast Texas while in his early teens. In 1971, the summer I was 18, I encountered Manuel buying gasoline at the Villagómez gasoline station in Rosenberg. I was struck by Manuel's presence. Even though we had met before he looked very different. He was very tanned and his wild curly hair had bleached out blonde. He had spent the summer working on a shrimp boat. Months later we talked about his genealogy. He had been told that his skin and hair were so light because some French soldiers had settled nearby. That was the reason why so many people from his city, General Bravo, had fair skin. Later I found a reference to what is called "the French Intervention."[2] People have told me that several men from Bravo participated in the last battle against Emperor Maximilian. They were supposedly among the men on the firing squad that executed the Emperor. At El Obispado, the Museo Regional in Monterrey, there is a group of rifles exhibited that are said to be the same ones used in this execution.

More than two decades later, in Monterrey, Alvarado told me a similar story about French soldiers in Villa de Santiago and Allende. He said that soldiers escaping execution had hidden away in these towns. Many of the young women became pregnant. However, since they did not marry, the names did not change.

Of the families that I actually met from Santiago and Allende, none told me specifically where the "French look" came from. It was very obvious, however, that these families for the most part were very different from other groups around Monterrey. On several occasions I attended the birthday parties of Karen Sepúlveda in Santiago and Allende. Although I was present and saw the other children, I was still amazed when I developed the black-and-white photographs showing children that looked like they were from the French countryside.

The other striking connection was the presence of the sanctuary of La Medalla Milagrosa. According to Doña Pepita Sepúlveda, the Virgin Mary appeared to a young French nun in 1839. The Virgin gave the girl a medal and said it would provide protection to whoever would wear it in good faith. The Virgin Mary is represented on the front side of the medal. The image of the Virgin, in this context, is that of a "white" Virgin Mary with blue eyes and fair skin. She is wearing a white robe and a blue mantel. This depiction is a complete inversion from the brown-skinned Virgin of Guadalupe that is seen all over Mexico.[3]

The issue of whiteness has permeated the cities of Allende and Santiago. Jorge Cavazos, who is now a student at the University of St. Thomas in Houston, lived in Allende as an adolescent. His blue-eyed father is from the "founding families" of Allende. Jorge told me that the "common" talk is for young people in Monterrey to say they want to find a spouse in Allende or Santiago because everyone is so "white" there.

While this discourse is not in most texts, it circulates among the people of northern Nuevo León. In August 1999, as historian Cristóbal López and I were walking around the main plaza of Santiago, we decided to visit the church, known as La Parroquia de Santiago Apóstol. As I entered I saw a man of African descent painting a mural. The artist and

Montalvo, the artist, painting murals for the church in Santiago with Cristóbal
López. 1999.

Photograph by the author.

Cristóbal knew each other. The artist, named Montalvo, was originally
from Cuba. The mural he was painting was of angels in heaven. The artist jokingly told us that he had originally painted the angels blonde but
then had second thoughts because of the already problematic attitude of
people in Santiago about being white. He said that blonde angels would
intensify the local people's image of themselves as white. Ultimately, the
angels would have no trace of indigenous features; however, their hair is
brown instead of blonde.

In what seemed irrelevant at the moment, I became involved in an interesting encounter with Montalvo and the church secretary. Cristóbal
and I had been having numerous intense discussions regarding a rumor I
had heard about an "underground city" in Monterrey. This rumor had
come from the documentation of tunnels existing under some cities in
Nuevo León. As we continued this conversation in front of Montalvo,
the artist said, "There is an underground chamber beneath this church.
I saw it once when they were remodeling the sanctuary area. I'm sure
there is an entrance to that room from the main floor." Montalvo then

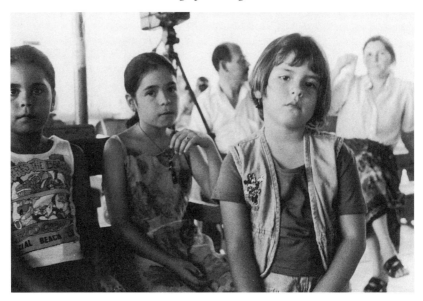

Children from San Francisco in Santiago, Nuevo León. At the birthday party of
Doña Pepita's granddaughter. 1998.

Photograph by the author.

went to the church office and asked about "the room." The secretary
said he did not know about an entrance. There had been a burial chamber for several centuries under the sanctuary, but it had been sealed off
after the remodeling was completed. The theme of another "layer" of
history or narrative existed in what Montalvo was trying to express.
There had been something "underneath" the church; he had seen it. Yet
the church staff said the space was inaccessible. At the same time, Montalvo changed the hair color of the angels on his mural. It was blonde;
then it was brown.

He also told us that he had lost his contract. Artists from Monterrey
learned of the generous fee he was being paid for his work. A controversy
ensued about how he was commissioned for the work. After this mural,
the work on the church was to stop. No one else would paint murals, at
least for the time. He said the issue was about *envidia* (envy). He was dismissed because he was being shown favoritism, having been paid more
than what some considered the norm for that type of work. Even so, according to Montalvo, as it happened, no other painters were able to obtain the contract to finish the murals in the Church of Santiago Apóstol.

Finding Pepita and the French Medal

Villa de Santiago
January 1998

Two kilometers from the church, Santiago Apóstol, on *la carretera nacional,* Alvarado's television crew is traveling through Villa de Santiago to Laguna de Sánchez. As we drive through the city, Alvarado tells me about the woman who always talks about the Virgin. We are taking the old road to Saltillo so that we can film the higher elevation of the mountains. It is January and very cold. This section of the road is narrow but in good condition. On each side are many houses, some with small shops in front that sell statues, large pots, and tables. They are made of *cantera,* a hard substance that is made with pieces of rock, concrete, and other whitish material that gives it the look of limestone. As the van moves past the curves in the road, our progression up the mountain becomes much slower. The road at times does not even look like a road. In the four hours we travel to our destination, he has much time to describe to me a woman who sounds as if she is some kind of mystic. From listening to him, I envision her as older (past seventy), somewhat haggard, and illogical in her conversation. I wonder if hers is one of the houses we just passed and imagine that she lives in poverty.

Alvarado was the first to give me one of Doña Pepita's medals near the end of the summer in 1997. I remember that I was sitting facing his desk, in my usual manner, waiting to see what he would tell me. He pulled out what seemed to be a tangle of metal chains. They all had medals that looked like sparkly charms hanging from them. The image on the medals was that of the Virgin Mary. In some she was looking to the side, while in others she faced directly into the observer's eyes with her arms wide open. Alvarado said that Doña Pepita gave him medals each time he visited the sanctuary. She wanted him to distribute the medals to his viewers. Carrying a medal provided the wearer protection from danger. He gave me one. I took the medal home with me, and asked the family I stayed with about the sanctuary and Doña Pepita. Yolanda Gonzalez told me that she had heard there was a woman in Santiago who always talked about the Virgin Mary. As Yolanda described it, Doña Pepita sounded as if she was mad. Yolanda did not actually meet Doña Pepita until the fall of 1997. When Yolanda's cousins were visiting from Houston, they drove south to Santiago to meet with Doña Pepita. Yolanda bought me a silver medal and gave it to me several weeks later as a birthday present. The medal showed the Virgin with outstretched hands and the date 1839 at the bottom of the front. On the back was an M with a † (cross) above it. *Italy* was spelled out (in English) at the bottom, even though Yolanda learned that the medal originally appeared to a nun in France in 1839. I only had the medal a few weeks before I lost it. Later when I told Doña Pepita that it had been lost, she said that it was Satan or evil forces that made me lose the medal.

May 1998

The spring semester had just ended and I quickly returned to Monterrey hoping to continue working with Alvarado and his television crew. The day I arrived at his office was the day he filmed his formal goodbye. The program had been cancelled after eighteen years. Now with even more resolve I was determined to find the sanctuary and meet with this woman who talked all the time of the Virgin. It was time to begin the second phase of my project.

On two occasions I tried to get Alvarado to make a trip with me to Santiago; however, we were not able to coordinate our schedules. I eventually traveled to the sanctuary with Yolanda's sister Rosalba González and their mother, Doña Soledad Villagómez. Alvarado told me to send Doña Pepita a message. He was unable to accompany me but wanted her to know that he had sent me personally to speak with her.

It seemed that we left early in the morning, but it was already about 9 A.M. Doña Soledad decided to go with us, which was unusual. She rarely went anywhere outside the house except to visit her sister across town. We had to wait until Doña Soledad made breakfast for her husband. When she was finished with this work, we dressed up as if we were going to church. We quickly took off on what is called *la carretera nacional* (the national highway), a speedy divided highway that goes south from Monterrey to Santiago and Linares, winding through the edge of the mountains of La Sierra Madre Oriental.

The scenery was picturesque. There were mountains on both sides of the highway. Halfway there was a market in the town of Los Cavazos. Both sides of the highway were filled with all sorts of shops that sold locally made furniture, jewelry, pots, statues, and many other things. A year later I found out that the market is over some high-risk pipelines. According to Felipe Montes, permanent construction was banned on the site. However, what appeared were hundreds of temporary shops, which ultimately became a gathering site for thousands of *nuevoleneses* every weekend.

By the time we reached Los Cavazos, the scenery had changed. There were many more trees, things were green, in contrast to Monterrey, which is dry and almost desert-like. The sign announcing the turn for San Francisco was covered by the branches of a large tree. We barely made out the letters and began winding up the town through the narrow streets, past houses that pushed up to the sidewalks and touched each other at the sides. They were painted white or cream, and many had bright blue, green, or red trim. The temperature felt noticeably cooler. About a kilometer down the road, we saw a blue sign that was somewhat rusty with the letters *Medalla Milagrosa* and an arrow pointing up. We continued to follow the road up to the *ejido* of San Francisco. At the center of the town, a small grocery store was situated on the corner across from a fruit wholesaler, which was owned by the same person, Don Hector. There was a yellow blinking light and signs that confused the driver as to which streets were one-way or two-way. We turned right and encountered a sharp curve. At this spot were large pieces of old car parts, fronts and ends of cars, doors, and grills. They seemed to be placed strategically on the corner in front of someone's house. Most of the car parts were used to hold baskets of fruits and vegetables. There were bright red tomatoes, avocados, limes, garlic, and other produce.

After the curve the road began to creep up again. We passed a few houses on the left and a store on the right. San Francisco's small church was located there, just where the large *quintas* (estates) began. We could see there was a change coming about in the landscape, but it was several months before I understood what it was about. Across the street from the church I saw several properties with new construction, houses as works-in-progress, which seemed to be very large and imposing compared to the little houses that already existed in San Francisco. As we moved farther up, the tracts of land became much larger; the houses sitting on the edge of the properties had large gates and fancy names. Finally we reached one of the last gates and from about half a kilometer we could see the statue of a woman standing out from the mountainside among the greenery. After this point, the visibility diminished and we concentrated on moving up the one-lane road with a sharp cliff on the right and no borders or protection for cars or people traveling up to the sanctuary. We began to see many artificial flowers, mostly roses that were once red, tied to the chain link fence. About ten minutes after leaving downtown San Francisco, we arrived at the gate of the parking lot. To the right was a line of portable toilets. To the left was the open lot with several stands that on Sundays sold canned fruit and spices.

The last gate before the sanctuary was large and painted yellow. We entered and saw to the left a stand in which medals and other religious objects were sold by Pepita's family. A few meters down the other side of the mountain was Doña Pepita's house. It had a large porch. There were many chairs under the porch. I found out later the chairs were for the people who listened to Doña Pepita talk of the Virgin.

She was an attractive woman. With dark brown hair and animated eyes, she was probably just over two meters in height. She wore a simple cotton dress and had on red lipstick. It was hard to say how old she might be, although she may have been in her seventies. Being sensitive about propriety, I never asked her age.

I introduced myself as we sat on her porch. I told her that Alvarado had sent me. She seemed aloof until I mentioned Alvarado's name. Once I told her of my connection to him, she became much more animated. She told me that she wanted to make a video of the sanctuary. Did I know anyone who could film a video for her? I said I could talk to José Cárdenas, the cameraman for *Reportajes,* to see if he would be interested in making the video. She said she would pay him for his services. In addition to the discussion of the video, she told me of the Virgin Mary and how everyone needed to wear "the medal," La Medalla Milagrosa (the miraculous medal). It was the same medal that Alvarado had given me at his office. She gave me several medals, rosaries, and some printed novenas.[4]

I returned to Santiago a few days later and began an association with Doña Pepita. She told me of her history, her background, her religious beliefs, and her family. Four or five days out of the week, I would make the thirty-minute drive up the highway to Santiago. I would usually arrive at the sanctuary around ten in the morning and stay with Doña Pepita until three or four in the afternoon. While I was at the sanctuary, we would clean and arrange the altar, sell medals and religious articles at *el puesto* (the booth where the medals were sold), take care of her two-year-old granddaughter Karen, eat lunch with her family, talk about the

Woman sitting in a chair in front of *el puesto* at the sanctuary of the Medalla Milagrosa. Behind the woman are the bottles of holy water that are sold at *el puesto*. 1998.

Photograph by the author.

Virgin, and do other things that Doña Pepita found interesting. This continued for two months. After that time, my visits became more intermittent, although we always stayed in contact.

History

As a young woman, Doña Pepita came in contact with a group of nuns whose convent was near her house in Monterrey. A friend of hers had become ill and had gone to see the nuns. The Order of St. Vincent de Paul maintained La Cruz Roja (the Red Cross) and provided medical care for those requesting services. Her friend was very ill, and Pepita made a promise to join the order should the friend be cured. When this recovery came to be, she left for the mother house in southern Mexico. She stayed for eighteen months. After that time, she returned home, telling me that her mother needed her to help with family obligations.

Man in a cowboy hat and other customers at *el puesto* in the sanctuary. 1998.
Photograph by the author.

Two men conversing in front of Doña Pepita's house. Here people sit on benches and hear Doña Pepita speak about the Virgin Mary or watch a video about the sanctuary. 1998.
Photograph by the author.

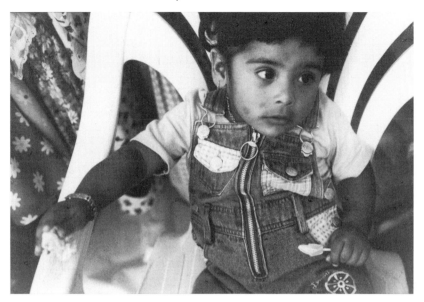

Doña Pepita's granddaughter, Karen Sepúlveda. 1998.
Photograph by the author.

Distribution of rosaries in front of Doña Pepita's house. Usually done after she
has spoken to the crowd. 1998.
Photograph by the author.

Statue of the Virgin Mary that has recently arrived from the state of Hidalgo. Her face is covered and hands dismantled to protect her from damage during the trip. This statue and others are sold at the sanctuary. 1998.
Photograph by the author.

As one can tell from her photographs, Pepita was a strikingly beautiful woman. On more than one occasion, she told me that one of the Maderos had wanted to marry her. The Maderos were an elite family from the neighboring state of Coahuila. Francisco Madero was president of Mexico when he was assassinated in 1914. Pepita's suitor was from the succeeding generation of Maderos, many of whom lived in Monterrey. She did not marry the young man. Although Pepita did not speak much of her private life, she told me that when she was young, her mother needed her to be available to help with the younger children in the house, Aquiles and Irma Sabina. By the time I met Pepita many years later, she was already a widow. She did not speak of her marriage but was devoted to her son, Alejandro, who lived with his wife and daughter in a house next to Pepita's on the grounds of the sanctuary.

The eighteen months in the convent left a profound impact on Pepita. The nuns from St. Vincent de Paul told her about the miraculous medal. The Virgin Mary had appeared to a young nun in France in 1839. As in other apparitions, the Virgin told the young woman that people needed to be more devoted to the Rosary. This was to become the main focus of Doña Pepita's life.

Some years later, a cousin of hers bought a piece of property in Villa de Santiago. The cousin asked Doña Pepita to co-sign the mortgage. After several months, her cousin defaulted on the note. Doña Pepita was left with the debt. In what she sees as a continuous string of coincidences, someone she knew offered to lend her the money, giving her sufficient time to repay the debt. This was in the 1960s. During the week she worked at a local *empresa* (corporation) in Monterrey. On the weekends, with her son Alejandro, she would make the trip to Santiago. She says she did it by herself. She began clearing the land, pouring concrete for sidewalks, and building fences. She would hire workers to help, but the responsibility was totally hers.

Neri García, who eventually became the daughter-in-law of Don Hector, was a friend and supporter of Pepita. She had recently become Doña Pepita's *comadre,* because Pepita and Alejandro had been the godparents of Neri's son, Guillermo.[5] Neri told me that she remembered Pepita coming up to San Francisco twenty years before in a little car. During that time it was extremely unusual for a woman to drive, much less to be traveling on a highway alone. Pepita would come to the site on Fridays, bringing Alejandro, who was the same age as Neri. He would play while Pepita would work at constructing fences, sidewalks, or roads. Neri was born in Laguna de Sánchez, a village that is at a much higher elevation and is more isolated than San Francisco. Neri's family moved to San Francisco when she was a small child. She said that she and the other children were fascinated by Pepita's beauty and sophistication. Neri remembers that Pepita always carried expensive purses. For San Francisco, which at the time was a rural, nondescript village, the presence of an attractive young woman, alone, who drove a car and used expensive purses created much conversation and gossip.

Early in the project, Pepita decided to place a large statue of the Virgin Mary at the top of the hill. Her sister gave her the money for the statue. Since there was no road or other structure, it was extremely difficult to transport the statue up through the trees and brush. It was seven meters tall and made of concrete. The Virgin was not Guadalupe, who is more commonly seen in Mexico. She was the blue-eyed Virgin, wearing a white veil and a sky blue mantle.

Eventually, the statue was positioned to overlook the village of San Francisco. This is when people say the miracles began to happen. As the sixties moved into the seventies, Alejandro grew older and Doña Pepita began to spend more time at the sanctuary. She built a small house on the property and eventually moved so that she could attend to the sanctuary on a daily basis.

By the 1980s, Alejandro was a grown man. He moved to Nuevo Laredo. He drove tractor-trailer rigs all over northern Mexico until he returned to work in nearby Allende. While he was away, he would send part of his salary to his mother. The money was used to continue the development of the sanctuary. Even so, the place remained mostly brush until the early 1990s.

In 1995 Alejandro met a young girl who worked for the Telmex office in Allende, fifty kilometers away. Her name was Mari Pérez. She was an attractive woman, fifteen years younger than Alejandro, very intelligent and quick-witted. She had not attended school past the sixth grade, but was naturally smart and agile. He told his mother that it was time that he married. They had a large wedding, and by the time I knew them I saw many large color portraits of Alejandro and Mari on their wedding day. They already had a two-year-old daughter, Karen, who would often pinch me and stick her tongue out at me.

A few months before I met the family, Alejandro began law school at night. When he was a young boy, with the help of Pepita's siblings, Alejandro had been educated very well in Monterrey. He was ready and motivated for school, as he told me. It made for an interesting dynamic. Every day, at about 5 P.M., Alejandro would leave Santiago and drive into Monterrey for class. This schedule left Doña Pepita, the daughter-in-law, and Karen alone at the sanctuary. Since he often did not return until after 10 P.M., the two women were left alone to deal with the normal tension between mother-in-law and daughter-in-law.

Pureza y Unidad con Dios—Purity and Unity with God

Villa de Santiago, Nuevo León
September 1998

Doña Pepita Sepúlveda has been looking for my phone number. It has been three weeks since I left Nuevo León. While I was there we talked for hours most every day for two months. I would travel south from Monterrey, about twenty miles, to her Santuario de la Medalla Milagrosa, which is located at the top of a small *cerro* (hill) on the outskirts of Santiago. She would tell me about La Virgen and about the miracles and medals. If a person wears the miraculous medal, the light from Mary's blessing blinds Satan, protects the wearer from all evil, and prolongs her life into old age.

Although Doña Pepita could not find my number, I also thought of her that day. When I called her, she was not surprised, since she was hoping to speak with me. I did not tell her that my daughter had been ill, yet she encouraged me to have my daughter "drink holy water, to make the child feel better." Doña Pepita believes in the curative uses of holy water. She sells hundreds of bottles of holy water every week. They sell for two pesos per bottle, about sixteen American cents. A young man named Juan fills the bottles and seals them with white caps. At such a minimal price, I am not sure that Doña Pepita benefits from their sale. Yet those who drink the water leave satisfied, sometimes taking three or four bottles with them.

At the top of the *cerro* are two statues of La Virgen Milagrosa. Her hands are outstretched, reaching towards the people below. There is a smaller statue of the Virgin of Guadalupe towards the back, and a large Christ on the Cross towards the front left. There are artificial flowers everywhere; they are brought by visitors. On weekends, Alejandro, Doña Pepita's son, pays a priest to celebrate the mass under a white canvas. After mass, Pepita speaks to the crowd from the porch of her small home, which is at the foot of the *cerro*. She uses a microphone. Later she plays a video of the "Medallas" story for those remaining. She gives away hundreds of medals and rosaries. Many more are sold along with the holy water at *el puesto,* fifty yards from her house.

On weekends, when Pepita was busy with the visitors, I would sit under a tree and watch people. They came in all types: some wealthy, many working class, some "white," and many dark. Buses would crawl up the one-lane road to the Santuario, their occupants having paid ten pesos to be brought from different towns in Nuevo León.

The townspeople generally do not visit the sanctuary. However, visitors arrive from all over northern Mexico to see the "white" Virgin. In Pepita's distribution of medals, water, and rosaries, she assists the people in their hope to achieve purity and cleanliness. Evil and Satan are moved aside with these practices. Pepita tells everyone that using the medals is a protection from witchcraft, another contamination.

The holy water that cleanses, spiritually and physically, is a tool of purification. Pepita's practices have numerous associations with the Catholic Church. The cleansing of evil and closeness to God and His Mother continue in the life of Nuevo León. Doña Pepita, a former nun from the order of St. Vincent de Paul, speaks in medieval tones about Satan and the thousand angels that surround the Virgin. The Virgin, European and white, existing before the brown Virgin of Guadalupe, has a connection to much earlier stories. The state of purity, which allows the lowly *ser humano* (human being) to be close to God and receive His blessing, removes the cast of barbarity. The pious man is not the wild man. Perhaps those that visit Doña Pepita's sanctuary seek to cleanse themselves of the contaminations inherent in living *en el norte;* for a moment they believe, and are blessed by God, the Virgin, and Doña Pepita. The medal they receive of the "white" Virgin may be a protection that continues after they leave the site.

MYSTIC

Místicos (delirios) . . . la creencia en la posibilidad de una unión íntima y directa del espíritu humano con el principio fundamental del ser (Diccionario taxonómica de psiquiatría 1993: 180). (Mystics (deliriums) . . . the belief in the possibility of an intimate and direct union of the human spirit with the fundamental principle of existence)

A House, Money, and Buried Treasure

The environment in Santiago is significantly different than in Potrero. Santiago is further inside the Sierra Madre mountain range. It is at a higher elevation. It is cooler, and there are many more trees and green vegetation. I was seduced by the imagery I encountered in Santiago. I seriously entertained the thought of renting a house in the city for a short while. I even fantasized about buying a small piece of property in the future. This was before I learned of the exorbitant prices of real estate in the area. On my third trip to Santiago, Yolanda González and I stopped at a house that had a sign announcing *terrenos de venta* (property for sale). Out of curiosity we wanted to see what a plot of land would cost. The woman was rather rude to us. I told her that I had been visiting with Doña Pepita Sepúlveda and that I liked the place so much that I was thinking of buying some property. The woman angrily responded, "Ask Doña Pepita to rent or sell you some property up on the mountain. She has a lot of property she could sell."

A few weeks later, as I continued to look for a house to rent, Doña Pepita recommended that I speak with Don Hector, who owned a small *depósito* in San Francisco. Don Hector appeared to be about sixty years old. He was a tall, attractive man who talked slowly and carefully. He showed me a small house about a block from the *depósito*. It had belonged to his mother. We walked to the place. It had a whitewashed front and looked like it had been part of a larger house at one time. I am not sure why I was not shocked or disgusted when I walked in. The front door had a few small holes in it. The living area did not have a window. The house had to be at least 100 years old if not more. There were holes in the interior wall. The ceiling was made of thatch. There were loose electrical wires hanging in each room. Don Hector had been using the place as a warehouse. Loose straw and pieces of trash were thrown about the house. The toilet was missing from the bathroom. There was no sink in the small kitchen.

Once we walked into the backyard, everything was different. There was still trash strewn around, yet the garden was remarkably green. There were plants, trees, and flowers growing without being tended. Once I saw everything, I imagined cleaning the place and making the garden a spot where I could write. Don Hector was aware of my enthusiasm. He said that he would rent it to me for 1000 pesos per month (about 110 dollars). However, I had to pay for all the repairs and after six months he had the option to ask me to move out. In my happy delirium I did not think that the proposal was somewhat skewed. A few days later when I came to my senses I told him that I could not invest in the property only to know it would be taken away in six months. He seemed very disappointed and tried to talk me into renting or buying a house he had in the country about ten kilometers away. He said that he was having financial problems because of an inconsistent and minimal cash flow. He told me that there were times that he just did not have any money.

My next attempt at finding a house in Santiago came to sound like an adventure novel. Easily sliding into the exotic, this story of buried treasure places the people and the place into an Other environment. It lures the story into the seductive magical real. At moments the story feels like an illusion because of the quotidian nature of the quest. I was simply looking for a house to rent while I did my fieldwork in Nuevo León. Even so, what lies behind the motives and the suggestions of all involved stems from many different sources beyond the search for a place to live.

There are innumerable examples of these fabulations in my conversations with people during the time I have spent in Nuevo León. A story about finding a renthouse is an example of what Stewart describes as a "nervous, overstuffed, insistent type of story" (1996). There was a house a few blocks from Doña Pepita's. One afternoon she was very insistent that I drive by the house. She wanted to see if I liked it. Indeed, it was very beautiful. It appeared to be from the colonial period, with a large front porch and a large yard. She said that no one lived there and the past few years it had been used only to store furniture. She then directed me to the owner of the house, a woman who lived near the main plaza of Santiago. I was not quite ready to go that far in my search, but she was so insistent I decided to visit the woman the same afternoon. After asking several people near the plaza, I finally found the house. It was truly elegant, very large, with stucco walls, neatly painted, and dark green trim on the ancient windows and doors. I approached the front door quite timidly. I did not know quite what to say to the woman. Doña Pepita had only told me that the woman was a widow and the owner of the property that I was considering renting. I knocked on the door for several minutes. I was puzzled because the windows were open, although there were wrought iron bars called *rejas*. I could hear a parakeet chirping. No one came to the door. I returned to Doña Pepita rather sheepishly and somewhat relieved. As our conversation went into the afternoon she explained to me the reason why she had hoped I would rent that particular house. There are ruins of a small building in the front yard of the house. Doña Pepita had been told that under the foundation of this building was buried treasure. If I were to rent the property, we could easily dig during the night. The money from the treasure would help finance Doña Pepita's sanctuary to the Virgin Mary.

This narrative tells of a history. It tells of daily life in which the past is buried yet remains alive. It produces a tight weave that interlaces the present moment of my seeking a place to live, the expected tasks of identifying the house and seeking its owner, and the underlying plot inside of Doña Pepita's directions. The search for buried treasure, as fantastic as it may seem, is not so unusual in the history of Nuevo León. Indeed, stories of buried treasure surface constantly in the region; the need to bury valuables inside walls, under foundations, and inside of caves was commonplace well into the twentieth century. The Mexican Revolution did not end until 1929. With the constant ruptures within the government and between the settlers and the Chichimeca, there was no sense of ongoing safety for anyone of any group living in Nuevo León and no guarantee of security for one's possessions. This instability lasted well into the 1940s.

This type of narrative is well-described by Luiz Costa Lima in his book *The Dark Side of Reason* (1992). He describes the suspension of a normalized perspective. To put it in the same terms Costa Lima uses, the story of the house and the buried treasure may be enveloped in the following manner: the "present" of the American (Mexican) anthropologist searching for a place to live near her interlocutor, the past of the (still) living "treasure" under the house, and Doña Pepita's pragmatic suggestion of "that house" for the purpose of excavating the treasure and using it for the Holy Virgin. To encompass these different moments and spaces, the narrator has to see things "outside the bounds of time and space" (187). The characterization of the particular moment (in linear time) and particular space (Villa de Santiago, Nuevo León) would only detract from the inherent evocation of the narrative. Costa Lima views this type of "temporal translucency" as less opaque than what he sees as the clearer "nature of imagined objects" (187). The focus of the narrative is the embedded nature of the "possible" with the necessary. The "possible" may also be termed the "Imaginary," the "fabulous," or the "far-out." This "possible treasure" wavers between many spaces.[6] While akin to a fairy tale, it also tells of how things are lost and found, of the probability of finding something valuable in any ordinary space. Tied in with "the necessary," which could be the parallel of the "material, historical reality," the narrative concerns the presence of the outsider seeking a place to live in the field, subtle issues of authority between the ethnographer and her interlocutor, and the awareness of discovery in the mind of the "foreign" ethnographer. Finding the treasure is not an economic necessity. Doña Pepita will continue to survive quite well without the imagined millions buried in the ground in front of the house. Yet searching for the treasure may be a necessity in the context of Doña Pepita's world. For what appears to be the benevolent opportunity of wealth is not easily dismissed. The real possibility of finding a treasure requires the initiation of a search. In other words, Doña Pepita would be a fool if she did not try to look for the treasure. The story informed her of a treasure that was buried under the foundation of the building in front of the house she wanted me to rent. For all practical purposes, the material traces of the treasure could be just where indicated.

While not relying on the factuality of documents (archives, newspapers, or land titles), the verbal narrative that indicates the existence of the treasure continues to focus on "material, historical reality" (188). In excluding documentary representations, the precise description that gives us chronology and spatial delineation is not present. Yet what remains is the body and form of the story as it travels from the local people of Santiago to Doña Pepita, who moved to the area in the 1970s; to the visiting ethnographer; to this text; to you, the reader of this text; and so on. The form is not static but remains alive as it passes from person to person. The way it molds and blends, diminishes, disappears for a time, and then resurfaces gives it the quality of a living myth. Yet it is not quite like a myth, because there are visible, factual aspects to the story. There is a house to rent, the owner of the house exists, and the foundation of the ruined building in front of the house is still there eighteen months after Doña Pepita told me about the treasure. Since she and I did not have possession of the property, we were not able to dig and see if there was something under the other building, yet the reality of Doña Pepita's desire is still present. To have the funds to further develop the sanctuary to the Virgin is a very realistic (and some would say noble) wish. Lastly, due to the nature of security, revolution, and revolt in the history of Nuevo León, the most fantastic aspect of the narrative is that it is actually probable that Doña Pepita would find something should she start digging in the yard of the house.

La Mujer Mística

The Mystic Woman

. . . metamorphosis is frequent among the mystics: the criterion of the beautiful replaces that of the true. It carries the sign from one

space to another, and it produces the new space. It is by this metamorphosis that a chart of knowledge is transformed into a garden
of delights. (de Certeau 1992: 58)

Doña Pepita Sepúlveda is a mystic. I find an intriguing semblance between what I know of Pepita and what Gershom Scholem writes in the
first chapter of *Kabbalah and Its Symbolism,* titled "Religious Authority
and Mysticism." I have used this text in searching for the movement and
thought in Pepita's "work." It is as if he is describing her as he writes on
mysticism. In this section I interweave Scholem's writing with Doña
Pepita's experience of mysticism.

Scholem's writing on religious authority and mysticism tells us that
mystic lives are "outside and above the historical level, that their experience is unrelated to historical experience" (1965: 7). And thus Pepita
lives in a surreal space. She is on the mountain, living in a house she built
for herself. She does not move forward in time as do other people. She
is submerged in the experience of the Virgin. She is often not aware or
interested in events outside her sanctuary. Her purpose is as Scholem describes—to communicate her knowledge of the divine to other people.
Her entire existence is based on acquiring and disseminating knowledge
about the Virgin Mary and of enlarging the scope of the sanctuary, its
physical space, and its mission. She is paradoxically conservative and radical at the same time. She chides me and other women if we wear dresses
that are more than four inches above the ankle. Yet, as a woman on her
own, she has managed to establish an intensely popular religious site in a
country where women are seldom taken very seriously. For Pepita,
woman is a sacred object, established for the purpose of serving God. For
her this service means physically working and verbally spreading the
messages sent from God (and His mother). This role for woman is not a
passive. Yet for Pepita, issues of sexuality and seduction are stratified in
mores of half a century before. According to Doña Pepita, while woman
must be active in her service to God, she is required to take a passive
stance regarding her sexuality and her relationship with men.

Inside this traditionalism she also promotes Marianism, which espouses devotion to Mary as the most important tenet of Catholicism.
This is somewhat radical in that there exists a large contingency in the
church that for decades has sought to diminish the importance of Marianism. Doña Pepita's promotion of the cult of Mary is related to her dis-
persion of medals. They spread her message. Scholem uses the analogy of

the saying that "mystics are always striving to put new wine into old bottles" (7). For Pepita, it is the traditional church structure that is the old bottle, fitted with certain gendered expectations. The tradition holds the pre-modern ideas of good and evil, God and Satan. The new wine contains two identified ingredients—the importance of Mary in the new millennium and the agency of the mystic who spreads Mary's message.

At the same time, Doña Pepita's specificity of mystical experience is illusive. Scholem continues: "The more intensely and profoundly the contact with God is experienced, the less susceptible it is of objective definition, for by its very nature it transcends the categories of subject and object which every definition presupposes" (Scholem 1965: 8). There are numerous possibilities for this ambiguous form. There can be descriptions from the mystic's "world of perception" or, at another level of consciousness, auditory or visual experiences that are not grounded in material reality. It is here that Pepita's discourse wanders from reason to the imaginary and from the material to a symbolic that cannot be demonstrated or explained.

As Scholem argues, the mystic is centered inside of traditional religious authority while she simultaneously de-limits the boundaries of the "word." Inside of what is taken as fundamental, the mystic begins to see that there may be another way of interpreting and pronouncing the text. ". . . the sacred text is smelted down and a new dimension is discovered in it. In other words: the sacred text loses its shape and takes on a new one for the mystic" (12). Doña Pepita locates her own wisdom inside of the text. It is used as a gate through which the mystic passes into the divine space. She does not have to "see" God. Similarly, as Scholem writes, the early Kabbalists in Languedoc "did not claim to have spoken directly with God" (19). There is no necessity of being formally "anointed." His description of Israel Baal-Shem, the founder of Polish Hasidism, parallels what I came to know of Doña Pepita: "His [Baal-Shem's] 'knowledge' in the traditional sense of the word was very meager; he had no teacher of flesh and blood to guide him on his way . . . In short, he was a pure lay mystic and lay mysticism was a vital factor in the development of the movement he founded. Yet this movement . . . won the recognition of the traditional authority" (26).

It is here that Scholem's description of the mystic moves exceedingly close to Doña Pepita's work. Although Pepita at times appears as if she has heard a "message," she denies ever having "spoken" to the Virgin. For this purpose she has brought in *videntes* (seers) who communicate with Mary and pass the information on to Pepita. There is no story of the Virgin ever appearing at the site of the sanctuary. It was merely Pepita's choice to use the land for that purpose. Most importantly, Doña Pepita was never formally anointed. Besides the eighteen months she spent as a novice, she has no formal religious training. She is clearly a "lay person" who took it upon herself to pay homage to the Virgin Mary.

Challenging Authority

When the large statue of the Virgin Mary was pulled up the mountain, there was no "official" approval given by the diocese. In contrast to the nuns in Mina who had the encouragement and approval of the Arch-bishop, Doña Pepita did not seek to be endorsed by any ecclesiastic source. She met with the Archbishop in Monterrey at different times over the thirty-six years of the sanctuary's existence. Only recently was she formally allowed to bring in a priest to say mass on the site. Masses are now being said on weekends and Holy Days. Priests from neighbor-ing parishes celebrate the mass. On a warm day, there would be as many as four hundred people at the 11 A.M. mass. In the summer of 1999, she was having a room built so that children could be baptized at the sanc-tuary. I did not ask her if the Diocese had given her permission to do so. From the time Doña Pepita decided to develop the sanctuary she always proceeded with her own best judgment, not with any guidance or per-mission from the church. Knowing what I already did about Doña Pepita's determined personality, I knew that she did not need permission from anyone to proceed with her plans.

The presence of the sanctuary also posed a challenge to the local "witches." On many occasions Doña Pepita would tell me or other people that dozens of witches would fly over the sanctuary and send evil in hopes of destroying everything. At other times, she felt that perhaps someone in the sanctuary itself was a representation of Satan. After all, she said, as others have also told me, Satan is always present alongside the divine.

After the battles with the church, witches, and money, the sanctuary managed to receive some type of approval by 1999. The local priests no longer confronted Doña Pepita. Clergy actually paid frequent visits to the sanctuary. There were no longer stories of witches flying overhead, although the story of the evil within remained. Most importantly, Doña

Pepita received a governmental endorsement. The governor of the state of Nuevo León owns a *quinta* in Santiago. While he was campaigning for office, Fernando Canales Clariond visited with Doña Pepita and requested assistance from the Virgin. When he won the election, he returned to the sanctuary and told Pepita that he and his services were at her disposal. The road to the sanctuary would be improved. She now had a direct connection to the governor. This was more than the Catholic Archbishop had ever attempted. However, the radical nature of her project made it likely that she would have support from the state before she received support from the church.

La Mística Ciudad—The Mystic City

Monterrey

May 1999

On a visit I made to El Museo de Historia Regional in Monterrey, I saw an ancient parchment book that was entitled *La mística ciudad* (*The Mystic City*). The title seemed vaguely familiar to me. The book, printed in Spanish, appeared to be from the early colonial period of New Spain. It was larger than a Bible. Because it was on exhibit at the museum, it was contained in a glass case along with other church artifacts.

A few days later when I visited Pepita, I remembered that she often spoke of *La mística ciudad*. I told her I had found a similar title. She asked me if I could speak with the curator of the museum to see if she could obtain a Xerox copy. I never carried out her request because I knew the director of the museum; we had already had a minor confrontation concerning a difference of opinion in regard to stories of a Jewish settlement in Nuevo León.

Doña Pepita had spoken repeatedly of what was written on the mystical city in the sixteenth century by Sor María de Jesús Agreda. It was a detailed account of the life of the Virgin Mary. The information had been divinely transmitted to this Spanish nun, who had documented what she heard. Agreda's work was banned by the Inquisition on several occasions. However, it is interesting to note that she became a confidante of Felipe IV and maintained a twenty-year correspondence with the king (Esposito 1990).

On many afternoons or early evenings, we would sit at Doña Pepita's dining room table as she would begin to tell me about the Virgin Mary. She discussed how the Virgin's mother, St. Anne, became pregnant well after she was into old age and how the Virgin was a brilliant and articulate child even before she could walk. Pepita explained how the Virgin and St. Joseph were married, how he managed the problem of her already existing pregnancy, and how the couple decided to live a "chaste" life.

As Pepita told me these stories, she would express herself with such emotion and in such a vivid manner that I became mesmerized. We would sit at her dining table. She had her special chair, which was nearest the door to the carport. I would sit facing her, perhaps drinking a Coca-Cola, hearing the same stories over and over again. It seemed to me that Pepita became inspired as she was talking. She told me that she had found the stories like those of *La mística ciudad* and had begun telling people about what she had found long before the church believed any of these stories to be important. She often talked of the apparitions at Lourdes and Fatima. Since the time I spent with her was close to the end of the millennium, there were many references to an apocalyptic event that might occur if people did not pray the rosary.

Although Doña Pepita came from a family that bore their civility proudly, she herself lived a very simple life. Her room was behind the kitchen of her small house. She slept in an antique brass bed that had belonged to her family. There were only two chairs in the room. Sometimes we would have conversations while she sat on the bed to play with her granddaughter and I sat in a chair next to them. Under the bed she kept boxes of prayers, cards, and brochures that told of the Virgin and her novenas. The house did not have an air conditioner nor did it have a heater. She did not have an automobile, although she did drive when she was younger. Her clothes were sewn by a local seamstress. They were plain cotton dresses. Her only extravagance was the red lipstick that she would wear on Sundays when the mob of people would arrive at the sanctuary and she stood for hours telling them of the Virgin and the miraculous medal.

In her interpretation of Agreda's text and in her purposeful dissemination of her divinely inspired message, Doña Pepita Sepúlveda broke through the socially expected limitations placed on women of her age and established a sanctuary and a voice that intersected with 100,000 people, easily, per year.

Milagros—Miracles

Neri García used to invite me to sit with her and her children outside their house, which was located on the top of large hill in Santiago. The house was small. There was a kitchen and one large bedroom. There was no living room. The oldest boy, who was about sixteen, slept in a room that was separated from the house. His room was burrowed into the side of the hill. Surrounded by plants she was growing or by clothes she had hung out to dry, Neri and her family sat outside on the carport on days with good weather. The view from the carport was spectacular. We could see as far as Monterrey, which was thirty kilometers away.

Neri really believed in the power of the medals. It was not so much that she had known Pepita since childhood, but was also that Neri's father had a near-fatal accident some years before. Neri believed that he had been saved by La Medalla Milagrosa. He had been driving a large tractor, which had some problems with the engine. Her father got underneath to see what the problem was. The tractor moved suddenly and rolled over the man's head. He was unconscious for a moment, but otherwise all he had were tire marks on his face. He was examined repeatedly by doctors and found to be in good health. Neri firmly believes that her father was saved because he carried a Medalla Milagrosa with him.

A few months earlier I was at Casa Enrique, a store in Monterrey that sells supplies to make handicrafts. The saleslady was wearing a Medalla Milagrosa. I asked her if she had been to the sanctuary. She said yes, but more importantly, her husband always carried a medal. A few months before, he had a very serious auto accident. Because the car was completely destroyed, she believes that such a crash would have killed him. All he suffered was a broken arm. She told me he survived because he had the medal in his pocket.

Doña Pepita and her son Alejandro sell the medals for about twelve pesos at their *puesto*. Over a period of a year, Pepita gave me hundreds of medals to give to people in Monterrey, Potrero, and Houston. She told me a story once that she firmly believed was true: during the Persian Gulf War, a young man who was originally from Nuevo León was sent into combat in the Persian Gulf. His wife visited the sanctuary asking for his safe return. Pepita gave the wife hundreds of little medals (those about ¾ inch long). The woman sent them to her husband, who had them thrown out of a helicopter. The war ended the next day and Doña Pepita was convinced it was because of the medals. She also reminded me on several occasions that President Clinton was exonerated by Congress after she sent him a medal. For this gift she received an official thank you note from the White House. Apparently a sincere admirer of Clinton, she used to tell me that Clinton's affair with Lewinsky was not adultery because the Clintons agreed to appear married but were in fact separated.[7]

Space of the Demonic

I am listening to Doña Pepita's stories of Satan and the power of the "Miraculous Medal." As she speaks of how Satan is blinded by the light of the medal, I think of her positioning as a "believer," her intense desire to speak to everyone, the intensity of her medieval perspective. When we are left alone, she smiles and tells me (again) that there is buried treasure in the *cerro* next to her house. At the moment that she utters these words, I sense I am entering the space where the subject momentarily disappears. For me there is no intellectual paradigm for the treasure on the *cerro* or for the blinding medals. Exegesis is not important, yet presence is a priority. I listen closely to the words that banish Satan and I wonder what Pepita is thinking at the particular moment that she is speaking. What language is she using? Who taught her this way of understanding? How does the real of her statement correspond to the real of the world outside her sanctuary?

It appears that Pepita genuinely believes what she says about the Virgin and Satan. Her language is colloquial, and all her visitors are easily able to understand her. She said she learned the ideas of God and the Virgin from the nuns of St. Vincent de Paul, although her siblings told me that their mother had been intensely religious. The real of her words parallels that of the outside world in that the Satan her visitors are facing is the corruption, the crime, and the economic problems faced by most people except the Monterrey Industrialists. At moments Satan is also a person's intimate family member, sister, brother, or best friend. Thus Doña Pepita conflates these relationships with evil that can destroy.

Pepita has never told me about Satan being in the Villa de Santiago, although numerous people, including Alvarado, have told me it is a "bad" place, and there is a "demonic" quality to the city. Perhaps it is seen this way because of all the wealth that has moved into the area. One afternoon, Neri, her children, and I traveled about Santiago looking at the large houses that were visible from the large gates protecting the properties. As we drove past one and another *quinta,* Neri named off the important people who owned the properties. It sounded like the Fortune 500 list of Monterrey. It seemed like the CEO of every major corporation owned property in Santiago. Very large properties, they had elegant landscaping and fences four meters high. Alvarado had told me that all the gay people in Monterrey had moved to Santiago. He spoke very badly of the place and said there were many murders. I had heard that the *narco-traficantes* often left bodies in open fields around Santiago or other cities nearby. There have been occasional reports of these findings in *El Norte,* Monterrey's newspaper, including a story several days ago about a man that had been missing for several months. His skeletal remains were found near Montemorelos, forty kilometers to the south. He was still dressed in his clothes and boots. He had owned a Casa de Cambio (money exchange) and had disappeared one night with thousands of dollars.

The day Neri and I were driving around Santiago, we passed by a very unusual house. I had seen the house several times before and had been fascinated with the architecture. Like many other *quintas* in Santiago, the house was like a wall itself, surrounding an inner courtyard. Neri said an uncle of her husband's had worked for the owners of the house. The interior was full of devils and demon-like images. Once a week, people came in the new cars from Monterrey and drove into the garage that automatically opened when they arrived. Several hours later all the cars would leave one by one, with the garage door seemingly opening by itself. Neri did not know the details of the group's activities, but she called them the "devil worshipers."[8]

As we talked of occult activities, Neri also told me the story of a house in the main plaza of Santiago. The local bank brought in a new executive and provided a house for the man's family. The man's wife found an underground passage one day as she was cleaning out a closet. The passage opened up to more rooms that were equal in size to the house above ground. Neri did not know what types of things had happened in this house. The banker's wife was completely surprised at the existence of these underground spaces. I had heard from other people that underground tunnels were common in Santiago as they were in Monterrey.

La Carretera Nacional

The National Highway

There is a store in Santiago that sells *piloncillo,* which is a cone of ground sugarcane and nuts. Their *piloncillos* are so famous, people say that even the presidents of Mexico have them sent to Los Pinos, the Mexican White House. The market surrounding Santiago has adapted to the demographic changes. There are scores of small shops selling everything from furniture to plants. The *piloncillo* and the markets draw people from all over northern Mexico. In the three years I traveled to Nuevo León I became one of those consumers. I would buy *piloncillos* and other small articles. I was one of the thousands of other motorists who traveled down the highway looking for goods to buy, tourist stops to visit, weekend homes to buy, or to visit the sanctuary of La Medalla Milagrosa.

On several occasions I found myself traveling from Santiago to Monterrey late on a Sunday afternoon. The first time this happened I thought there had been a serious accident on the highway. The traffic looked like a Houston traffic jam. The cars were bumper-to-bumper the entire way. Police were stationed every kilometer or so to watch the traffic. I later realized that it was Monterrey's middle class and affluent who were clogging *la carretera nacional.* Santiago and beyond were the escape. Many had weekend homes, desperate to get out of the city. These were the people who lived in the big empty *quintas* that Neri showed me as we drove around Santiago.

While most of the people who visit Doña Pepita are working class, they, also, try to escape from Monterrey when they can. The differences between this working class and Monterrey's middle class are striking. On numerous occasions, I found a couple walking up the steep hill towards the sanctuary. They had taken the *camión* (the bus) to Santiago and could not (or would not) hire a taxi for the last four kilometers. I often gave them a ride, feeling guilty for the privilege of having a car.

Perhaps there is also a mystical aspect to the environment of Villa de Santiago. It drew Doña Pepita and scores of affluent *regiomontanos.* It has lured the wealthy and the clandestine. The poor go to see Doña Pepita, and the rich go to their *quintas.* The rest go to look and to buy.

PART FOUR

LOCATIONS OF *LE RÉEL*

Le réel, the space between the tangible, holdable reality and the moment inside the mind of the witness, cannot be cited. It is ineffable. The trance-like state experienced at the instant of what de Certeau terms *ravishment* is the delirium located between the moment of experience and the moment of scriptural documentation (1988). This ineffable quality parallels the lack of citation/documentation in the history that has created this *réel.* The documents have been burned, purged, lost, stolen, sold. They are burned ashes that have floated above the skies of Monterrey or sit in a vault at the Benson Latin American Library at the University of Texas. There are stories circulating in Nuevo León that a certain prominent historian from Monterrey sold numerous documents from the regional archives. These were reportedly purchased by the University of Texas. These claims are unsubstantiated, yet were repeatedly mentioned during conversations I had with *regiomontanos.*

The Scriptural Economy, whether connected to power or money, has left Nuevo León's archives bereft of information regarding the region's early post-conquest history. What is left is our imaginary. The narratives people tell about Jews, Indians, and lost documents have no material basis, although it is worth mentioning that, if we take seriously the viability of archives, we may also question their truth. Even so, the written link to the past is missing. In its place has emerged a multitude of phantasms, probably affording more interesting and imaginative narratives than if the history of reality would still be present.

The *réel* in this section is found in the lost archives documenting the Jewish settlement, the tunnels of Monterrey, the underground city, the people buried under foundations of buildings, the insides of walls, the secrets that are "known" but cannot be told.

CHAPTER VII

The Discourse of Illusion: *Los Sefardíes*

The Statue

The first time I spoke with Aquiles Sepúlveda, in July 1998, he told me that a statue of Alberto del Canto, the Portuguese founder of Saltillo, was lying among old and wrecked automobiles somewhere in the city. In 1995, when Monterrey was celebrating its 400th year, the newspaper *El Norte* published a photograph of the forgotten statue. The newspaper was looking for stories that would tell of Monterrey's history. Once the condition of the statue was made public, there was no movement to salvage del Canto from the wreckage of autos. I asked Aquiles if he did not want to remove the statue and perhaps place it in his garden. He told me it would be dangerous. Besides settling Saltillo, del Canto was the first European to make note of Monterrey. Yet del Canto lacks significance in the late twentieth century. He is relegated to the refuse. Aquiles believed that anyone who shows an interest in the statue may be placed in an undesirable position and end up like del Canto, lying face down in a space designated for damaged and unusable objects.[1]

It is a Saturday afternoon. Aquiles wants to convey to me a significant aspect of *norteño* history. As he describes the fate of the statue, he plays music recorded in a Mexican synagogue—*Cantos judeos/Jewish Cantos.* He then plays music written by a Mexican composer, classical, with a touch of regional sound. One of the pieces sounds like a *Canto.* This juxtaposition of name and sound leaves me thinking of other possibilities. After the sixteenth century, the name *del Canto,* to my knowledge, has not appeared in other texts regarding Nuevo León's history. Yet there are thousands of persons descended from a family in northern Mexico by the name of "Cantú." Although I have heard explanations for those named

Cantú being French (this is still a possibility), I also wonder about del Canto, and any need or desire to have altered a name that evokes a resemblance to one of the *Cantos judeos*.

When I first met him, Aquiles asked me not to identify him in my writings. It was a caution associated with what he perceived as the danger surrounding the Jewish narratives. This explained his reluctance in rescuing the statue of del Canto. It resonated with a secrecy necessary to protect him from harm. Aquiles reminded me that it was a common story that northern Mexico was settled by Jews. What he told me was not new information. Yet he believed that the text resulting from our conversations could cause him harm. As time passed, he became more open and less cautious in his conversations with me.

Correlaciones — Conexiones

Correlations — Connections

Nuevo León is a historical site that can be studied by locating the placement of entities—events, people, and confrontations. As Foucault (1974) writes, history can be understood as an archaeological site to be studied by analyzing the spatial and interactive relationships between events, coalitions, confrontations, and violence. The different pieces create a schemata that provide the historian a sense of what may have transpired during particular phases of the region's history. The intense ruptures between the settlers and the Chichimeca paradoxically created a fragility within the new "state" while simultaneously forcing the settlers to take on the role of the "invincible" Spaniard. The confrontations encountered in El Nuevo Reino were of a different character yet no less violent and bloodthirsty than what they escaped when they left the Iberian peninsula.

At the time that Carvajal was given the territory of El Nuevo Reino, Spain and Europe were in the midst of numerous conflicts and transitions. There was significantly more occurring than the problem of the Spanish crown needing funds to continue operating. The Reformation was already entrenched in France and England. The Catholic Church was being challenged to its core. Spain responded with its Inquisition, which also assisted in delineating the criteria for the "pure" Spanish citizen and strengthening the ideology of the solid Spanish nation. Carvajal formed

El Nuevo Reino de León less than one hundred years after the expulsion of the Jews from Spain. Those who remained behind as *conversos* and their descendants continued to live precariously, whether or not they secretly practiced Jewish traditions.[2] The Inquisition seemed to attack indiscriminately. In this risk, paradoxically, was also the possibility of wealth. Many *conversos,* such as the Carvajals, who moved about the Spanish Empire, amassed riches from the slave trade and other commercial exploits.

In studying the narratives regarding del Canto, Carvajal, and Montemayor, it is necessary to consider that they were migrants. They were leaving one world for another that in many ways was unknown. What little information they had indicated an inhospitable place that posed significant physical danger. Numerous texts propose that these three men were descended from Portuguese *conversos,* which was said to be the group that held on to their Jewish practices much more strongly than Jewish descendants from other Spanish regions (Caro Baroja 1996). I believe that the eventual displacement of Carvajal as governor and the annihilation of his family are closely related to the "secret Jewish stories" often told in present-day Nuevo León. This secrecy is intensified by the contradictions of history and remaining ambiguity regarding the current-day presence of Jews in the world. The sense of danger regarding disclosure as well as the narrative's pairing with heresy placed it in a discourse of the Other.

The discourse of Jews in northern Mexico is somewhat akin to a diabolical discourse. When a discourse becomes diabolical, de Certeau tells us in *The Writing of History* (1988), "Its language changes status." Significantly, during the time when El Nuevo Reino was established, the Enlightenment was taking hold over Europe. During this period, the "world is transformed into *space;* knowledge is organized around a *looking-over.*" Thus there is a problem of truth when it assumes the form of an unstable place such as El Nuevo Reino. "A 'truth' becomes doubtful." It is not possible to discern if these signifiers that have transformed themselves from words to spaces are in the category of truth or of falsehood, "if they can be ascribed to reality, or to the imagination." The discourse regarding the Jews becomes a "language of illusion."[3]

The ruptured society that del Canto, Carvajal, and Montemayor were leaving behind most likely created a need to continue the language of illusion. This language became even more necessary after the death of Carvajal and his family. De Certeau reminds us that a truth becomes doubtful when there is no stable basis for knowledge.

Antecedents

What is essential . . . is . . . the foundation of a field in which specific procedures will be developed: a *space* and an *apparatus* . . . The reinterpretation of the tradition is characterized by an ensemble of processes that allow language to be treated differently. (de Certeau 1992: 14)

En el discurso de los tiempos la pequeña aldea judía de San Luis se transformó en la industrial, rica y progresista ciudad de Monterrey. (Robles 1938: 107) (As time passed, the small Jewish village of San Luis was transformed into the industrial, rich, and progressive city of Monterrey)

There is a tension in the traces of history that accompanied del Canto, Carvajal, and Montemayor on their travels from El Valle de Estremadura in Portugal to El Valle de Estremadura in New Spain. The timing and the actors are worth noting. El Nuevo Reino de León was founded during the Golden Age of Spain, which occurred only two centuries after what is known as the Golden Age of Spanish Judaism. The first sections of the Kabbalah were written in Gerona and Toledo during the twelfth and thirteenth centuries. Its mysticism and profound erudition made it a fantastic document that continues to be significantly misunderstood in the late twentieth century. Two centuries later, three significant bodies of written work appeared. From Spain's late medieval period, they were also associated with the Jews. The most noted, of course, is Cervantes's *Don Quijote de la Mancha,* which is considered to be the first "modern" novel. The other two are by religious mystics—Santa Teresa de Avila and San Juan de la Cruz. All three authors have been said to be the descendants of *conversos,* Jews that had converted to Catholicism (Caro Baroja 1961; Peña 1975).

Teresa of Avila, considered to be Spain's greatest saint (Caro Baroja 1961), was the daughter of a rich merchant. Her brothers were dispersed throughout the Americas after a failed attempt at clearing their name of *limpieza* accusations. In an earlier generation, her paternal grandfather, Juan Sánchez de Toledo, was tried by the Spanish Inquisition. Caro Baroja states there are indications that some of her family members continued to practice Judaism in Spain and in the Americas (1961). Another great Spanish mystic, John of the Cross (also known as Juan de Dios), was the dispossessed grandson of a rich *converso.* De Certeau describes the issue of dispossession as evident in the saint's mystical writing, which exemplifies a "negative theology" that signifies by what it "takes away" (1992). St. Teresa and John of the Cross were Carmelites. The faint link to Judaism lies behind the connotation of the name *Carmelite*. There is "a Palestinian and biblical institution; a place, Mount Carmel, a physical and mythical presence to which the entire Western and Eastern monastic tradition was related since its origin, a fortiori the Carmelites born on its slopes in the thirteenth century; and also a long line of Jewish contemplatives" (134). An ancient definition of the term *Carmel* is that of "circumcision." Within the context of the Carmelite Order is the transfiguration between three forms: the Jewish contemplative, the *converso*, and the Christian mystic.

In de Certeau's *The Mystic Fable* (1992), he argues that both John of the Cross and Teresa of Avila were mystics whose work emerged from a sense of loss. Initially he associates the loss with their family's diminished social status. Yet I believe there is also the connection to loss in reference to the Kabbalah, which is often said to be a discourse on the Jewish diaspora (Bloom 1975). With the initiation of *limpieza de sangre,* there is an additional displacement. This loss is the Hebrew connection with God. De Certeau describes the words of Teresa of Avila and John of the Cross as cutting "the body of the mother tongue." The shift from Judaism to Christianity creates a *réel* that remains alive in its pieces after it has been cut away from its home. The words of these two mystics form a paradoxical separation, which at one level delicately exhibits the split from Judaism, in which the mystic is submerged in the Christian "truth of God," while at the same time venerating the old connection. The circumcision, the allusion to Mt. Carmel, is a constant referent to the "mother tongue" that has been cut.

Comida Alterada—Food of the Other

Cabrito—Baby Goat

In the large windows of El Rey del Cabrito on Avenida Constitución in Monterrey, are a number of baby goats that have been lanced and are standing with their limbs outstretched and their open ribs showing through the glass. It is a tradition for eating places in northern Mexico that serve *cabrito* to exhibit their "delicacy" in this way. Pepe Quijano, owner of the Café Infiniti, a few blocks from "El Rey," told me in the spring of 1999 that the *cabritos* on display reminded him of Jesus on the cross.[4]

Cabrito asado—Nuevo León es una tierra apta para la producción del cabrito y sus habitantes son grandes consumidores de esta cría, pero la manera en que se selecciona, limpia y prepara inevitablemente evoca costumbres sefardíes.

La forma en que se deguella al animal, la cuidadosa extracción de cada uno de sus órganos y la limpieza exhaustia de ella antes de cocinarla es parte del rito judío. (Campoy, *El Norte,* December 3, 1999) (Barbecued Baby Goat—The land of Nuevo León is an apt environment for the production of goats. The inhabitants of the region consume copious amounts of *cabrito.* The manner in which *cabrito* is selected, cleaned, and prepared evokes Sephardic customs.

The manner in which the animal is slaughtered, the careful extraction of each of the animal's organs and entrails and the exhaustive cleansing of the animal before it is cooked are parts of the Jewish tradition.)

RECIPE FOR *CABRITO ASADO* [ROAST YOUNG GOAT]

1 small young goat, headless

4 tablespoons margarine

6 tablespoons butter

4 garlic cloves

6 bunches fresh thyme

10 leaves fresh sage

2 lemons (juice only)

⅓ cup oil

12 peppercorns

Coarse salt, as required. Rub young goat inside and outside with salt, crushed garlic, and mixed herbs; pour oil into deep roasting pan, and fit in prepared meat. Pour lemon juice evenly over meat, top with butter and margarine cut into small bits, and sprinkle with

peppercorns. Roast young goat in preheated oven at low temperature, basting frequently with juices in pan. When slightly browned,
cover with greased waxpaper, and continue roasting until done.
(Ferriera, *The News,* May 13, 1999)

Minor literature is completely different; its cramped space forces
each individual intrigue to connect immediately to politics. The
individual concern thus becomes all the more necessary, indispen-
sable, magnified, because a whole other story is vibrating within it.
(Deleuze and Guattari 1986: 17)

After speaking with Quijano, I consider the idea of the goat, its meaning in history, and the comments I hear from *regiomontanos* about what
the image evokes. I begin to think that the visual image of a *cabrito* with
its body flayed and exposed is in some ways like the written story. The
slaughter, the blood, and the point of exhibition are all in the narrative.
The personal injection of the ethnographer's experience is an attempt to
correlate the immediacy of the *cabrito* without its skin with the story of
the Jews in Nuevo León. The narrative of the *sefardíes* "vibrates" within.

Laredo, Texas 1958

The *cabrito's* tongue

The day after driving from Houston to the Mexican border almost 300
miles in a car, my mother predictably took my grandmother and me
across the international bridge into Nuevo Laredo, Tamaulipas, to buy a
cabrito, baby goat, which is considered a delicacy in northern Mexico.
We would go to the market where the meat was sold. The *cabritos* were
mostly red and pink, rather small, hanging from lines stretched across the
walls of *el mercado.* They had no heads; those were stored separately in
refrigerators with glass fronts like those in American meat markets. The
surface of the bodies and the heads looked like peeled potatoes, only
pink. The eyes of the heads peered out, often scaring me if I wasn't prepared to look at them. My mother would purchase the *cabrito* and have
it wrapped in white paper; then we would rush home so that my grandmother could prepare it especially for us.

I remember sitting at the table in the green kitchen of my grandmother's house as I looked at a cooked head of *cabrito.* It was now brown,

with a juicy covering, its eyes still glaring at me. I used to eat the *cabrito's* tongue. It was grayish brown and tasted quite good.

Now that I travel frequently to Nuevo León, my mother has asked me to bring her a *cabrito*. People in Potrero, a village eighty kilometers north of Monterrey, tell me there are no *cabritos* this year (1998) because of the drought. Perhaps there will be in the spring. My grandmother has been dead twenty-two years. She did not teach my mother how to prepare a *cabrito*.

Doña Elena tells me that many *cabritos* are born in the spring. Perhaps then I can take my mother a newborn goat that has only had mother's milk. That is the requirement for an appropriate *cabrito*. In Potrero, at the house where I stay, which is the home of my grandfather's niece, Doña Magdalena Vásquez de Villegas, there is a black *cabro* behind her house. He is tied to the outdoor restroom. He is a beautiful black animal, maybe four feet tall. I ask Doña Elena what his name is, but he has no name. He is used for mating purposes with *las chivas* (female goats).

Nuevo Laredo, Tamaulipas

1998

A handsome man with the feet of a goat (who is really the devil) has appeared for centuries throughout northern Mexico and south Texas.[5] As recently as April 1998, in a western club by the name of Silverado, in Nuevo Laredo, Tamaulipas, 210 kilometers northeast of Monterrey, there was an "appearance" by a handsome Mexican cowboy, who lost his boot riding the mechanical bull; it is said that he had a hoof instead of a human foot.

The goat, an animal that thrives in desolate landscapes, is an interesting companion to the dryness and negating climate of Nuevo León. Doña Magdalena's husband, eighty-two-year-old Jesús Villegas, walks up the mountain behind Potrero every day with his *chivas*. They do well on the mountain grass. The drought may affect their fertility, but they continue to live and thrive in most any type of weather. Prepared as a delicacy *en el norte,* the *cabrito* conflates widely varying practices into a meal, which has supported an expensive chain of restaurants in Monterrey named El Rey del Cabrito.

Fifteen years ago, while having conversations with persons doing genealogies in northern Mexico, I was told of the significant Jewish influence in the early settlements of Nuevo León. At the time, I was told that the flour tortilla was related to Jewish cooking practices, the dough for the tortilla being called *masa,* which sounds like *matza.* The manner of slaughtering livestock had a strong similarity to the kosher style of preparing meat.

The traditions in Nuevo León adapted themselves to the environment. The *cabrito,* after having been drained of blood, was either cooked over an open flame on a stake or cooked in a large pot. The blood drained from the body was combined with oregano, salt, and pepper, and made into *sangrita,* a sauce that is poured over the meat when the *cabrito* is served.

The process of conducting a kosher slaughter is inconsistent when the animal's blood is used as the basis of a sauce. Perhaps distance from more populated areas and contact with an indigenous people who consumed human blood could lead to this practice. Regardless, the narratives of the *sefardíes* do create a paradox of purity and contamination in the *cabrito's* preparation. The contaminated blood is removed from the carcass of the goat, yet it is saved for mixture with oregano, salt, and pepper, making the *salsita* to enhance the taste of the meat.

Limpieza de Sangre

La historiografía al uso parte del supuesto de que la sangre, su transmisión a lo largo de las generaciones, determina la esencial constitución del hombre hispano . . . (Castro 1962: 5) (Historiography assumes that a man's blood, its transmission through the generations, determines the Hispanic man's essential constitution)

Textual history describes the centuries that separated the Kabbalah and the works of the Spanish mystics and intellectuals as catastrophic for the Jews. The Reconquista, Spain's push to reclaim its territory on the peninsula, was finally successful in the late fifteenth century. The Inquisition was established in 1478; its stated purpose was to cleanse Spain of heresy and evil. The first Inquisitor General, Tomás de Torquemada, himself the descendant of *conversos,* convinced the monarchs, Fernando and Isabela, known as Los Reyes Católicos, to expel all the Jews who refused to convert to Catholicism. The first statute of *limpieza de sangre* was implemented in 1547. During the reign of Los Reyes Católicos, several hundred thousand *conversos* were burned at the stake by the Spanish Inquisition in what history books describe as a "pre-modern" holocaust. Most of the Jews in Spain were eliminated from the peninsula. Horrifying legends proliferated throughout the country. The Jew was said to be the son of the devil (Netanyahu 1995) and was blamed for many outbreaks of the plague in Europe. Some said the Jews poisoned the water in the cities and placed spells on the people. Benzion Netanyahu writes in *The Origins of the Inquisition* that narratives were also published concerning Jews murdering Christians. The killings were carried out as part of a desperate need to "remove the blight of a terrible curse," which the Jews received when Christ died and they shouted, "His blood be upon us and our children." The guilt of deicide was passed to their descendants and their blood became diseased, which created a physical torment for the Jew unless he admitted his share in killing Christ. It was said there was a Jewish prophet at the time who declared they could be cured "with the use of Christian blood" (1995: 823).

There are varying perspectives regarding the Reconquista. Américo Castro, among others, wrote of Spain's need to strengthen the "Spanish identity." The obsession with *limpieza de sangre* was an ideological manifestation that focused on the purity or essence of the Spanish citizen. There are others who argue against this interpretation. Historian Aniano Peña writes that there were no true Spaniards, not even the Goths who invaded Spain before the Moors (1975). Maravall proposes that the obsession was not with pure blood but with the development of the Spanish nation-state (1975). This is also Peña's theory. Yet it was the search for the "purest blood" and the elimination of the "stain" that became the tools for the development of the modern Spanish state. According to Peña, the statutes of *limpieza de sangre* and, subsequently, the establishment of the Holy Office of the Inquisition had more to do with strategies of power carried out by the Spanish monarchy. There were numerous inconsistencies. Many of the Inquisitors were descendants of *conversos* (Castro 1962; Peña 1975; Caro Baroja 1961.) Castro writes, "*[T]odavía en 1491 Fernando el Católico protegía a los judíos de Zamora contra las predicas de los domínicos, confiaba a hebreos la administración de la Santa Hermandad, los utilizaba como embajadores, etc.*" (1962: 53) (In 1491, King Fernando still protected the Jews in Zamora against the sermons of the Dominicans, trusted Hebrews with the administration of the Holy Brotherhood, and utilized them as ambassadors, etc.) Much of the Spanish nobility had intermarried with *conversos*. Fernando is said to have been descended from *conversos,* through his grandmother Raquel, wife of Alonso VIII (Caro Baroja 1961; Peña 1975).[6]

A significant portion of the nation's wealth was held by the families of its *conversos.* For those expelled or executed, the Crown received all their assets. For those who stayed in Spain and those who traveled to the new territories, the money paid to the Crown for these privileges supported the economic needs of the monarchy (Caro Baroja 1961).

> *¿Quisieron Carvajal y los suyos hacer en grande un ensayo de colonización judía para huir de la intransigencia religiosa europea . . . anticipándose así a lo que hicieron cuarenta años más tarde los peregrinos del Mayflower?* (Robles 1938: 101)
>
> (Did Carvajal and his followers plan to create a Jewish colony so that they could escape from religious persecution in Europe as the Pilgrims on the Mayflower did forty years later?)

There are two people who told me that a group of Jews in Spain formulated a plan for the Jews to settle in the north—antiquities collector and artist Aquiles Sepúlveda and historian Amado Barrera. These conversations occurred in 1998. I spoke with Barrera first. Saying the historian had substantial information, Alvarado had suggested I call Barrera.

At the time, Amado Barrera was the Director of the Museum of Monterrey. The museum is housed in a colonial building that had once been El Palacio Municipal (City Hall) of Monterrey. It is painted bright yellow; because of its color, Barrera tells me, it is impossible not to find it. I arrive early, hoping to view the exhibits on display. There is a large exhibition of abstract photography by a German artist. In a gallery with no visitors besides myself, there is abstract art by a Mexican painter with whom I am not familiar. Inside the reception room of Barrera's office, there are books on Hasidic Jews.

He talks to me over a two-hour lunch at the Americanized Sanborns located near his museum. He is interested in art and history. For many years he had been the director of a museum in San Pedro Garza García, an area of Monterrey known for its *nouveaux riches.* Slightly embarrassed, yet acknowledging the conveniences of a tightly secured, upscale neighborhood, he admits he still lives there.

Animated because of the opportunity to talk about Nuevo León, he speaks of the myth of purity that is located throughout the region. Just about everyone says they are only of Spanish blood. I ask questions, being curious after seeing large groups of blonde, blue-eyed children in

Villa de Santiago and Allende. He does not deny that there are many people of "fair complexion." He emphasizes that in a recent demographic study done in Nuevo León, almost all the families interviewed admitted to having at least one member who was of African origin. He then begins to tell me the Jewish stories. From what people know now, he says, it appears there had been a plan; Carvajal, del Canto, and Montemayor were all *conversos* from Portugal. They came in separate groups to the Americas; Luis Carvajal y de la Cueva was designated as the first governor of the new "kingdom."

Barrera told me that the best history on Nuevo León was written by Eugenio del Hoyo. The book was first published in 1972 in two volumes by the prestigious "Tecnológico" (Instituto Tecnológico y Estudios Superiores de Monterrey). Hoyo gives an exhaustive account of the first Spanish settlers, whom he believed to be Sephardic Jews.

Aquiles Sepúlveda discussed many of the same topics as Barrera. Sepúlveda considered himself an "insider" since he is descended from the first post-conquest settlers of Nuevo León. He said he was sure that the Jews had made a plan in Spain to establish a place for themselves, a sort of late medieval Zion. The isolation of the mountains and the distance from the center of government was ideal for them to continue their lives with regular ease. Historians Eugenio del Hoyo and Vito Alessio Robles both suggest a plan in their texts on Nuevo León's history. Robles asks himself about the possibility of a pre-existing design in a well-circulated essay he wrote in 1933. He also asks if these ambitious Jews dreamed *"de tan magna empresa labrarse una nueva patria, formando un reino independiente de España?"* (1938: 101) (of forging a new nation out of such a monumental enterprise, creating an independent kingdom.) Hoyo writes that when Carvajal was in Spain negotiating with the monarchy, he used the information given to him by four Portuguese men already in El Nuevo Reino—Alberto del Canto, Diego de Montemayor, Gaspar Castaño de Sosa, and Manuel de Mederos. Hoyo found it "extraordinary" that Carvajal encountered Montemayor in a remote area such as the mines of San Gregorio and was so easily able to convince del Canto to let him take over the city of Saltillo and in essence betray the government of the Nueva Vizcaya, which had already established jurisdiction over the city (1972).

Aquiles's interest in the Jewish narratives had led him to develop a collegial friendship with local rabbi Moises Kaimen.[7] Aquiles and the rabbi had been meeting regularly for several years. From these conversations,

Aquiles believed he could make several inferences. For example, Sepúlveda's grandmother was a Santos Coy. The rabbi told Aquiles that Coy was a derivative of Cohen. The practices of intermarriage among the "founding families" were widespread, since the beginning of El Nuevo Reino. This practice, combined with the distinct separation from the local indigenous population, created what Aquiles sees as an unquestioned bloodline. He discussed this idea with Kaimen and felt the rabbi was in agreement with him.

Sepúlveda had a special interest in two books on the Jews. One is a book I found at a used bookstore in Monterrey. It was written by Eva Uchmany and is titled *La vida entre el judaísmo y el cristianismo en Nueva España* (1992). He borrowed the book and kept it for several weeks. When he finally returned it, he said it was the most detailed and comprehensive book he had seen on the subject. After reading the book, he told me he wondered how anyone could doubt the presence of Jews in New Spain. Uchmany's book details the history of the Díaz Nieto family. The details of how Jews traveled from Spain to Portugal to Spain again, to Italy, and finally to Mexico are written in Uchmany's book. Also included are details of Carvajal's *proceso* (interrogation by the Inquisition). The publisher is Mexico's official Fondo de Cultura Económica. It is thoroughly documented and researched. After reading Uchmany's book, Aquiles was even more certain that the Treviños lived in Italy before arriving in Mexico.

In my conversations with Aquiles Sepúlveda, we often speculated on the demise of the Carvajals. The question remained ripe because we could not think of a specific reason why someone would want all of the Carvajal family to die. Aquiles would remind me that in Spain not all *conversos* and heretics were burned at the stake; politics and economics determined who survived. After speaking with Taussig, I was even more intrigued about the elimination of Carvajal's family. I read publications of Carvajal's *proceso,* yet realized that these testimonies actually told me very little. The duress of those speaking and the violence of the event of torture keep me from accepting those words as fact. Historian Rolando Guerra told a history class at Monterrey's History Museum that the most famous of all *nuevolenese* historians, Israel Cavazos Garza, known as El Cronista de la Ciudad de Monterrey, told everyone that in fact there were no Jews because there are no archival documents. Alex Saragoza, a professor at the University of California at Berkeley, said in a conversation in September 1999 that the documents do not exist; he had been told, he said, that many of the state and national archives containing information about the Jews were confiscated during the Mexican Revolution. Vito Alesso Robles attributes these missing documents to an unnamed Brazilian Jew. Robles also notes that the Mexican National Archive does not have any royal decrees before the year 1609 and that the correspondence between the monarchy and the Viceroys before 1775 is no longer in the archives. In his essay, "La judería de Monterrey," Robles writes, *"En esos [documentos entre el Virrey y la Monarquía] . . . se encuentra, indudablemente, toda la historia antigua del noreste de México, hasta ahora borrosa y llena de lagunas y sombras"* (1938: 422−423). (In those documents between the viceroy and the monarchy there can undoubtedly be found all the early history of northeastern Mexico, which even yet today is cloudy and full of lakes and shadows)

CHAPTER VIII

Inquisition: The Present

Monterrey, July 1999

It is necessary to examine the hidden alliances between mysticism
and torture. (de Certeau 1986: 40)

. . . a (public) secret may . . . be defined as that which is generally
known but cannot be spoken. (Taussig 1999: 50)

Historian Rolando Guerra contends in his essay "¿Cual cultura e identidad norestense?" ("Which Northeast Culture and Identity?") that
whether any stories of origin from northern Mexico are true is not the
issue. He believes they are, more importantly, part of an ideology that
forms what people see as the personality of Nuevo León (1995).

These various forms that Guerra mentions are those that have been
addressed throughout this text—the Jewish, the indigenous, the barbaric. Based upon Foucault's notion of the archaeological field site, what
can be found in the history of twentieth-century Nuevo León are constant verbal narratives regarding the possibility of a Jewish settlement,
contrasting assertions by local historians, a denial of any type of indigenous history, and a play on the barbaric which at times is an embarrass-
ment and at other times is touted as an asset. Physically located among
these narratives in 1999 was the presence of a museum exhibit that stirred
the interest and curiosity of the people of Monterrey.

In July 1999, a new exhibition opened in Monterrey. It was held at El
Museo Regional de Nuevo León in the Obispado, the site of one of the
oldest churches in Monterrey. The exhibit was announced with bright
red banners that were placed throughout downtown Monterrey. They
were lined in gold, announcing "The Tools of the Inquisition."

On a Sunday afternoon, a former student of mine, Agustín Loredo, who was visiting relatives in Monterrey, accompanied me to the exhibit on the Inquisition at the Obispado. When we arrived there were about fifty people waiting in line outside the museum. By the time we left the exhibit there were more than one hundred fifty. The courtyard was full of people of all ages. Many were young couples and many were young children and infants. Inside, filling the inner courtyard, were numerous "instruments of torture." "The rack" was there, and so were several chastity belts, although I am not sure what they have to do with the Inquisition. There were tools that tightened around a person's head and tools that held a person in a seat and dropped them down upon a spike. A few of the pieces looked like they might have been authentic. There were some that listed their origin. However, most were reproductions that had been made out of roughhewn wood. They were stained with an oil-like substance, which made them look old to the naïve observer. The charge for viewing the exhibit was twenty *pesos*. The man at the *taquilla,* which is slang for a toll booth, overcharged me, but I didn't realize it for several minutes. By that time, I knew it was too late to ask for a refund.

I looked over the pieces rather quickly and was irritated when I realized they were mostly reproductions (even though the brochure lists the collections from which they came). After a few minutes, I sat on a step away from the lines and waited for Agustín to finish looking. I began to get nauseated. I left the courtyard and asked if I could enter the other part of the museum. I was not allowed because it was almost closing time. I stood at the door of the museum, waiting and watching the people enter. Mostly middle class, they appeared fairly well-dressed. They looked content. There was much conversation and frequent laughter.

The "tools of the Inquisition" that I saw at the Obispado stayed on my mind for many days. I began to think of other issues regarding Jews and the Mexican Inquisition. Some months before, the subject of Jews in Nuevo León was discussed in a lecture I attended at Monterrey's Museum of History. I had enrolled in a *diplomado,* a continuing education course at the Museum. The dialogues that I witnessed during the seminars of the *diplomado* made the exhibit at the Obispado seem out of sync.

The Symbolic

The goal of torture, in effect, is to produce acceptance of a State discourse, through the confession of putrescence. (de Certeau 1986: 41)

While admittedly I did not seek out the organizers of this exhibit to question their motives or "official statements" regarding the exhibit, I did visit the site. I believe that the choice of objects and the symbolism they connote betray the existence of some type of memory or idea regarding the Inquisition in modern-day Nuevo León.

An image that comes to my mind is a lithograph of Isabel de Andrade de Carvajal standing with bared breasts in front of her inquisitors. This image, originally published in *El libro rojo* in 1870, has circulated widely. There is a second image of Mariana Nuñez de Carvajal shortly before she was burned at the stake. She is standing with her hands tied together and her body being strapped to the stake. She is wearing the pointed hat of the penitent; her head is facing the ground. A few feet behind Mariana Carvajal, the body of another penitent is already burning; smoke from the fire is floating up into the sky. The images of Isabel and Mariana Carvajal have had wide circulation. Vicente Riva Palacios, the director of the national archives of Mexico, was the editor of *El libro rojo,* which described the "great tragedies" in Mexican history.

In Eva Uchmany's *La vida entre el judaísmo y el cristianismo en la Nueva España,* the author reproduces numerous images of the Carvajals and the Inquisition (1992). One of these is that of Isabel Rodríguez, a family friend of the Carvajals, being tortured on *el porto* (the rack). Uchmany also shows the garrote, *el tormento de rueda* (the torment of the wheel), and several different photographs of *el porto.* Under the lithograph of the garrote, Uchmany uses the description: "*Instrumento para dar garrote*" (95). I recall the word *instrumento* is used in the title of the Monterrey exhibition: *Instrumentos europeos de tortura y pena capital.* The distinction "*europeos*" (European), which designated these "tools" as European, is added. Because the Carvajals represent the founding of El Nuevo Reino de León, and it was Mexico's version of the European Inquisition that eliminated them, the vivid images of the Carvajals being tortured present striking symbols.

There is a direct association between these surviving (and spectacular) narratives and the spectacular exhibition. Whether directly intended or not, the connection between the instruments of torture used on the Carvajals in the sixteenth century and the imitations on display at the Museo Regional de Nuevo León is too close to deny.

Denegar—Disavowal

A voice comes through the text, a loss transgresses the ascetic order of production . . . the sign of a death is traced upon the display windows of our acquisitions. These noises, fragments of strangeness, . . . scattered as memories always are, dislocated, but still relating to the substantive figure of the past that furnishes them with the reference point and name of what has disappeared. (de Certeau 1992: 78)

In April 1999, I was attending the third session of the *diplomado*. The topic was colonial Nuevo León, and the lecturer was Rolando Guerra, a noted academic specializing in regional ecclesiastic history. Having heard the Jewish stories for the two years I had been in Nuevo León and read about them in Alvarado's book on the history of Monterrey, I was completely surprised at what Guerra told us. He said that the constant story about the first Spanish settlers being Jews is an "ideological myth." He said the story of a Jewish origin is not true. Although Guerra acknowledged that Luis Carvajal was the son of Jewish *conversos,* Guerra told his class that *there were no other Jewish settlers.* Guerra was emphatic. "There is no documentation," he said. He also cited Israel Cavazos Garza's statement that there are no archives to substantiate the presence of the Jews in Nuevo León. As Guerra spoke in the opulent auditorium of the city's largest museum, the students began to stand up, barraging him with questions. "How could this be possible?" they asked. "Isn't it logical that the Jews would leave no documentation because of the continuing vigilance of the Inquisition?" Guerra was firm in his response: "No Jews, no documentation." When I raised my hand and asked him what the purpose of this ideology was, he listened to my question, but did not respond to me.

Guerra is supported by others. In July 1999, in a personal conversation with Claudia Lozano, who was director of education at the Museo de Historia de Monterrey, she also told me there were no Jews in Nuevo

León during colonial times. Lidia Espinoza, the director of El Museo de Historia Regional, also lectured during the *diplomado* regarding the "lack" of Jews in Nuevo León. Historian Santiago Roel echoes the words of Guerra and Espinoza. Roel concludes,

> *Hay quienes suponen que entre los primeros pobladores de Monterrey hubo muchos judíos, . . . y que llegaban hasta practicar sus ritos y ceremonias con toda libertad. La suposición no tiene fundamento alguno. El gobernador Carvajal había abandonado el judaísmo desde su juventud y era católico ferviente desde mucho antes de venir a estas regiones; y por lo que hace sus familiares ninguno residió en el Nuevo Reino, salvo Luis, su sobrino, quien lo acompañó por breve tiempo en su campaña de conquista.* (Roel 1977: 23) (There are those who assume that there were many Jews among the first settlers of Monterrey, and that they came to practice their ceremonies and rites with total liberty. There is no basis for this assumption. Governor Carvajal abandoned Judaism since childhood and was a fervent Catholic long before he came to this region; and for what his family did, none of them resided here, except his nephew Luis, who only accompanied the Governor for a short time during the campaign of conquest)

With the Inquisition exhibit still on my mind, I thought about conversations I had with Aquiles after hearing about the "myth" of the Jews at the Museum. Aquiles reminded me of a story he had told me some time before. His Jewish friend, Radko Tichavsky, who is the Consul of Czechoslovakia, once asked for Aquiles's position on the Jews. Radko said, "Either you are a Jew or you are a Nazi." When Aquiles told me this anecdote, I asked why the response had to be so extreme. His point, Aquiles told me, was that "there was still fear." He and Tichavsky thought it was dangerous to get involved in issues regarding the Jews even in late twentieth-century Monterrey.

In 1933, just as Hitler came into power in Germany, Vito Alessio Robles wrote a newspaper article titled "*La judería de Monterrey.*" It was printed in various locations, including Monterrey, Mexico City, "the provinces," and "other countries," according to Robles. Five years later it was published in a book of Robles's essays. He begins the article with a reference to Hitler: "*Con motivo de las persecuciones desencadenadas por Hitler en contra de los judíos de Alemania, resulta interesante exhumar en estos momentos algunos datos relacionados con la judería establecida en . . . Monte-*

rrey." (1938: 96) (In reference to Hitler's persecution of the Jews in Germany, it would be interesting to exhume at this time some information
related to the Jews who settled in Monterrey)

Rethinking what Aquiles had told me, I thought again of the exhibit
at the Obispado and wondered if the Inquisition or the Holocaust were
still alive at some level in Monterrey. Also, I wondered how Lidia Espinoza, who was director of the museum, could remain coherent while
she displayed tools used to torture Jews and simultaneously claimed there
were none to be tortured.

The uncertainty surrounding the polarized stories that are very much
alive but also very much dead became even more salient as I continued
to read Robles's essay, *"La judería de Monterrey,"* especially its opening
footnote. While the author, Robles, seems awed by the Jewish mystical
practices he does believe existed in Nuevo León at the time of Carvajal,
the first page of the essay provides a jolting disclaimer: ". . . *algún igno-
rante, con la aviesa intención de zaherir a los hijos de Monterrey, les llamó descendientes de judíos, ignorando . . . que la mayoría . . . fueron quemados vivos
en el auto-de-fé de 8 de diciembre de 1596. . . . entre los nuevos pobladores no se
encontraba ninguno de los judíos de Carvajal"* (1938: 96–97). (. . . someone
ignorant, with the bad intention of censuring the children of Monterrey,
called them descendents of Jews, ignoring that most of Carvajal's people
were burned alive in the auto-da-fé (public execution) of December 8,
1596. . . . none of Carvajal's Jews were among the later settlers)

The controversy still lingered thirty-nine years after Robles first published the essay. Hoyo addressed the issue in *La historia de Nuevo León;* in
his chapter entitled *"Las gentes de Carvajal"* (Carvajal's People) (1972),
Hoyo wrote that Robles "agitated the problem" regarding the authenticity of the Jewish narratives and was criticized publicly by historian
Santiago Roel and other local citizens. *"[Robles] se desató de la polémica"*
(Robles removed himself from the controversy) by writing the disclaimer
in the beginning footnote of *"La judería de Monterrey,"* denying that any
Jews existed after the death of Carvajal (Hoyo 1972: 200).

Hoyo ends his chapter on the Carvajal family with a citation from
David Cossio's massive history of Nuevo León. *"Los judaizantes, . . . no
dejaron de seguir trabajando subrepticiamente en este territorio . . . En el mayor
secreto eran celebrados los ritos judaicos"* (272). (The Judaizers . . . continued
to work secretly in this territory . . . The Judaic rites were celebrated
with major secrecy.)[1] Cossio limits his references to Jews to Carvajal and
the later notation, cited by Hoyo, that is several chapters later in a sec-

tion on the seventeenth century (1924). Faced with a paucity of what is considered legitimate documentation, Hoyo wrote that the most fortuitous alternative would be to conduct an intense study of the region's folklore. He had already found some "curious and significant" correlations between the folklore of the *nuevoleneses* and those of the Mediterranean *sefardíes*. Here again, I find a connection between de Certeau's writing and what people/academics/texts say about Nuevo León. De Certeau proposes that the mystical constitutes "a specific *historical reality*," albeit a reality that appears in the form of an absence (1992: 9). It is the historical reality of what is lacking. There are traces of similarity to the past that can be correlated with numerous forms of practice in the present. Yet the absence of the central character (the Jew) makes the quest impossible. Carvajal's descendants have vanished. What are left are pieces and memories of the everyday such as "sensations . . . meetings or daily tasks" (10). "The mystic (fabled) discourse transforms the detail into myth; it catches hold of it, blows it out of proportion, multiplies it, divinizes it. The transformation creates its own kind of historicity" (ibid.), a delirious type of story that leaves confusion in its wake. It leaves a history that is situated in what is not. The legitimate story that is written in the history books on Nuevo León leaves out the Jews. This is done purposefully. The lack of documentation defines the lack of reality for the narratives and leaves those written stories that have expulsed the Jewish narratives as accepted, legitimated history.

This historicity has also become the narrative of *renunciación* (giving up by formal declaration). The literal analysis of *renunciación* is abandonment, yet what may seem like delirious rejection may be an act of loyalty and respect. *Renunciación* may be a way of maintaining the secret for protection; it could be related to issues of conversion. In converting to Christianity, Jews were required to publicly renounce their religion. Most frequently it was to prevent the death of their family or themselves. As de Certeau proposes, traces of correlation create a history; the trace of *renunciación* continues in Nuevo León.[2]

In an effort to acknowledge the lack of "proper history," Hoyo proposes that future researchers develop an erudite analysis of the folklore of Nuevo León and that of the *sefardíes*. Hoyo was aware of the "lack or ambiguity of meaning" in mythical history as described by de Certeau. Whatever would be found in the comparative analysis between the *nuevoleneses* and the *sefardíes* would be significantly remote from what Hoyo sees as the current state of understanding.

Descubrimiento—Discovery

The Ghost of Mariano Treviño

I want to add to this observation my idea that this [sacredness] is achieved through a *"drama of revelation"* which, like unmasking, amounts to a transgressive uncovering of a *"secretly familiar."* (Taussig 1999: 51)

According to legend, Monterrey was founded in 1596 by *conversos*—Spanish Jews who had converted to Christianity but still feared persecution by the Inquisition that was gaining momentum 600 miles away in Mexico City. (*Los Angeles Times,* October 22, 1991)

Muchos de los primeros habitantes de Monterrey fueron judaizantes españoles. Por conveniencia y temor al medio social se hicieron bautizar . . . Descendientes de estos judíos españoles, por la rama Treviño, que originalmente se escribia con las letras "g" y "n" en vez de la "ñ"—Trevigno—, fueron los González Treviño . . . Entre sus ancestros se encuentra uno que se llamó Joseph Alexander de Trevigno y Gutiérrez . . . (Aguilar 1970: 264–265) (Many of the first inhabitants of Monterrey were Spanish Jews. For convenience and fear they agreed to be baptized as Christians. The descendents of these Spanish Jews, through the Treviño name, that was originally written with the letters "g" and "n" instead of the "ñ"—Trevigno—were the González Treviños. . . . Among their ancestors there is one who was named Joseph Alexander de Trevigno y Gutiérrez)

As I repeat the story of my research project to colleagues and friends, I am often told that the stories sound more like fictions than ethnographic narratives. Aquiles Sepúlveda has been described to me by a colleague as "a character out of a García Márquez novel." What is magically strange is made familiar in the stories that Sepúlveda and his sisters have told me. They are a "'history' that one tells" (de Certeau 1988: 346). The absent narratives about Jews are occasionally mentioned in passing texts such as an American newspaper or the memoirs of a wealthy woman from Monterrey. For Aquiles Sepúlveda, the story of the missing Jew was almost an obsession. In every conversation we had, such as the one in late August 1999, he mentioned it to me.

A few days before I left Monterrey for the summer, I visited with Aquiles Sepúlveda. As usual we sat at the dining room table, with the light from Arreola street coming in through the window. He was sitting directly across the table from me and asked, "Why are you so interested in the Jews?" I responded by saying it was an interest I had all my life. In our many conversations he had told me that he was Jewish. While not a practicing Jew in terms of religion, he was descended directly from Jews and belonged to a family that had not intermarried with any other group. Aquiles's mother's surnames are González Treviño. His father's are Sepúlveda Gutiérrez.

The previous summer, in the second conversation I had with Aquiles, he told me, "You are Jewish." I told him that I had heard of the Jews in *el norte,* but did not believe myself to be one. He listed aspects of my appearance: skin color, curly hair, and facial structure. Then he walked into another room and returned with an old photograph. There were three women in the picture. One appears to be the mother, an older woman; the other two are younger. He told me one was his grandmother and the older one was his great-grandmother. Their name was Treviño. He said they were Jewish women from one of the richest families in Nuevo León. He told me I look like the older woman in the photograph.

During that conversation in August 1999, after he was satisfied with my explanation regarding my interest in the Jewish narratives, he brought out an ancient parchment Bible. He said he had bought it from the estate sale of a professor from the TEC (the Instituto Tecnológico, Mexico's version of MIT), although he could not recall his name. It was in Latin. I thought I saw that it was published in Italy, but later Aquiles said it was published in France. Inside the front cover in handwritten script is what appears to be the name *Mariano Treviño.* On the next page, under the title and publication credits appears Treviño's handwriting, with the year "1688" written underneath the printed date of 1680. I started searching through the book, hoping to find some notes or special sections. I remembered reading that Luis Carvajal el Mozo (the younger) learned much of his Hebrew teachings from a Catholic Bible (Liebman 1967). The back section of the book was more worn than the others. It looked like a mouse had nibbled at the edges of the page. Aquiles said it must have been the oil from hands touching the pages. After the Old and New Testaments were sections I did not recognize. On page 462 of the Bible was the following: *PRÆ fatio, Sancti Hieronymi, Presbyteri in Penta-teuchum Moysi Ad Desiderium.*[3] Sepúlveda told me that he had not seen the back sections of the Bible. He said he was as surprised as I was. A few weeks after I left, he made an appointment with Rabbi Kaimen. He said the rabbi was stunned when he saw the Bible. Kaimen said, "Like this one there is no other," and initially encouraged Aquiles to contact someone in Jerusalem. In a later conversation, the rabbi was less enthusiastic. Aquiles felt the rabbi was insinuating that it was better to leave things alone.

In the meantime, Sepúlveda and I separately began research, seeking the name of *Mariano Treviño*. Neither of us could find the name in any document. Sepúlveda speculated that Mariano was either the youngest son or a grandson of Joseph de Treviño. Yet we could not find the name in any list or genealogy. Aquiles contacted several local historians who were not able to help him. Eventually I found a list of Treviños in a book by Tomás Mendirichaga Cueva (1982). There was a woman, a Mariana Treviño, who would have been an adult during the time the Bible was used. She appears to have been a granddaughter of Joseph Treviño. Yet the name on the Bible looked like it ended with an *o* rather than an *a*.

What Aquiles could tell me was that for a person to own such a book, he or she had to come from substantial wealth. At the time, the cost of a Bible of this sort was beyond the means of almost anyone in New Spain. During a telephone conversation he reminded me that Joseph de Treviño came to El Nuevo Reino de León with unlimited wealth. I asked Aquiles if he knew from where the money had come. He did not know.

A companion volume which Sepúlveda bought with the Bible was a Spanish-Latin dictionary, also ancient, made of parchment. Treviño's name was written inside the front cover. Sepúlveda and I both concluded that perhaps Treviño used the dictionary for assistance in reading the Bible. After months of searching genealogical records, I began to wonder if Treviño had only written 1688 on the Bible in hopes of transcribing the roman numerals. Perhaps he was one of the several Mariano Treviños who lived in Nuevo León in the nineteenth century. There is a distinct possibility that Sepúlveda had more information on the previous owner of the Bible but refused to tell me. Now that Sepúlveda is deceased, the search for *Mariano Treviño* has ended. In addition, the rabbi's change in attitude does not encourage further investigation on the authenticity of the Bible. The possibility exists that it is not a Jewish book as the rabbi first claimed. Since Ofelia Sepúlveda, who is now the owner of the Bible, has removed it from the premises, there is no way to verify its legitimacy. I no longer know where it is. It has vanished along with *Mariano Treviño.*

A Respectable and Hardworking People

El judío respetuoso de aquello que dice, "Ganarás el Pan con el Sudor de la Frente," es trabajador y considera el descanso como algo impio a excepción de día obligatorio de descanso. . . . Nuestra gente como los sefarditas, rinden culto en la noche sentándose bajo las estrellas y a meditar en su soledad . . . (Alvarado 1995: 64). (The respectful Jew says, 'You earn bread with the sweat of your forehead,' he is a [hard] worker and considers his rest something impious unless it is his obligatory day of rest. Our people, like the Sephardic Jews, demonstrate reverence in the night by sitting underneath the stars and meditating in solitude . . .)

Two years before Aquiles showed me the Bible, Alvarado told me the story of a Jewish settlement. He had written about it in his book, *Textos para conocer la historia de Monterrey 400* (1994). In June 1997, the first time I accompanied him on a day of filming, the crew traveled thirty kilometers north of Monterrey to the town of Zua Zua. Alvarado interviewed a woman named Rosa Alba Martínez, who cooked the traditional foods of the region. She prepared a large meal and transported the food to the nearby Ex-hacienda de San Pedro. The Hacienda was built by the Lara Gutiérrez family in the seventeenth century. It was purchased and restored by the local state university, the Universidad Autónoma de Nuevo León. According to Professor Celso Garza Guajardo, the restoration was as close as possible to what the existing archives described the place to be. In the massive kitchen, on the second floor of the Hacienda, Rosa Alba Martínez presented her food in traditional style. The film crew taped Alvarado, Señora Martínez, and I as we discussed the origin of the foods she had prepared. Alvarado told his audience that the foods were of Sephardic origin. After the interview, we divided up the food for each of us to take some home. Two items I recall were the *semita* and the *empalmes*. Covered with a sweet crust, *semita* is an unleavened bread made with sugar and molasses. I had eaten it before in Laredo, Texas, where *semita* is very popular, though the recipe in Laredo also includes pecans.

Empalmes are corn tortillas covered with a heavy dose of shortening. Two of these tortillas form a type of sandwich with different types of spiced meat inside.

As the crew loaded the camera equipment onto the van, Alvarado sat with Rosa Alba Martínez near the chapel of La Ex-hacienda de San Pedro. They had an animated conversation with much laughter and interest. I could tell that he enjoyed talking to her. In all the time I have known him, I have rarely seen him converse in such an animated manner. Due to Alvarado's uncommon animation, I visited with Rosa Alba later in the summer in the hope of learning about Zua Zua, the Martínez family, and the task of having a business in a small town in Nuevo León.

Rosa Alba is an attractive woman in her early fifties. She is about 5'9" tall; her hair is salt-and-pepper and curly. She keeps it short. She does not wear makeup. She is direct, assertive, and not coy. She is a serious businesswoman. She runs her business and her family. She did not marry until the age of forty. Her husband is also a Martínez, probably a distant relation. They have a teenage son, a tall and lanky boy who looks like he could be from the American Midwest. Rosa Alba works sixteen hours per day, seven days per week. Her business, Antojitos de Tía Rosa Alba, is located in a stucco building painted bright green. It sits at a major intersection in the small city of Zua Zua. During the three years I traveled to Nuevo León, I visited Antojitos about five times. It always had a crowd of people coming and going.

Rosa Alba Martínez reminds me of the women Alvarado describes in his book. He writes, "*Aun nuestros tiempos en algunos pueblados del Noreste de Nuevo León . . . vemos matriarcados en las familias, la abuelita maternal tiene gran autoridad.*" (1994: 64) (Even in our times, in certain communities of northeast Nuevo León . . . we see matriarchies in the families, the maternal grandmother has great authority.) He believed the matriarchy was based on Jewish tradition.[4]

He also said that many regional expressions were also based on Sephardic practices. One in particular that I remember was the word *guerco*. I had always heard the word *guerco* when I was among my Spanish-speaking relatives in Texas. It was a term for a child or young adolescent. It also connoted a mischievous or bothersome child. In a conversation I had with Alvarado in the summer of 1997, he told me that the word was used by the Crypto-Jews to describe a child who had not been told the secret of the family's religion. In accordance with what I had found (Liebman 1967), the children of Crypto-Jews were not told that the family still believed and practiced Judaism until they reached a certain age. When they became adolescents, they were told the family secret. Until then, according to Alvarado, they were known as *guercos*.

The correlation with mischievous behavior belies the ambivalence and *renunciación*. The *guerco*/child who does not know the secret is the child who is bothersome and not well-behaved. It is this unreliability that poses danger. A child could tell the truth of the secret more easily than an adult who has learned the necessities of misrepresentation.[5] Yet the impossibility of this position is apparent. Old narratives from the Inquisition remind one that if the child knew, he could die.

El judío rico—The Rich Jew

> For decades, Monterrey residents have been the brunt of jokes by other Mexicans that poke fun at their thrift and dedication to making money. (*Los Angeles Times,* 22 October 1991)

> "You are so tight with your money, sometimes I think you are Jewish."[6]

In November 1999, Aquiles told me for about the fourth time in sixteen months that I needed to read *The International Jew,* a multivolume work by Henry Ford. The books I found in Houston made no mention of Henry Ford. Instead the citation listed *The Dearborn Independent.* I went up to the fourth floor of the Rice library and sat on the floor of the aisle as I searched through the four volumes. The books were small. Three appeared rather old. One seemed new or at least republished recently. As I opened them, one by one, I found they had been published in 1920. The subtitle of the series is *The World's Foremost Problem.* While still not clear on Sepúlveda's intentions or interest in *The International Jew,* I found that the series focused on what the author perceived as the problem of Jews taking control of the international market, which, according to the author, could signal the demise of capitalism and the American way of life. The introduction tells the reader:

> This question reaches down into South America and threatens to become an important factor in Pan American relations. It is interwoven with much of the menace of organized and calculated disorder which troubles the nations today. (*Dearborn Independent* 1920: 5)

The writing was dated, inflammatory, and brazenly anti-Semitic. Like the film *Birth of a Nation,* the books concerned the birth of the United States; focused on Jews rather than African Americans, however, the books argued that the nation's lifespan would be limited should the Jews be permitted continuing prosperity. I was surprised the books were even in the college library. I had never expected to find them. The second volume was a new copy. The new volume did not list a publisher. However, there was a gold sticker on the first page announcing *Americana Books:* "Write for a free list of books on Race, Communism, Zionism, Philosophy, Ideology, Politics, WWII, Survival, and Self-Defense."

When I returned to my office with the books, I found it hard to read past the first page of the first volume, which read like something out of Nazi Germany. It seemed like such a paradox to me. Aquiles spoke proudly of his Jewish heritage in our first conversations, yet he told me it was of utmost importance to my research that I read *The International Jew.* I recalled that each time he mentioned Ford's work our conversation centered on issues of capitalism, money, power, and control. He told me from the beginning that he was convinced the Jews in the United States had sent me to find information in Nuevo León. At first I worried about his state of mental health, but over time I found that he was quite rational. He firmly believed in the far-reaching influence of American Jewry. He believed there was a controlling aspect to their influence that was felt throughout the world. As much as he felt proud of his Sephardic ancestors, he also thought that the American Jews were dangerous and manipulative. He believed what was written in *The International Jew.*

Having heard of Henry Ford's notorious anti-Semitism, I hesitated to follow Aquiles's suggestion. Certainly this anti-Semitism is evident in *The International Jew.* Eventually I got past the introduction to the first volume and, surprisingly, found numerous references to financial and economic issues that resonate with oral and textual narratives told about Nuevo León. During the time I was reading *The International Jew,* I telephoned Aquiles to ask him how he found the book. He said he saw it in a bookstore in Monterrey when he was nineteen, which would have been in 1955. It had been translated into Spanish and published in Argentina. I asked him why he wanted me to read the book. He said it was because there were many similarities between *nuevoleneses* and the Jews described by Henry Ford.

The author of *The International Jew* gives the reader this preliminary generalization:

The single description which will include a larger percentage of Jews than members of any other race is this: he is in business. (10)

It is a curious dilemma when a reader is confronted with devaluing stereotypes that reverberate in her surrounding environment. I am repeatedly told that the wealth in Monterrey is directly related to the Jewish ancestry of the *regiomontanos*. The confusion is more of an ethical one. The stories of rich Jews in Nuevo León abound. Aguilar Belden, in her memoirs of growing up in Nuevo León, describes her family's business and their Jewishness. "*Los hermanos de mamá fueron grandes comerciantes. Operaban aquí en La Laguna, en Matamoros y en Chihuahua, bajo la Firma Jesús González Treviño, Hnos. El vulgo, como pasa muy a menudo, les cambió el significado de las iniciales, y los empezaron a llamar Judíos Grandes— Todos Hermanos.*" (My mother's brothers were great businessmen. They operated here in La Laguna, in Matamoros and Chihuahua, under the name of Jesús González Treviño and Brothers. After a number of years, the name of the company was vulgarized. The meaning of the initials changed and they began to be called The Great Jews—All Brothers) Hearing this story from her father, she asked him if his uncles were offended. He responded by saying, "*Noo ¡que va! Al contrario, eran los que más festejaban su nuevo nombre.*" (1970: 265) (No way! On the contrary, they were the ones who most celebrated their new name)

In our conversations, though he did not reveal his source, Sepúlveda mentioned that the most powerful synagogue in Spain helped finance the *conversos'* first ventures into El Nuevo Reino de León. He said this was specifically for the establishment of a congregation in the Americas. The author made reference to this in *The International Jew:*

. . . a great block of wealth in America was made possible by the lavish use of another block of wealth from across the seas . . . certain Jewish immigrants came to the United States with the financial backing of European Jewry behind them. (12)

Aquiles told me specifically about a prominent Jew who emigrated from an Eastern-bloc country in the 1980s. The man had been provided financial backing by "powerful Jewish men." In addition to the financial support, he was required to marry a Jewish woman as part of the arrangement. When Aquiles mentioned this story to me, he also reminded me to read *The International Jew*. Similarly, *nuevolenese* historian Eugenio de Hoyo tells of how Carvajal was supported by his family in purchasing his territory, title, and permission to take approximately one hundred *conversos* to New Spain (1972).

As I continued reading the books, I found other connections between what was claimed by the *Dearborn Independent* and what I had heard and read in Nuevo León. In the summer of 1999 I visited Irma Salinas Rocha, the widow of Roberto Garza Sada. During our long conversation, I also met her granddaughter, Aileen Garza Sada. Aileen told me of El Grupo Monterrey, a conglomeration of industries established by her great-grandfather, the elder Roberto Garza Sada, and his brother Eugenio Garza Sada. She said it was basically a practical matter. The family established a brewery and needed glass, so they established a bottle manufacturing company. In *The International Jew,* Ford again wrote of these "observations:"

> Another modern business method whose origin is credited to Jewish financiers is that by which related industries are brought together, as for example, if an electrical power company is acquired, then the street railway company using the electricity would be acquired too, one purpose being in this way to conserve all the profit accruing along the line, from the origination of the power down to the delivery of the street car ride. (20)

This idea is further evidenced by Rojas and Rodríguez; in a sociological study on Nuevo León's industry, they discuss the creation of Garza Sada's Hojalata y Lamina (HyLSA), which ultimately became the most important fabricator of ironworks in Mexico. HyLSA was initially created as a project to provide sheet metal for the caps of beer bottles for Cervecería Cuauhtémoc (1988). These types of collaborations continued as other aspects of production and delivery were created. By the late twentieth century, the family company grew into a Fortune 500 corporation.

Although Monterrey is not a company town per se, the *empresas* (corporations) have always been farsighted in attending to the production and consumer needs of Nuevo León. The Garza Sadas have placed themselves in all aspects of Monterrey's urban life. In his work on the social history of Nuevo León, historian Juan Mora-Torres writes of "interventions" by *las empresas,* which moved local residents toward the middle class. Educational programs, support for property ownership, and worker advocacy groups were established long before other Mexican corporations considered such options. Mora-Torres believes these benefits were not only to provide trained workers for their *empresas,* but also to build a financially stable consumer market that would purchase their products (1990).[7]

Almost every family I have met in Monterrey has at least one family member who at one time worked for Cervecería Cuauhtémoc. Yolanda González told me that the *empresa* was instrumental in providing needed services to the community. She said that Eugenio Garza Sada, who managed the company during a significant part of the twentieth century, was seen as a generous and sensitive man who was always concerned about his employees. Employee benefits still include free medical services, home loan assistance, further training and education, and scholarships for employees' children.

In an interesting twist to the proclamations in the *Dearborn Independent,* Irma Salinas Rocha writes of the entrepreneurial Garza Sadas and how "certain" families in Nuevo León changed their names in order to avoid being identified as Jews (1970).[8]

Ambivalence—Ambiguity—Creativity

> The meeting of the two religious traditions, one removed to an inner retreat, the other triumphant but "corrupted," allowed the new Christians to become, to a great extent, the creators of a new discourse, freed from dogmatic repetition, and, like a spiritual Marranism, structured by the opposition between the purity of the "inside" and the lie of the "outside." (de Certeau 1992: 23)

The distance between a mystic and an entrepreneur is vast. However, de Certeau has related the two in his search for the place in-between, where mystic, heretical, and/or "different" thought has arisen. In *The Mystic Fable,* de Certeau writes of the Jews in nineteenth-century Germany. Their story could be a parallel to the spectacular success of Nuevo León: "Just as the massive adoption of German culture by the Jews in the nineteenth century made possible theoretic innovations and an exceptional intellectual productivity, the upsurge of mystics in the sixteenth and seventeenth centuries was often the effect of the Jewish difference in the usage of a Catholic idiom" (1992: 23). The correlation between de Certeau's words and the situation in Nuevo León is striking. First, there are situations of conversion, be they stories or documented events. Second, both have become locations of industrial capital. In Nuevo León the success of the industries is referenced with the stories of Jewish ancestry in Nuevo León. The "Jewish narratives" are about the real or imagined relatives of these early *converso* mystics who may have founded El Nuevo Reino de León. In this real/imaginary epic, their descendents four centuries later have continued the "massive adoption" with their own unique culture that may have been instrumental in forming their "exceptional" industrial and capitalistic success. A "different way of thinking has permeated" the work world of Nuevo León (ibid.). Aguilar writes of this difference in her memoirs: Monterrey "*. . . vale por su gente franca, llana, [y] tesonera*" (1970: 264) (. . . has value because of its people who are plain folk, steadfast, and frank).

Although the Carvajals were executed by the Inquisition, it is notable that there were no subsequent problems in Nuevo León regarding *conversos*. Historians Espinoza and Roel say Carvajal was the only one, "the only Jew." Numerous other verbal narratives and texts state there were many other Jews. It was commonly known that anyone from Portugal was considered to be a *converso* (Liebman 1967; Hoyo 1972). Carvajal, Montemayor, and del Canto were said to be from the region called La Raya de Portugal, known for its significant percentage of *conversos* (Hoyo 1972). After Carvajal's death, Montemayor became the second governor of El Nuevo Reino. Montemayor is credited with re-populating the region and founding the city of Monterrey.

There are numerous connections that do not specifically prove the narratives true, yet create questions regarding these conflicting stories. Santiago Roel's negation of stories regarding the Jews' freedom to practice their religion for many years after the initial settlement is telling. While he denied the existence of these practices, the mere presence of the narratives in local folklore is significant.

The Establishment of the In-between

De Certeau describes the German Jews as being in that space "in-between" (1992). The people of Nuevo León are in a similar space. The stories of industrial and financial success in Germany and in northern Mexico have numerous similarities. The embracing of American culture with its capitalistic thrust while maintaining a Mexican identity has placed *regios* in a space that is neither. De Certeau offers three possible circumstances that allow for this positioning: separation (being far away in the barbarous north), collusion with the corrupt to achieve success (involvement with materialistic American society), and the juxtaposition of the good and evil existing in these spaces. These three issues, all of which correlate with Nuevo León's legendary Jewish history and the state's current success, assist in defining the unique location of Nuevo León's culture and economy.

Historically, Nuevo León's social and geographic existence is joined with an act of withdrawing. For de Certeau, the act of withdrawing, which is related to the "segregation of a place," is counter to the "docility" or "compliance" of "State-connected religious institutions" (1992: 21). Nuevo León's geographic location is central to any narrative regarding its history. As is told in the narratives regarding the location of the first Spanish settlement, Amado Barrera and Aquiles Sepúlveda both indicated that the choice of location was significantly influenced by its isolation and separation from Mexico's center of power.

For two centuries, the church's authority over the ecclesiastical life of Nuevo León was located in Guadalajara, 600 kilometers away. After the death of Carvajal, there was no authorized Viceregal presence for more than a quarter century.[9] Even so, the Franciscans made significant inroads into *nuevolenese* culture; Lidia Espinoza, for instance, believes the culture they brought was more influential than that of the Jews. Yet, de Certeau reminds us that the Franciscans were an order that was not as rigid about *limpieza de sangre* as were the Benedictines and the Dominicans (1992). Aquiles Sepúlveda told me that he believes the church was replete with *conversos,* perhaps even Crypto-Jews. He mentioned on two occasions a story from the 1940s of the priests at Monterrey's Cathedral reading the Kabbalah in a room under the church.

The first church in Monterrey, interestingly called El Templo, was El Convento San Francisco, which was founded by Franciscans in 1612. Since most of those in power lived in rural areas with limited access to the city in order to tend their *encomiendas,* there was little contact with structured Catholicism. In a strange event occurring in 1914 that could have been a scene from a film about the American Wild West, General (later Governor) Antonio Villareal is said to have charged into El Con-

Photograph of Irma Sepúlveda and Juan Rulfo. *El Excelsior,* Mexico City.

vento San Francisco on horseback and shot up the religious statues inside the church. The expression used in this instance is that Villareal *balasió los santos* (shot the statues of the saints). The word *balasiar,* however, means more than shooting a gun; it also connotes rage and lack of control. The interior of El Convento was then sacked; the statues and other artifacts were thrown into a cart and taken to the northern edge of town, where they were burned in a large bonfire (Arroyo Llano 1996).

Although Espinoza espouses the strong influence of the church in the north, it is a common belief that *norteños* are distanced in practice and belief from the Catholic religion (Guerra 1995, Nuncio 1997). In the north, piety and religious devotion is demonstrated in a much more personal and individual way. These practices are focused on folk beliefs more than tenets of the Catholic Church as an institution. In Mexico, which is a country that is overwhelmingly Catholic and intensely devoted to the Virgin Mary, the north's "separate" position vis-á-vis the church places that region in a polarized position with regard to the country's national identity.

Nuevo León is separate geographically, ideologically, and culturally. The region exemplifies de Certeau's argument about a separation of ideology, practice, and policy. The historical narrative of Nuevo León also encompasses the "segregation of a place" (1992: 21). Analogous to *conversos* establishing a settlement far away from the Inquisition, de Certeau writes of this separation: "The regular life, the religious congregations . . . and the popular missions were all responses to the prime necessity of a rupture that organized (after the manner of a "departure," a wall, a social selectivity, a secret, etc.) the circumscription of a field for specific practices." It is about "the *passage* from one sociocultural economy to another." For Nuevo León, this passage has taken it from *"la miseria,"* as Hoyo describes, to the focus of Mexico's economic power (1972). Monterrey has become the bridge between Latin America and United States capitalism.

In a paradoxical manner, de Certeau's description resonates with the topography of Nuevo León. This "in-between" and "different place" "favors concrete modes of relations to money, . . . to sexuality, . . . and to power." It is about places and "social categories" that have gone into "socioeconomic recession, disfavored . . . pushed aside by progress." While recent economic success portrays Nuevo León as indeed First World, the region itself has been designated as Other. As previously mentioned, a citation from the *Los Angeles Times* claims, "For decades, Monterrey residents have been the brunt of jokes by other Mexicans." (22 October 1991). Sara Aguilar Belden, as a young girl, writes that she asks her father, ". . . *Monterrey . . . es bastante feúcho, ¿verdad?* (1970: 264) ("Monterrey . . . is very ugly, right?"). Lidia Espinoza found in her historical research that colonial Nuevo León was considered the modern-day equivalent of "hazardous duty." The benefits of settling the area in relation to taxes, governmental support, and freedom were augmented because of the inhospitable landscape. The winters are harsh and extreme, as are the summers. For four centuries, the image of the *nuevolenese* was of an uncivilized person, which was an image in accord with the uncivilized landscape.

De Certeau explains that the place of the in-between conveys the presence of a loss. Home no longer exists, yet the "new" is not quite embraced. This became apparent to me while I worked with Alvarado on his television program. The primary thrust of the program appeared to be about "the return." Celso Garza Guajardo, author of a biography of Alvarado, perceives *Reportajes* as an attempt at return to a narrative and place that existed before "the change." In our conversations, Garza Guajarado told me that much of local culture deals with loss. This premise is significant, given that *Reportajes* was on the air for over seventeen years. Everyone over the age of ten knows the face of Alvarado. While the reasons behind this attachment to nostalgia are numerous, the connection to de Certeau's concept of loss and the space in-between is compelling. Nuevo León is literally situated in a geographical in-between. With the exception of a thirty-mile buffer zone provided by the state of Tamaulipas, Nuevo León is the connector between the United States and Mexico. The high-speed toll road that charges eighteen dollars to take the motorist 200 kilometers from Monterrey to Nuevo Laredo, which is the border to the United States, makes the back and forth movement of Nuevo León's economically privileged a conductor for cultural practices and money.[10] It is a space where identity escapes. Pieces of American practices return to Monterrey with every family that pays the second eighteen dollars to race down the *autopista* (toll road) after buying all they can in the malls of McAllen and Laredo, Texas. Newspaper advertisements placed weekly by Texas merchants in *El Norte* lure *regios* to buy as often as their economic situation allows.

The movement consists not only of cultural identity but also of people. The flow of migration from Nuevo León to Texas since the nineteenth century, legal or illegal, has been massive. Solís explains in *El mexicano del norte* that *norteños* have generations of people who have been *despadrados* (without fathers) because of the father's need to seek better employment. The more subtle issue of loss concerns what is seen as the original identity, the Jewish identity that is ambiguously detained inside occasional stories. The repetition of loss is related to the ongoing need to officially camouflage their stories of origin. These factors have left the *nuevolenese* in a space in between identities. They are "maybe" Jews; they are "maybe" Mexicans; they are "somewhat" American.[11]

While the stereotypical narratives about rich Jews may seem like childish folktales, the description of the pure, honest, hardworking, hard-saving *norteño,* which was evoked in many of the conversations I had with people from Nuevo León, remains alive. Perhaps this theme is the thrust behind the television narratives of Horacio Alvarado Ortiz. The purity is maintained by the histories presented in each filmed segment. The feeling or possibility of evil is eliminated from public discourse. It is unusual for the media to comment on the Jewish legends. Occasionally there is an exception. Ana Campoy's article in a December 1999 issue of Monterrey's newspaper, *El Norte,* for instance, directly addressed the stories of a Jewish settlement. Campoy interviewed Monica Montemayor Trujillo, who had been researching Monterrey's "cultural traditions" for over twenty years. Montemayor insisted that numerous practices, recipes, and festivals were directly related to what she believed to be the presence of Jews in early Nuevo León. It is a confusing presence. The chaos around this confusion came to the surface in the lectures at the Museo de Historia, when scores of people from the audience insisted that the Jewish stories were true while the lecturers vehemently denied their validity.

This confusion leads me to consider de Certeau's writing on "secrecy," which "is not only the state of a thing that escapes from or reveals itself to knowledge. It designates a play between actors. It circumscribes the terrain of strategic relations between the one trying to discover the secret and the one keeping it, or between the one who is supposed to know it and the one who is assumed not to know it" (1992: 97). The actors are not the historian at the museum and I. While I am the ethnographer who is ignorant, and the historian is the informant who believes she knows the secret, there is a much larger context. Connected to this secret is the self-proclaimed identity of many middle-class *regiomontanos.* Their intense reaction to the historian's denial at the museum was an indication of how important these narratives are to this population. When confronted with these denials, they are faced with an unknown that seems valid at one moment and invalid the next. Thus the cinematic tension heightens. Hearing these inconsistencies, I question the permeability between clandestine stories of contamination and the hard-driven movement toward production that seems so non-Catholic.

The existence of these narratives leaves the sense of another ideology. The Jewish narratives of these "original" Spanish settlers, ancestors of the wealthy industrialists, may have augmented the intensity of their displaced Protestant work ethic. Because the state and national archives regarding the Jews are missing, the most respected form of "evidence" is lacking. All that we have are the agony-filled transcripts of El Santo Oficio (the Inquisition), a Bible that sat on the shelf of Aquiles Sepúlveda's study for twenty-five years, traces here and there of some Jewish tradition, and stories telling of Jewish ancestors. Even so, as previously mentioned, the awestruck rabbi is no longer enthusiastic about the discovery of these possible Jewish documents. Yet Aquiles continued to discuss his theories about the Jews. These conversations only ceased with his death.

In Monterrey, there are many conversations regarding a hidden "social network." For those *regiomontanos* in power, the tightness is a long-standing narrative. "The secret binds together . . . those who hunt for it, keep it, or reveal it. It is the center of the spider web spun around it by lovers, traitors, jealous protagonists, pretenders . . ." (de Certeau 1992: 97). When I speak to persons living in Nuevo León or who are acquainted with the power structure of the region, they often tell me, "The place is controlled by a few very tight-knit families." Irma Salinas Rocha has written extensively on this subject. Her position in the pinnacle of Monterrey society (even though her family was Baptist) and her marriage to a Garza Sada made her privy to the secret underworld of "the family group." Indeed her book, *Nostro grupo,* is a sprawling memoir centering on the assassination of Eugenio Garza Sada, one of the founders of El Grupo Monterrey and the TEC (1970). As mentioned previously, Garza Sada and his older brother Roberto were the force behind the successful conglomeration of Monterrey's industry. Salinas Rocha likens the family to a mafia-like operation with its clandestine movements and unexplained murders. The possible secrets that could be told by *Nostro grupo* were soon sealed away. Soon after publication, the book was confiscated from where it was warehoused and never became available to the public. A few copies are circulating around Monterrey and can be discreetly bought (with photocopied pages) for about twenty American dollars.

Salinas Rocha, Mora-Torres, Saragoza, and Nuncio (among others) have broached the subject of the Garza Sadas with varying success. Nuncio reports having been harassed by a federal police agent after meeting with Salinas Rocha (1982). Saragoza no longer studies Nuevo León. After the publication of *Nostro grupo,* Salinas Rocha was forced to sequester herself within her home for over a year for her own protection. These authors used assorted terms to describe the network of powerful *regio* families. Their descriptions explained intricate networks, structured by endogamy and *compadrazgo,* that could be likened to a system of interweaving webs.

On the first page of *Nostro grupo,* Salinas Rocha tells her reader that many *regio* families are of Jewish origin. Thus, she immediately establishes the connection between the Jewish narratives and El Grupo Monterrey. These narratives have a woven feel about them. By intermarriage or collaboration in business, the ties between and among families are at times like straitjackets, as Salinas Rocha learned. In the search for history and myths about the *sefardíes,* however, what has tied everyone together more profoundly has been the search itself. I remind myself of Aquiles's question, "Why are you so interested in the Jews of Nuevo León?"

The secret evil that is juxtaposed with what is pure could be the stories of a corrupt economy or the "secret" contamination of a Jewish ancestry (if one takes the Inquisition and Henry Ford seriously). It could also be the decision to lie, or rather, to represent "something else." As a man from the audience at the Museo de Historia told Rolando Guerra about the history of the Jews, "How can there be any documentation, if they would be killed if anyone found out?" Guerra had no answer for this question. Yet the dialogue is telling. The secret must remain because, as the First World and the Third World know, history has often shown us that Jews in different eras have been surrounded by danger.

History: The Official Myth

In his book, *The Culture of Literacy* (1994), Wlad Godzich, the well-respected editor of the University of Minnesota series on literary criticism, writes that he was conceived and born in a Nazi concentration camp. In a chapter titled "Paul de Man and the Perils of Intelligence," Godzich responds to revelations concerning de Man's "wartime journalism," pro-Nazi writings published by a Belgian newspaper. Godzich tells his reader that although four members of his family died because of Nazi persecution, there were others who collaborated with the enemy. He continues: "It is not simply a matter of clan loyalty but a recognition that we are never in another person's shoes, no matter how close we may be to them, and we cannot tell whether we would do otherwise were we in their specific place, were we they" (1994: 135). Godzich believes that Americans forget how "pervasive anti-Semitism was in Europe, or indeed in the United States, before the war" (136).

As I read Godzich, I am reminded of my role as ethnographer and recall the denials of a Jewish history in Nuevo León. Those who insist that this "history" is a myth include the "official" historian for the city of Monterrey, the "director" of the state's regional museum, and a historian with close ties to the Catholic Church. It could be that these individuals represent the structure of governmental power with regard to "official history" in Nuevo León. Again I look at Godzich's words: "Once legitimated by the power of the government, however illegitimate

that government may have been, it could affirm itself without the deco-
rum of shared deprecation" (1994: 136). Do these "dissenters," using the
legitimacy of archival history, actually speak for the government or
someone else in power who is ordering them to publicly state that "these
people did not exist"?

The question that surfaces in Godzich's essay on de Man is the relationship between the person and her words, what she speaks. Perhaps she
is aware that the "truth" she believes is a "verbal construct," made up, a
lie. She realizes that her statements may not be true according to "new
rules" (not the government's), yet she continues her treatise because she
has come to terms with the "fundamentally falsifying nature of language"
(1994: 140). She opposes "a local . . . truth to a larger falsehood." The
local truth is the existence of the Jewish narratives that are very real for
many *regios*. The larger falsehood represents the larger power that dictates
what she may say. The narrator now says to herself: "I know that what I
am saying is false in an absolute sense . . . but it is nonetheless true in a
punctual sense" (137). The echo of historian Israel Cavazos Garza is
formed here. He is saying there were no Jews, because there is no archival documentation. I think of this statement as I read what Godzich says
about de Man: "He had learned that it was all too easy to stand by one's
statements and one's actions; it was far more difficult to examine them
critically" (144).

On May 16th, the last class of the *diplomado* at the government-
financed Museo de Historia, Lidia Espinoza was lecturing. At the end of
the session, I stood up and said, "I understand from what you and the
other historians have said, that there is no documentation regarding the
history of the Jews in Nuevo León. Yet I would like to know why in
every session of this series, the students have asked numerous questions
about the Jews." She then cut me off in mid-sentence and said with a
shrill voice, "There were no Jews!"

Espinoza's vigorous disavowal of the Jewish narratives leaves me pon-
dering the question of intent. Foucault proposes that intent is not important in the analysis of a situation (1974). Using Foucault's argument,
whatever Espinosa was thinking as she heartily reacted to my question is
insignificant next to her obvious rejection of the "Jewish Story." The denial itself is placed in a moment before and after the consequences and
movements that have surrounded a controversial narrative. The confusion surrounding the "reality" of the narrative has existed since the time
of Carvajal. Espinoza's interesting response allows us an indicator as to

the intensity of the polemic surrounding the Jewish narratives. Her own individual ambivalence regarding the questionable stories cannot be understood in light of the vehement emotionality in her reaction. After the lecture, I approached her with certain questions regarding the settlement of the Jews and the legendary destruction of El Templo San Francisco. She denied both ever occurred.

CHAPTER IX

La Sultana del Norte:
The Second Nuevo Reino[1]

Monterrey

Los dueños de Cementos Mexicanos o de Alfa [de Monterrey] hoy podrián responderle a Felipe II [de España] que, efectivamente, en sus dominios tampoco jamás se pone el sol. (Nuncio 1997: 121) The owners of Cementos Mexicanos or of Alfa [of Monterrey] can advise Felipe II [of Spain] that their dominions are so vast that the sun never sets on them, as was the Spanish Empire in the sixteenth century.

This chapter is about the city of Monterrey, Nuevo León, known as La Sultana del Norte, the most successful industrial city in the north of Mexico. It is about how a very modern city is facing its past, which in a sense has been placed underground, beneath the facade of a "Macro Plaza" that encompasses 242,000 square meters and is constructed over the ruins of Monterrey's oldest neighborhood (Nuncio 1982).

As I have proceeded through the project, I have come to realize that this "macro-cover" is actually a metonym for the hidden and deflected histories that I have inadvertently encountered in my travels through Nuevo León. Finding innumerable stories that bordered on the Imaginary, I searched through the work of Brazilian literary critic Luiz Costa Lima and found that his work on the Latin American Imaginary closely fits the history of Nuevo León and Monterrey. Costa Lima's project on the Imaginary has led him to see what is not considered a logical part of reason has to be controlled, hidden away, in the space of the Other, to serve the purposes of those in power, those with the "appropriate reasoning." As part of his trajectory, he has studied a number of Latin American authors, including Juan Rulfo, Irma Sepúlveda's mentor. As Costa Lima travels to the interior of Rulfo's work, he finds a strange

Templo San Francisco before its destruction.
Photograph by Refugio Z. Garcia. 1914.

Graffiti on the Macro Plaza in downtown Monterrey. 1999.
Photograph by the author.

Bridal store on the Macro Plaza. Agustín Loredo
traveled with his mother, his fiancée, and her mother
from Baytown, Texas, to Monterrey to buy a wedding dress at this store. 1999.

Photograph by the author.

illumination that is not often seen in other writing that pertains to what
is commonly called "the magical real." Rulfo's characters speak; whether
they are living or dead, he amplifies their voices. There is a tension and
an "unknowing," uncanny quality about Rulfo's narrative. Reality is not
quite located. The reader is left to distinguish her own perception of the
réel. Costa Lima comments, "This is a story of the dead who never leave
the earth" (1992: 87). According to Costa Lima, the voices of the half-
dead, half-alive are somehow trapped in Rulfo's narrative. It is difficult

to tell from what side (life or death) the voices are coming. These representations remind me of the voices of those buried underground, under the Macro-Plaza, who fight to communicate their intentions. In these particular narratives about the "macro-cover," the boundary between reality and the imaginary is blurred. There is no other possibility of explanation. There are no documents to assist the archivist in determining a truth. The excess stemming from the lack of "documentation" is located in the phantasmic surrounding the concrete cover hovering over downtown Monterrey.

In this text, which has located itself in the idea of the production of history, the underground city is akin to exhuming what historiography "cannot know." Similarly, Tom Conley writes in the translator's introduction of de Certeau's *Writing of History* that "historiography must exhume what it cannot know, or dig up whatever it can muster, to have a fleeting grasp of the present" (1988: xix). As I ask different people what they know of the tunnels and those persons buried inside of walls and under houses, I feel like I am metaphorically "digging up what I can muster" to have a "fleeting grasp of the present." The stories of the women buried in walls or buried in their underground houses tell me that the Other has been sealed away to keep a secret. What is enclosed in secrecy naturally creates curiosity and interest. At a certain moment, a story is told; the words form exciting sounds. The listener straightens in her chair. The drama sounds fantastic. The storyteller recounts the event in such a way that his descriptions sound like daily life. Yet the border around reality dissipates when what has died is brought to the world of the living.

Sealing Away the Imaginary

> . . . the crucial feature here is the off-kilter, creepy feeling of the uncanny due to an unstable and uncapturable blending, . . . of concealment and revelation of a secret that for all its secretness is not really a secret . . . but what we might call the public secret. (Taussig 1999: 50)

During the prosperity of the early 1980s, Monterrey, the state capital of Nuevo León, went through a transformation. In 1981, the three-hundred-year-old houses near the city's cathedral were torn down for the construction of a new, modernistic "Macro Plaza." From the edge of downtown that bordered El Río Santa Catarina on past El Ojo de Agua, where Monterrey was founded, everything imaginable was destroyed. Abraham Nuncio describes it as the result of a compromise between the Garza Sadas and the governor, Martinez Domínguez. He likens the result to the Holocaust: "*[E]l centro de la ciudad rememora en muchos de sus rincones a Nuremberg de postguerra. La demolición de los viejos edificios y casas ha sido mas eficáz que un bombardeo*" (1982: 113). (The center of the city recalls many of the corners of Nuremberg after the war. The demolition of those old buildings and houses was more efficient than a military bombing). In an essay on Monterrey, Eduardo Reineri writes of the aftermath: "*Primero fue una rapina organizada, como de terremoto: . . . ventanas, puertas, muebles sanitarios, dinteles [estan tiradas donde quiera]. Finalmente, llegaron los trascavos, parecia . . . Hiroshima . . . la mañana siguiente*" (1994: 135) (First it was an organized rape, like an earthquake: windows, doors, toilets, door frames were scattered about. Finally, came the tractors; it looked like Hiroshima, the day after). Citlalli Hernández Rosales lived nearby. She tells me of this destruction. There was a night in which she found herself walking home after a late appointment. Only about ten blocks from her home, she thought that the walk would be brief. She had forgotten that she had to cross the area of construction for the new Macro Plaza. Before she realized it, she was in an area that seemed like a war zone. There were no lights. There was no moon to light the streets. There were holes and rocks everywhere. She was not as afraid of being assaulted as she was afraid of the mist, the dark, and the holes in the ground. The mist seemed to rise from the ground with a slow movement towards her. She sensed a diabolical quality in the haze that was quickly surrounding her. She began to run. There were no taxis nearby. For what seemed like several kilometers, she kept running until she arrived home out of breath and exhausted.

It was this conversation with Hernández Rosales that led me to the focus of this chapter. Her story was emotional. It left us both wondering about the purpose of the destruction. What did the broad concrete Macro Plaza cover up? Perhaps her fear of "the mist" betrayed a somewhat superstitious nature, yet there was no denying that the darkness in which she found herself appeared dangerous. There were no people around and no street lights; there were only disjointed pieces of buildings, openings in the ground, and a dust that settled in the air and traveled with the breeze as far as Bustamante ninety kilometers away (Reineri 1994: 135).

Hernández Rosales informed me of a "legend" that is told about Reineri's neighborhood. Throughout the center of Monterrey there are a series of tunnels. Also, there are numerous verbal accounts of "underground houses." In the late 1980s, Hernández Rosales was teaching in a *secondaria* (middle school); in response to a citywide contest of "the best" myths and legends in Nuevo León, one of her students wrote a story often told in his family: "*Until the early twentieth century, living in the houses underground were women and children. Mistresses and 'hijos naturales' (illegitimate children) of Monterrey's priests. When the man tired of his 'underground family' he had the doors of the house sealed, with the occupants unaware of their impending deaths.*" Hernández Rosales was further convinced of the veracity of this story when a number of skeletons appeared near the edge of the Macro Plaza. During construction, workers found skeletons of women, children, and infants; the skeletons were not in any orderly form but were randomly scattered, suggesting that the site was not a cemetery. The local newspaper stated that the disorderly location of the bodies suggested an "earthquake." There have been no significant earthquakes documented in northern Mexico.[2]

The Purpose of Stories

It is the story of the women sealed in their underground houses that leads me to my question. Where is the issue of "sealing bodies away" placed in a world where bloody, public execution is the recent norm? How does this story (and others that are similar) continue to live in late twentieth-century Monterrey? The city is the most modern in Mexico, as is evidenced in the fact that it is the home of the TEC (Instituto Tecnológico). Monterrey, with its broad base of concrete that covers much of a neighborhood once named Los Dulces Nombres (The Sweet Names), is said to have the largest downtown plaza in the world. What is the "macro-cover" doing for Monterrey? What was sealed in the underground houses? What secrets did these *queridas* (mistresses) maintain with their silent deaths? Why were these women killed and occulted in comparison to the public, dramatic killings of Mexico's *caudillos* (political leaders)? De Certeau's approach to history is a "diachrony within synchrony"

(1988: 348), which references Freud's work in *Civilization and Its Discontents*. Freud was speaking of Rome in "supposing an image, coming from nowhere, in which incompatible places would coincide, 'in which nothing that has once come into existence will have passed away and all earlier phases of development continue to exist alongside the latest one'" (312).[3] Thus events are layered as different moments that do not dissolve into the past but spill on top of one another (1988). De Certeau's description resonates with Monterrey's layers of bodies underground. The curiously placed cover serves as a concrete seal for the past. The layers continue to pile on top of one another. At moments of construction or excavation, traces of these former layers are exposed. What exists in the present is not the same as what existed in the past, yet a semblance of previous lives and places sprouts as the tractors move about the spaces of Monterrey's downtown. More powerfully, what is imagined still to exist belies any claims of a past that has disappeared.

Mujeres Emparedadas—Women Buried in Walls

When I told Aquiles Sepúlveda that I wanted to know about the underground tunnels in Monterrey, he responded by telling me stories he heard from a friend who had been an altar boy at the Cathedral during the 1940s. The boy witnessed numerous "strange events." He followed the priests as they descended into the tunnels to rooms where they had secret meetings. They spoke Latin and discussed the Kabbalah and issues regarding exorcism. Yet the most grotesque adventure was the boy's witnessing the discovery of a woman buried in the wall of a building near the Cathedral. She was wearing a wedding dress.

This conversation with Aquiles occurred in the summer of 1999. A few months earlier, his sister Ofelia had told me a similar story. For twenty-five years, Ofelia Sepúlveda was the headmistress of a girls' school next to the Cathedral. The building was very ancient and had three levels of underground basements. On the first level, the school had a kitchen. Most of the school staff congregated in the mornings to have coffee in this room. Someone had been excavating between her school and the next building, right at the wall of her school's kitchen. The excavating was a search for buried treasure, a common occurrence in Nuevo León. According to Ofelia, the men who were tearing the wall apart found a woman's body perhaps about one hundred years old. I asked her if she saw the body. She said she was irritated with the workmen because they did not notify her until the body had been removed. She was sure this delay was because they had stolen the jewelry on the corpse. All they showed her were some flowers from the dead woman's dress. Afterwards some of her staff would often remark excitedly that for years they had been having coffee in the kitchen while the woman in the wall was right next to them.

Curious about this story, I asked other people I knew if they had heard of women buried in walls. I was told of men being buried in the walls of houses in rural areas after burying treasure[4] and of young children being buried alive in the corners of lakes so that the children's souls could warn the nearby village of impending floods. There are also stories of children buried in the corners of churches, their spirits supporting the construction. Two churches in Monterrey, one being the notable "El Roble," had collapsed because "there were no children buried in the corners of the buildings."[5] There are also many stories of people being buried "under" houses. In the 1960s, one family I came to know very well found the body of a man under the floor of a house they were demolishing for new construction. This body, also, was in the area near the Macro Plaza.

In searching for the "buried women," I found there were many forms of entombment for many types of people. Yet what seemed common to all of these narratives was that the person being buried was "the Other": the child, the woman, or the weakest man of the group. There are no stories of *caudillos* being buried in walls or underground. Those murders have been reserved for the open, the daylight, the obvious.

Showing or Hiding Bodies

In 1999 Mexico experienced a series of public executions. Perhaps the most notable was of Paco Stanley, a sort of Mexican Johnny Carson. In the early afternoon of June 7, 1999, Stanley was leaving a downtown Mexico City restaurant and was killed by several gunmen as he approached his car. The response to the murder was profound. I heard the news as I was driving to Monterrey from Laredo, Texas. The radio station I was listening to was going back and forth from Frank Sinatra–type Mexican music to "live reports" from the scene of the crime. The television stations preempted all programs and were permanently situated on the theme of Paco Stanley's murder. Three months later, Monterrey's newspaper, *El Norte,* continued to publish stories on Paco Stanley, the latest being that he had an eleven-year-old son from a relationship outside his marriage. The child's mother appeared in order to claim his inheritance. The murder was public; moreover, the mourning and the family scenes were all held in front of a curious nation of TV viewers.

On September 17, 1973, when the most powerful and famous Monterrey industrialist was publicly murdered, it was the same. The city was hysterical. Thousands attended the funeral, including the President of Mexico, Luis Echeveria. The eighty-five-year-old Eugenio Garza Sada was killed at 9 A.M. at the downtown intersection of Villagran and Quintanar. He was gunned down while driving his black, late-model Ford Galaxie.

In the cases of Stanley and Garza Sada, it was necessary for the assassins to publicly eliminate their victims. As in the assassination of presidential candidate Luis Donaldo Colosio in 1994, there was no ambiguity in their elimination.

In contrast, no one knows the identities of the women discovered in the walls of the buildings near the Cathedral. There are no photographs, and there were no funerals. As Ofelia remarked, by the time she was notified, "The body had been disposed of."

Women in the Dark

The origin of the presumption that those entities, which are really fictitious, are in fact real is lost in bygone ages, when a supposed equivalence between the real and the existence of a name for it was concretized. For it is the name that created the presumption of reality "between the idea of a name and that of the reality of the object to which is was applied. . . . sprung a very natural propensity . . . That of attributing reality to every object thus designated . . ." (Costa Lima 1988: 35)

There are moments when the ethnographer hears a story so fantastic that the reason she needs to write it down is forgotten as quickly as the storyteller tells it. It took two months for me to realize the significance of this story, which was told to me by Artemio Villagómez, a schoolteacher originally from General Terán, Nuevo León.

His great-uncle, José Cano, was a soldier in the Mexican Revolution.

During the eighty-five years since the story had transpired, the name of Cano's *comandante* had been changed to Emiliano Zapata, who actually was never in Monterrey.

The troops had already taken over the city of Monterrey. The year was most probably 1915. They had gathered at El Obispado, a foothill west of the city, at the site of a three-hundred-year-old church. Entering an underground opening, they proceeded with their horses through a tunnel. Afterwards, Cano was released to visit his family in General Terán. He was able to talk of the tunnel and the people inside. It was so large that a horse and wagon could pass through. It was so wide that there were houses on each side. There were women and children there. Cano told his family that the women were Catholic nuns. The children were the offspring of the nuns and the local priests. Cano's sister told the story to her grandson Artemio forty years later.

At the age of fifty-six, Artemio Villagómez lives about fifteen kilometers from the tunnel. As he tells the story, he is sitting at his kitchen table. The story emerges after we eat dinner at a restaurant named El Portón. His cousin Yolanda González is with us. They spend over an hour talking about the marriages, divorces, and births in their family. I am so bored I am ready to go home. They decide to continue the conversation at Artemio's house; the talk then shifts from secrets in the family to secrets in the city. The nuns/mothers with their children sounded so fantastic that I hesitated to take the story seriously. Eventually, however, I made note of what he said and began searching for information regarding the tunnels.

The narrative of the women living in Monterrey's underground city opens the discourse of this study into the space of the ambiguous, the secret, the clandestine, the covert, and the sexual. It stands at the door of this text that intends to present and analyze the history of women who were forced into spaces underground, at times sheltered and at times murdered. Yet the image I retain as I recall the words of Artemio Villagómez is of the dark, the huge tunnel, horses and carriages running through, and women and children standing in front of their underground houses. In my imagination, the tunnel, lit by torches, is only partially visible.

After José Cano left his family in General Terán, he was never seen again. It is likely that he died during battle and was buried in some unknown grave. When I finally realized the significance of José Cano's story, I began to ask everyone I knew in Monterrey about the underground "houses." I asked Alvarado, thinking that surely he would be able to give me some information. He responded by saying he had filmed the large tunnel that runs from the Obispado to the Cathedral. Yes, it was very large; a horse and carriage could easily drive through the tunnel. As for houses, no, there were no houses and no city. At the end of our conversation, he did add, "Well, during the revolution, there were a few girls who were hidden in rooms in the tunnels; the families were trying to keep them away from Pancho Villa."[6] This information was all he offered me.

Don Ceferino, who sells used books in his shop on Guerrero Street, was more helpful. He is an acquaintance of Aquiles Sepúlveda. Don Ceferino was previously a college professor. During the previous thirty years, Aquiles and Ceferino continuously bought and sold books from each other. I had gone to visit Ceferino in search of Irma Salinas Rocha's book, *Nostro Grupo*. Don Ceferino seemed to relish intrigue. Waiting for his other customers to be out of earshot, I whispered to him that I was searching for Salinas Rocha's book. I also asked him about the tunnels. He did not mind telling me about the underground houses inside the large tunnel between the Obispado and the Cathedral: "There was an 'underground city' that was active for centuries. What you tell me is true. The problem is that the church and the local powers have decided to occult the existence of the 'underground city.' It is not so much the government, it is the local corporations. They have more control than the government because they are so wealthy. They have colluded with the church, perhaps because the church would lose significant status if the stories of the 'nuns with children' would circulate publicly. The local media is controlled by the corporations which have stymied the publication of these stories."

In what seemed like an attempt to help me in my search, Don Ceferino called his friend Abel Moreno for information. According to Ceferino, Licenciado Moreno had a great deal of information on the history of Monterrey. While I stood by his desk in his store, Don Ceferino made several calls to Moreno's office. The Licenciado works for the PRI, the political party that lost control of Mexico in 2000 after being in power over eighty years. Moreno's position made me rather uncomfortable. I asked Don Ceferino if Licenciado Moreno would be open to speaking about the tunnels. I was assured that Moreno would be very helpful. After about twenty minutes, during which time I went shelf by shelf through Ceferino's bookstore, I finally was able to speak to

Moreno. I said, "Licenciado, I am researching the history of Monterrey and am looking for information regarding the tunnels and what may be an underground city inside of them. Do you have any information on this?" He responded by saying: "What I have is a book on the geology of the tunnels but nothing more." I thanked him for taking the time to speak with me. Afterwards Don Ceferino took the phone and said he would be expecting the Licenciado to come by the shop. Two weeks later I asked Ceferino what Moreno said when they talked. Moreno knew nothing of the tunnels. As Ceferino spoke, I realized that the PRI now knew I was looking for something.

In a curious combination of medieval belief and modernity's technological control, the stories of women entombed and the resultant censorship of references to these events creates a unique space for the understanding of how the citizens of Nuevo León have dealt with their genealogy, their "questionable origins," and their future as a people. De Certeau (1988) looks at what is hidden or covered up as more powerful than what is openly discussed. When a piece of history is occulted, the repressed finds its way back into the space of the present, leaving clues and tensions in many places. Perhaps as an indication of this tension, the traces of repressed *nuevolenese* history have remained inside the myths and legends of the city. Censorship, however, has made almost impossible the location of specific information that substantiates the underground city, the women in the walls, or the even older "stories" that still proliferate among the *regiomontanos*. In consideration of this problem, I will focus on the reality of the narrative event, which is that the stories are being told. Veracity is not the issue. For the purposes of this project, the "real" concerns what is "said," not what is written.

A few months later, I am walking around the Macro Plaza in the late afternoon while taking photographs with historian Cristóbal López. We both see a group of women running. They appear indigenous. Cristóbal remarks that they are the *vendedoras* (street vendors) who sell candy and soft drinks on the plaza. We have just bought a Sprite from one of them a few steps from the city's theatre. The women run into an underground opening about sixteen meters from us. Soon after, a group of about seven men pursue the women down the stairs. The men appear to be in their twenties and thirties; many are wearing white T-shirts and jeans. They all have cell phones or pagers clipped to their belts. I tell Cristóbal that maybe we better leave. Always looking for controversy (in the introduction of his book he quotes Subcomandante Marcos), he goes toward the opening and begins to film the encounter with his video camera. A man comes up and tells Cristóbal something. The man covers the lens of the camera with his hand. Cristóbal is not allowed to film. After Cristóbal returns to where I am waiting (and hoping not to be noticed), he tells me that the women were at the foot of the stairs. The men were plain-clothes policemen enforcing the rule of no *vendedoras* in the Macro Plaza. When Cristóbal was told to leave, the police were on the verge of beat-ing the women.

The stairway from the Macro Plaza leads to a large subterranean park-ing lot. Although the parking lot is lit, a person driving her automobile needs to turn on the lights to see well enough to drive. The *esta-cionamiento* (parking lot) has several levels and is usually where the middle and upper classes park their cars when they go to downtown Monterrey. Public transportation in the city is rarely used except by the working classes. The women running from the police in the Macro Plaza appeared to be "Marías." They ran underground in an attempt to escape. Their running underground reminded me of something I had heard a few weeks before. In my conversation with Citlalli Hernández Rosales re-garding the underground tunnels and houses, we both speculated on the use of the tunnels. In other conversations, Ofelia Sepúlveda had told me many times that the tunnels were used to protect the city's inhabitants from attacking Indians. Hernández Rosales had other conjectures. What else happened in the tunnels? What could have been hidden there? Is it possible people who were trying to escape something else would have descended into the tunnels in order to keep their private activities oc-culted? Alvarado had said there were rooms used to protect the young women of Monterrey from Pancho Villa. Aquiles Sepúlveda told me about rooms that were used by priests for reading the Kabbalah in Latin. How far-fetched would it be to wonder if there might have been rooms in which other types of rituals were conducted?

Containing and Colonizing Fecundity

The Production of Genealogy and Nobility

. . . micro-sites [are] where designations of racial membership were subject to gendered appraisals and where "character," "good breeding," and proper rearing were implicitly raced. (Stoler 1995: 11)

Un mestizo—What Alvarado told me about my father ˆwhen I showed him a photograph of my family. (1997)

Central to this project is the question of origins. "Where one comes from" is pivotal to the mythology of entitlement and power. From the divine right of kings to the genealogy of nobility, the identification of the original parents is central to the right to power. The narrative of the powerful Aztec nation, which supports the current ideology of the Mexican nation-state, is not the same narrative that is used by the middle and upper classes in the north. As Abraham Nuncio aptly mentions, the only statue representing Mexico's indigenous population is that of Cuauhtémoc, which stands outside the Cuauhtémoc Brewery. Nuncio is convinced that if it was not for the brewery, the Aztec leader's statue would not exist in Monterrey (1997). This disconnection with the ideology of origin with the Mexican state creates a continuous polemic for *norteños.* It feeds the myth of their own illegitimacy vis-à-vis Mexico, the mother nation.

Considering the illegitimacy of the Jewish narratives in Nuevo León, for the *nuevoleneses,* there is also no secure comfort found in saying its ancestors were Jews. Creating a form of "making do," as de Certeau would say, the Jewish narratives have creatively embedded themselves into the modern story of origin in Nuevo León. The story of origin has become the story of the founding of El Grupo Monterrey. The ten or so families that are reported to have been part of the initial "group" are seen as the originators of Monterrey. This originary status, of course, is not in the literal, biological sense. However, since these families were those who began the "second kingdom," they are seen as the nobility.[7]

In a conversation I had with Cristóbal López on a Tuesday afternoon in the cafeteria of El Museo de Historia in Monterrey, we discussed the question of origins. I told him I had been thinking about the early postconquest history of the region and that it seemed there was no publicly accepted ideology regarding the origins of the people of Nuevo León. Cristóbal agreed. It was an issue he had been analyzing for some time in his studies on the folklore of northern Mexico. The indigenous history was erased; the Jewish history was not taken seriously by those "in authority;" and the "white" people, considered to be descended from the original Spanish settlers of Nuevo León, were known as barbarians.

The *Original* Newscaster

In the time I came to know Alvarado and two of his sons who worked on his television program, I also learned of his wife and children. One morning, a year after I first began working with him, I arrived at his office to find a different set of photographs on the wall. I asked him who the people were. They were his grandparents and his in-laws. He described each one in detail, telling me about his relationship with them and how they had influenced him. I was rather surprised that his wife's parents were included. His mother-in-law had died before Alvarado married.

His wife's surname is Genesi, but he did not tell me this fact. I already knew, since his sons use the surnames Alvarado Genesi, as is the custom in Mexico, where the mother's surname is listed after the father's. The Genesis migrated from Italy. The mother died early and Alvarado's future wife took charge of numerous younger siblings. She knew how to cook and manage a home. When he made his choice, Alvarado was sure that she would be the best mother for his children. As he told me about this decision, I thought of the ramifications. The children would have an Italian last name, would be fair-skinned, and would have a mother who already had experience with children.

This choosing of "the mother" resonates with the concept of bio-politics which Foucault addresses in his series *History of Sexuality* (1990). Such bio-politics involves the efforts of those in power to further strengthen their coalition by producing "the best" offspring. These are the physically strongest, the most intelligent, the "better strains." Alvarado's offspring attest to such efforts. His oldest, Eduardo Alvarado Genesi, is tall, blonde, and attractive. At forty-five, he is the news director of Monterrey's Televisa affiliate. Another son, Pepe, is a local corporate executive. A daughter, Teresa, is the wife of a wealthy industrialist in Puebla.

The stories of marriages in the history of Nuevo León are replete with these types of planned unions. Marriage between first cousins is very common. Intermarrying to preserve land ownership and local power is reminiscent of medieval unions within the European nobility. As Nuncio argues, *Los apellidos notables se cruzan y vuelven a cruzar en las actas de matrimonio y en las escrituras constitutivas de las sociedades anónimas que dan cobijo a cada vez mas diversificados giros comerciales e industriales* (1982: 32). (The notable surnames cross and cross again in marriage certificates and documents of corporations that each time give cover to more diversified commercial and industrial movement.) The "background" means prestige and inclusion in certain important social lists (ibid.).

Alvarado, in describing his background, is in accord with Nuncio's observation:

> . . . *aquí en La Purísima teníamos un nivel social; . . . Pero teníamos aquí a la gente pudiente en la Colonia Mirador, la gente de cultura, de cierto nivel, de cierta educación . . . familias muy respetables . . .* (Garza Guajardo 1993: 24) (here in La Purísima we had a certain social class; . . . However, we had nearby, powerful people in La Colonia Mirador, people of culture, of a certain social class, of a certain education . . . very respectable families)

Proper control of reproduction maintains the prevailing social order. Alvarado is a significant regional personality. Felicitos Leal writes in the introduction of a biography of Alvarado: *"[el ha] hecho . . . para fomentar nuestra esencia y proteger nuestras raices"* (Leal 1993: 13) ([he] has helped define our essence and protect our roots).[8]

Alongside this quest for "good genes" is another type of control. It is "la casa chica," which is still very common in Nuevo León as in other regions of Mexico and Latin America. It is discussed publicly. In a recent conversation at "La Prepa 15" in a journalism class, the students discussed the tradition of having a "second family." It was expected, if the man had the economic means to do so.[9]

During the revolution, when José Cano saw the houses in the tunnel, he saw *"las casas chicas"* of the priests. These were the *"casas chicas"* that were sealed with the occupants trapped inside, according to the story presented for El Concurso de Leyendas in 1989. The idea of these homes being underground, occulted, and secret was to keep the "Other/contaminated women/children" away. In the present day, they are in "other neighborhoods," away from the first family. The women of the *casa chica* are usually (but not always) of a lower class than the man. A recent newspaper article on Paco Stanley's *casa chica* describes the child and his mother: *"El niño está igualito a Paco Stanley, su cara y sus cachetes, pero no tiene los ojos azules,"* dijo un amigo de la familia que lo ha visto. *Durruti es una mujer de casi 35 años, morena clara y con el cabello negro."* ("The boy is just like Paco Stanley, his face, his cheeks, but he does not have blue eyes," said a friend of the family who had seen the child. Durruti [the mother] is a woman of about thirty-five years of age, who is somewhat dark-skinned with black hair.)

The father maintains control over this second family by providing financial support. The "honorable" man provides enough so that the woman does not need to work. This support prevents the woman from seeking a more "respectable" relationship with someone else. The off-spring develop ambivalent ties to their father, yet are stymied by their half-caste position in society.

There is something reminiscent in this arrangement to the children of American slave owners and their female slaves. The resulting child is "lighter skinned" yet trapped at a level lower than her father and half-siblings. The question is whether the children of *la casa chica* become anything similar to the "house Negro" of the American south. In a recently broadcast telenovela, the illegitimate daughter of a wealthy woman actually becomes the maid of the house.

Risking Burial

[Leonora] tendría apenas diez y seis años. Era muy bella y con su alegría llenaba la casa . . . sus padres . . . como solía ser en aquellos años, la tenían comprometida con don Joaquín . . . quien . . . tenía . . . vastas posesiones y . . . próspero establecimento comercial . . . Sus pretendientes hubieron de resignarse, excepto Manuel . . . [quien] concibió la idea y la logró de conseguir empleo en la hacienda. Fue de este modo que consiguió estar cerca de su amada y mantener una oculta relación . . . Nadie sabe lo que pasó al ser descubiertos, pero doña Leonora no se vio más en la hacienda . . . don Joaquin explicó que habla emprendido un viaje a Europea de varios meses. Pero doña Leonora jamás volvió . . .

Ancianos de la Villa del Carmen, cuentan que cuando eran niños oían decir que doña Leonora había sido "emparedada" pero que entre los muros que iban cayendo, jamás se encontró su cuerpo. (Villanueva de Cavazos 1988: 73–74) (Leonora was only sixteen. She was very beautiful and her happiness filled her home. Her parents, as was done in those years, had her promised to Don Joaquin who was a wealthy businessman with many holdings. All of her suitors resigned themselves, with the exception of Manuel, who thought of finding work at the hacienda. Thus he was near his lover and was able to maintain a secret affair. No one knows what happened when they were discovered, but Leonora was never seen again at the hacienda. Her husband, Joaquin, told everyone that she had gone to Europe for several months. However, Doña Leonora never returned. Older people from Villa del Carmen say that when they were children they heard that Doña Leonora had been buried in a wall of the hacienda. In later years, as the walls of the hacienda began to fall, her body was not found.

This legend about a woman from Montemorelos tells of an arranged marriage, an illicit affair between the young wife of the *hacendado* and a working-class man. The consequence of transgression was death. Leonora rebelled against what was normally expected of her. Her liaison with another man who was her husband's employee created a double transgression. This type of situation is described by Ann Laura Stoler (1995) in her work on Foucault's *History of Sexuality* (1990). Stoler recounts how legislators in colonial Maryland focused on the "unmanageable desires" of European women by regulating interracial unions. The use of law in the service of sexual control is an indication of a potentially dangerous practice that could be a "threat" to the social body of the colony. In the legend of Leonora, there is no indication of Manuel's racial status. However, the difference between Manuel being called by only his name and the husband, "Don" Joaquin, having the honorific "don" indicates that Manuel was of a lower social class.

The reasons for this type of "burial" seem to be numerous. Ofelia Sepúlveda tells me that she spoke to *un vidente* (a seer) about the woman who was found in the wall of her school. The seer told her the woman was buried in the wall about a hundred years before; she had been killed because she had approached someone requesting payment of monies that were owed her.

The friend of Aquiles who saw the woman in the wall wearing a wedding dress did not give any details or reasons behind the discovery. Yet for the *emparedada* to be wearing a wedding dress is enough for anyone to question the relation between the dress and her death.

The risk continues. Since I first spoke with Aquiles, who was the brother of Ofelia and Doña Pepita, he always urged me to be careful and not to develop notoriety. He urged me to take seriously the risk of death.

The stories of the women in the walls are from another century, and I found it difficult to bring the risk into the present. Yet his most striking argument concerned his sister, Irma Sabina.

Irma's first two books, *Agua de las verdes matas* (1963) and *Los cañones de Pancho Villa* (1969), focus on rural people and their quotidian existence. They concern the witches, ghosts, farmers, and children of Potrero. Her third book is different. Sepúlveda's short stories, which are published in *El agiotista,* humorously criticize the city's middle class. A banker is blackmailed by nuns after he has an affair with his secretary; two elderly women lose their life savings to gypsies; a beautiful blonde woman, appearing chaste and attractive, is really promiscuous. Blanca Montemayor, a writer from Monterrey, wrote of Sepúlveda's work and life; alluding to "family problems," however, she provides no further information on the author's life. In the essay, Sepúlveda is shown to have "a predilection for those who are marginal," perhaps because of her own marginality as a writer. Montemayor is most probably representing the "local talk" regarding Sepúlveda. The third book is not about those who are marginal but about the urban professional class and their misguided lives. The politics of Montemayor's essay is interesting; she is a *becario,* a writer who has received a scholarship, special recognition, and training from El Centro de Escritores de Nuevo León. Montemayor's essay omits Sepúlveda's national recognition and association with Juan Rulfo. Montemayor, however, does corroborate the harsh criticism of *El agiotista:* *"[E]s para mí el menos afortunado de los tres [libros]"* (is the least fortunate of the three [books]) (ibid. 247). The phrase "least fortunate" was another way of saying that people were offended. The book was harshly criticized. Aquiles tells me Irma's mistake was speaking with such candor about the people in the city. It was acceptable for the rural people to be seen as superstitious and petty but not the people of Monterrey. Soon after the release of *El agiotista* (1970), Irma went into seclusion in the Sepúlveda home. For the next ten years, she did not leave the house. Some people have told me it was because she had a severe weight problem. Aquiles is sure that it was a *maleficio* (some type of spell). She was punished for saying too much and perhaps for being too successful. In 1988 she died at home of cancer. She never told her family the nature of her illness. She left behind numerous unedited manuscripts of short stories and theatrical pieces.

Irma's body was not placed inside a wall of a colonial building. Yet she was entombed in a different sort of way. The possibility of the continuation of a brilliant career ended after the publication of *El agiotista*. At this time, there is no way of knowing what her motivation was in locking herself away. Perhaps in her numerous unpublished manuscripts and letters there might be some indication of her motivations behind the decision to seclude herself.

The narrative that her brother Aquiles presents is that of a woman entombed for not containing herself, for letting her pen flow too easily. It was in this same way that he told me many other stories. The context was often dramatic, with a hint of secrecy or intrigue associated with everything he said. There was often a dual meaning in his narratives. His interest in folklore as well as the history of his family and Nuevo León joined with his superb storytelling abilities. He told me stories of Potrero, Mexico, the errant priest in Villaldama, and my own family. He made his storytelling into an art form. Yet inside the creativity of expression was the constant word of caution. Each story had a meaning and a purpose, resonating closely with the nature of folktales but even more exciting.[10]

Irma also had the gift of narration, as I could clearly observe from reading her stories. Yet the difference I saw between Aquiles and his sister was that she allowed her stories to circulate. She seems to have been freed from the caution that he said was necessary for survival.

Speaking From the Other Side

There are many stories of people buried in different spaces in Monterrey. There are conflicting narratives about the cemetery that belonged to the now destroyed Convento San Francisco. It has often been said this site was where the indigenous were buried, yet Lidia Espinoza told her audience at the Museum of History that people of both races were buried in that cemetery. Ofelia Sepúlveda told me a most surprising story of numerous people being buried or trapped inside the basement of her school building, which was located next to the Cathedral downtown. She has always had a practice of lighting a candle to the Virgin Mary, whether at home or at the school. According to Fela, the candle to the Virgin attracted the ghosts of the people who were buried in her building. Ofelia said there were many people buried underneath. The candle let the ghosts know that Ofelia had good intentions and that she was trying to help them escape with the light from the candle. Once, another *vidente* told her that a ghost was requesting "American coffee." Ofelia obediently made some American coffee and placed a cup full near the candle. The next day, when she arrived at the school, a male colleague who was accompanying Ofelia chided her superstitious nature. They were both shocked to find the cup empty. She believes that the ghost drank the coffee.

In a convolution of past and present, reality and the imaginary, Ofelia tells me that the present owner of the building is Raúl Salinas Gortari, the imprisoned brother of former Mexican president Carlos Salinas Gortari. In the same breath, she also tells me that one member of the Salinas family married into her family. She says the Salinases "are not that bad; it was politics that corrupted them."

While the connection in mid-sentence between the ghosts and the Salinas family may seem extreme, there is actually a link between the two. The Salinas family, in their reign of spending, murder, and billions of dollars in laundered money (not unusual for Mexican politics), are symbols of the corrupt secret in Mexico. It is required to stay underground. When the secret is told, even though everyone already knows, there is again an implosion. In early March 2000, the head of the Partido Revolucionario Demócrata (PGR), one of the opposition parties, was accused of having embezzled millions of dollars. The next day he was found shot to death in his car near his home in Mexico City. In 1994 Francisco Ruiz Massieu, a Salinas brother-in-law, was also murdered. This man's brother was recently found dead in his New Jersey apartment, where he was under house arrest. Many of these deaths have been ruled suicides. Like Ofelia's ghost who likes American coffee, the ghosts remain underground, keeping the secret safe but occasionally wanting some of the modern conveniences. Not all that is hidden is about the distant past. It also concerns the hidden present.[11]

Analysis of Women in the Tomb

A tomb is a container. In Spanish it is referred to as *el ataúd* (the casket) or *el cajón* (the box). It contains the contaminated remnants of the dead. What is most striking about the *mujeres emparedadas* and the women who were trapped in their underground houses is that their death was their entombment. The men who were assassinated had a clearly defined space in which their lives were publicly extinguished, somewhat reminiscent of the public executions of the eighteenth century. The women went straight from life to entrapment. There was no space for discourse. Now, in the late twentieth century, the Macro Plaza further seals their history. The broad expanse of molded concrete seals away any semblance of the parallel world. The realities of their experiences are erased in the silent protection of *las empresas* (the corporations). The modernity that has brought Monterrey to the forefront of Mexican capitalism carefully pushes down traces of those last gasps of breath.

When Citlalli Hernández Rosales described to me her own feeling of entrapment within the devastation of the barrio of Los Dulces Nombres, I started wondering about the need for Monterrey to "entrap." A lone, unaccompanied woman who found herself late at night in a space of devastation was against the code. As Sara Aguilar Belden writes in her memoirs of Monterrey, a woman had to appear chaste at all times; her conduct was of utmost importance (1970). It is no surprise that Citlalli was severely reprimanded when she arrived home. While she was still gasping for breath, her parents were reproaching her for having been out so late alone and in such a "dangerous place." Citlalli, then thirty years old, was a married professional woman with two children.

The tomb, therefore, may not necessarily be to contain death. It may also be to contain life. The ancient myth of woman as bearer of nature, children, and evil is manifested in this need to entomb. During our conversations, Don Ceferino told me that Monterrey was a highly technological city full of shamans. Most are women. Most of the clients are women. There is no distinction in social class. There are shamans/curanderas/healers all over the city. There are also temples throughout Monterrey that have no connection with the Catholic or Protestant Church. These places, many of which are named "Oromu," are where mostly women congregate to talk of a magical spirituality and to worship on the day of the equinox. This spiritual discourse, which describes the "knowledge of the woman," is firmly embedded in the life of Monterrey. There exists a clear and separate boundary between this talk and the boardroom activities of the Monterrey industrialists. The only image of woman that crosses the boundary is the Virgin Mary, who is at times the blue-eyed Mary and at other times the brown Guadalupe. The pure, unadulterated Mary presents a divine magic that can heal and change. What she offers has its safety. Her chaste nature leaves no danger of contamination.

There is an ambivalence in how Monterrey sees its women of nature.

There seems to be a fear that the woman will lose control and contaminate what the *caudillos* have so carefully put together. The woman's lack of control can affect the purity of the blood in her offspring. She can place a *maleficio* and ruin a man's life. She can dishonor her family by refusing her father's or brother's control. If she places a spell on him, he is helpless in resisting her. All it takes is the man's photograph and a helpful *bruja* (witch). The spell, called a *trabajo,* requires a photograph of the person being bewitched. The witch uses the image as a representation of the person who is to receive the "energy" from the *trabajo.* From my conversations with *regios,* I found it very easy to locate a person who would perform (for a fee) "a *trabajo.*"

The cap of the Macro Plaza is a superficial cover that leads Monterrey into another form of make-believe. It pretends to have lost the flavor of the baroque world of El Nuevo Reino de León. The sleek lines of the new architecture and the modernistic statues smooth out the bumpiness of the past. Yet, as in the afternoon that Cristóbal López and I witnessed the *vendedoras* running across the Macro Plaza to hide from the police, it is clear that there is no way to dam the flow of what came before.

Even as much of the population "appeared" white (before the mass migration from the south in the 1980s), there is a sense of devaluation in how La Patria views the north. It is at this point that the issue of class enters the polemic of impurity. Nuevo León's distance from Mexico City, the nation's "center of culture," also presents an ideological distance. The north is caustically seen as a wasteland of white people. Stoler reminds us that the tension in sexual politics is not always drawn on racial lines. Vasconcelos identified the white men of the north as "common." This places the common men of the north into a space where "European men of lower-class were repeatedly accused of giving in to their biological drives at the cost of empire" (Stoler 1995: 179). This submission to "biological drives" meant not only a lack of sexual control but also a problem in the control of violent urges. This discourse justified the designation of who had the "right to rule." Stoler continues: "It divided men of 'character' and reason from men of passion" (1995: 182). The questioning of who was the "authentic" civilized man left the *norteño* lacking. The questionable *converso*/Catholic and the "common social base" did not leave those in the north much in their defense. Because New Spain had been a possession of Spain, which despised those who were born in the colonies even if they were of "pure" Spanish blood, the history of this disdain is not completely erased. The faint vestige of the incapable, indolent *criollo* remains, especially in a population that "appears so white." This memory creates a polemic. The "white" *norteño* wants to be *criollo,* yet does not want to be indolent and lazy, which is the stereotype of the colonial Spaniard in southern Mexico. Hence the possibility of a "work-obsessed" population arises with the success of the industrial north. The most striking way for the *norteños* to make themselves different from the *criollos* of the south is to be the opposite of indolent.

The American facade of success is situated inside the structure of the modernistic Macro Plaza. In keeping with de Certeau's notion of "repressed history," the history that is held in check by Monterrey's power brokers was placed underground. The ghosts that were seeking to approach Citlalli Hernández Rosales the night she found herself caught in the upheaval of the destroyed barrio of Los Dulces Nombres, are reminiscent of Costa Lima's regeneration of the ghosts from Rulfo's novel. The ghosts of the women buried in walls and under the streets cross over into the world of the living and tell the story from the "other side." The stairways that lead down from the Macro Plaza allow a space for movement. After being sealed away by the concrete, the ghosts found a way to move upward. They take the stairs to the outside, just as the *vendedoras* take the stairs down when they need to escape from the police and from modernity.

CHAPTER X

La Joya: The House on Arreola

The House on Arreola

Bachelard proposes that houses contain the space of daydreams, childhood memories, and the universe remembered (1964). An imaginary world could be described in the house on Arreola. Yet the house, its occupants, and its contents actually existed. Aquiles Sepúlveda once told me that he had never been able to go to Europe, but Europe had come to him. What he and his sister Ofelia placed inside of the structure in which they lived was a narrative in itself. This house embodied the history of the Occident as it was contained and hidden. For numerous reasons, decades passed before its existence was disclosed. The stories of what the house contained transcended reality. I cannot say if what Aquiles told me is totally verifiable. In Bachelard's terms, all these stories in fact come from objects and events that actually existed and occurred, yet the narratives about how they came to be in the house on Arreola transpose them to the level of a dream.

Le Réel

Layers of meaning and living are sometimes repressed for other reasons than what is viewed as unacceptable or primitive. Sometimes the secret can also be a treasure. The home of Aquiles and Ofelia Sepúlveda is such a secret. The house is painted a light creme. It sits on the block between Cuauhtémoc and Pino Suarez, the two most important streets in downtown Monterrey. It has wrought iron on the front door and windows.

When a visitor arrives, she rings a doorbell to the right that calls someone to the door. The front is always locked.

The ceilings of the house are very high—at least six meters. In the
coldest time of winter, the house is warm with only minimal heating. In
the summer when it is more than 44° Celsius, the interior is fairly cool;
a fan is sufficient to keep a small breeze. When you first walk in, there is
an entryway that goes directly to the patio. Off each side of this entrance
are different rooms. To the immediate right is a large dining room and
anteroom with a piano, an old television, and old books. Behind that
room is a small kitchen and bathroom. To the left is the sitting room, full
of elegant furniture, a grand piano that is at least 200 years old, other antiques, and many family pictures. Behind the sitting room is what appears
to be a study. It is full of hundreds of old books. Just to the right, once
you enter through the door, is a small desk, which is where Irma
Sepúlveda wrote her short stories and other literary work. Behind Irma's
room are several more bedrooms; a cage full of thirty canaries; and another, larger kitchen. The patio parallels two-thirds the length of the
house. Outside there is a well, rocking chairs, tables, many plants, and a
number of full-grown trees. In addition to antiques, family photographs,
and books, the house is full of all types of artwork, ranging from the Renaissance to the early twentieth century. I had never before seen anything
like the house on Arreola Street.

The neighborhood has changed significantly since the house was
built. At one time, it was one of the most fashionable areas of Monterrey. The neighborhood is known for La Alameda, which is a block away.
La Alameda is a plaza that was once the center of many musical concerts,
gatherings of family or friends, children playing, and young couples
courting. It has been several decades since the Alameda lost its brilliance.
However, the Sepúlveda family has continued to live for sixty years in
their house on Arreola Street, even though there is now a toy store at the
corner, an alterations shop across the street, and a hair salon.

Antepasados—Ancestors

The Sepúlvedas are descended from one of the early governors of Nuevo
León. This is a story that Doña Pepita neglected to tell me during our
many conversations early in the summer of 1998. Pepita was focused on
her work at the sanctuary and was not very interested in her family's his-

Statue and painting from Sepúlveda home. Monterrey.
1999.

Photograph by the author.

tory. At least not the history before she was born. Months later, after numerous conversations with her brother Aquiles, he explained to me that
the family was probably descended from Capitán Joseph de Treviño.

Joseph, Jusep, or José de Treviño (he has been known by all three
names) is said to be descended from a *converso* family. In the first decades
of the seventeenth century, according to scattered textual information,
he came from Mexico City and arrived in El Nuevo Reino de León with
1,000 head of cattle, which indicates an extreme amount of wealth for
that era.

Aquiles told me about the Sepúlvedas' various ancestral links to the

236

early Spanish settlers of Nuevo León. His maternal grandparents were both Treviños, the grandfather being from an extremely wealthy family. They were first cousins. Aquiles listed other names to me: *Gutiérrez,* from Gutiérrez de Lara, who had established La Ex-hacienda de San Pedro in Zua Zua, and *Santos Coy,* which Aquiles was told really was the surname *Cohen.* The name *Sepúlveda* came from Martín de Zavala y Sepúlveda, an early governor of El Nuevo Reino de León. The governor is said to be the illegitimate son of another *nuevolenese* governor, a wealthy Basque miner who had established his fortune in Zacatecas. As a boy, Martin was favored by his father and sent to Europe to study. He returned an erudite man and is known as the most prodigious governor in Nuevo León's history.

Divination

La Vidente—The Seer

. . . the credibility and the impossibility that make the visions what they are, this proper material (as Vico would have it) of the poetics of the imagination, is inevitably a joint construction brought about by the coming together of shaman and patient. The former brings mute certainty, the latter uncertainty but voice. (Taussig 1987: 462)

A most salient connection between the three Sepúlvedas I came to know was their caution. I became much more aware of this caution after they had me meet Fela Hernández. After I had been visiting Doña Pepita for over a month, she suggested in a friendly way that I meet with Fela, whom they described as a *vidente* (a seer). Pepita and Ofelia had known Fela for over thirty years. They started consulting with Fela after their mother died. They had found the consultations very helpful and supportive. Fela never charged them anything. In return, Fela's daughters, Ana, Soledad, and Rosalba all attended Ofelia's school, El Instituto (the Institute) without charge. For consultations, the arrangement was that Fela would take a bus from her home on the northern side of Monterrey and meet with them in their house on Arreola Street. It would take Fela about two hours to make the trip. She came any time Ofelia would request a visit.

Doña Pepita vaguely told me that it would be good for me to speak with Fela. Perhaps Fela could tell me something. I wondered at the moment what it was that Fela could say. I did not hesitate taking the opportunity, because I was interested in learning about how esoteric practices continued to exist in late twentieth-century Nuevo León. Doña Pepita called her sister, Ofelia. Ofelia telephoned Fela's neighbor, leaving a message for Fela to come to the house on Arreola Street the following Saturday.

A few days later, at 8:30 A.M., I drove expectantly down Revolución, going north from El Cerro de la Silla, where I lived. I exited on Constitución and turned right on Cuauhtémoc, at the exact same spot where El Templo San Francisco once stood before it was demolished in 1914. I drove another ten blocks, turned left on Arreola, and parked right in front of the house. I rang the doorbell. A few seconds later, a woman who appeared to be in her seventies answered the door. It was Ofelia. Because she had never married, she preferred for me to call her Señorita Ofelia. She had short, dark brown hair and olive skin. She smiled as she spoke. Wearing a cotton housedress, she looked very comfortable. She introduced herself to me and said she was relieved that her brother Aquiles was not at home. He always wanted to know everything that she and Pepita were doing. She also told me that he often criticized his sisters for their opinions and their actions. She was glad that he had gone to Potrero for several weeks.

She escorted me into the dining room, offered me a soft drink, and asked me to sit at the long dining room table. I sat facing the window that opened to Arreola. There was a slight breeze. Even though it was July, it was still fairly comfortable, because it was nine in the morning. That particular chair, which situated me to the right of the window, came to be the place I would always sit whenever I visited Ofelia and Aquiles.

On the wall facing me as we spoke were two pencil drawings that have the look of the 1920s. One was an image of a flapper with short hair. The other was a landscape. Hanging in the middle of the two was a large Renaissance painting. Not wanting to appear invasive, I did not ask about the drawings. I looked around me. Sitting on various pieces of furniture were small statues that looked to be hundreds of years old.

The doorbell rang, and she attended a visitor. In the meantime I stood in the hallway looking at a life-size painting of an indigenous man, a red-striped *sarape* draped over his shoulder as he stands next to a large archway. It was a painting, circa 1920, by Carlos Sáenz. The man in the painting rang the bell for the Cathedral in Monterrey. Perhaps because of its size, the painting made the man appear actually present in the room. I became aware that I wished I could take the portrait home. Trying to suppress this impulse, I realized that Ofelia and her brother would be in danger if the public in Monterrey knew of their art collection.

I returned to the dining room and looked out the window. I saw a short, dark, indigenous woman crossing the street towards the door. It was Fela. I did not expect that she would appear so indigenous. There was a striking difference between Fela and Ofelia, which surprised me, because I had imagined that someone who had become so close to Ofelia and Doña Pepita for three decades would have been from their world. From appearances, the relationship was extremely asymmetrical. There were differences of color, social class, and "heritage."

As Fela entered the room, Ofelia embraced her and quickly left. Fela sat at the head of the same dining table. A glass of water, which Ofelia had brought, sat on the table. The water was Fela's instrument for divination. Fela said the credo, made the sign of the cross over the glass, and looked inside the water with intense concentration. She told me I would be successful in my work and would have many little books of writing. She said a virgin had led me to Doña Pepita and that I was to do some good with the knowledge I obtained from my travels. She then said I was of the same family as the Sepúlvedas. After a few minutes, I gave her 150 pesos (about nineteen U.S. dollars at that time), which she resisted accepting. I quickly left as Ofelia made arrangements for Fela's lunch.

When I visited with Pepita in Santiago the next day, she could not wait to ask me what Fela had said. Although I felt reluctant to take Fela's declaration very seriously, I told Pepita that I was supposed to be from the same family. Doña Pepita, however, said that Fela was almost always right and thus it was very possible that somehow we were related.

What occurred to me after a period of time was that the invitation to speak with Fela was not totally altruistic. Without even realizing it, I was entering deeply into the lives of Doña Pepita and Señorita Ofelia. Fela was able to give them a reference: Could I be trusted? Was I honest? What were my motives? This suspicion was never discussed directly with either woman. However, I became more aware of this issue in a recent telephone conversation with Ofelia (February 2000) in which she told me that "you don't often meet people that won't talk." She meant that most people do not hold confidences. She also, I believe, referred to the issue of "propriety." According to the rules of her family, a person does not gossip or tell others what they have seen when they visit another person's house. She was right about my own "propriety;" I rarely spoke to anyone of what I saw in the house on Arreola. Yet, paradoxically, as I write this ethnography, I am not only "talking" but also am describing with intimate detail Ofelia's house.

El Tesoro—The Treasure

I had a glimpse of the house on Arreola Street the day I visited with Fela. Just past the front door in the foyer was a Renaissance oil painting of St. Joachim. To the right of the door was an object placed in a frame. Upon closer inspection, I saw that it was a dagger. It was almost destroyed by rust but still maintained some of its original shape. Months later, Aquiles told me that the dagger was from the tomb of Governor Martín de Zavala y Sepúlveda. Upon the governor's burial, the dagger was placed on top of his coffin. Aquiles never told me how he came to be in possession of this dagger. Further down on the same side of the hall was the portrait of the man with the *sarape*.

Aquiles once told me that he believed Ofelia was too naive. He thought she was not cautious enough with her friends and acquaintances. At the time, he was somewhat correct in his observation. Although he was not aware of it, Ofelia had lent several of Irma's original (and unpublished) manuscripts to a friend in 1998; they had yet to be returned. Since Aquiles's death, however, she has been extremely cautious regarding her ownership of the antiquities and documents.

I was taken aback by Ofelia's openness on my second visit. She showed me the entire house. I had caught a glimpse earlier of the sitting room with its square piano. Yet even this room, with the Victorian furniture and the old photographs, was no preparation for all the other things I saw.

A few days later, I returned to visit Ofelia. She allowed me to enter the other rooms. It was like entering a tomb that had not been touched in centuries. While this description of the experience is perhaps morbid, visiting the rooms reminded me of what I had read about exploring ancient tombs. It was the moment of discovery. Walking into room after room had a surreal quality. I saw so many objects that my mind could barely integrate every vision. There was a smell of enclosure—not necessarily unpleasant, just closed off, away from the world. Ofelia did not turn on the lights as we moved to each room. I could see by the sunlight entering through the windows that some rooms were darker than others. I could sense the layer of time over every object. The dust was not from lack of cleaning but from objects being situated in the same place for years and years.

The small desk where Irma wrote was dark and had a glass over the top. Small photographs of the family's children were under the glass. I also saw my business card next to the pictures. Behind the desk was a glass cabinet full of old books. There were layers and layers of books, row behind row. In later months, there were moments that I sat at the desk and became mesmerized by all the titles jumbled together. I tried to imagine Irma writing while enclosed in the dark room. On another occasion, Ofelia and I went through two other bookshelves on the other side of the room. We pulled out text after text in English, Spanish, and French. Some of them were useless, some important. Ofelia treasured all of the books. The day we organized the bookshelves we ended up with several piles of books more than a meter high that Ofelia thought I might want to read. She also found a box with some of Irma's personal correspondence. There were many newspaper clippings and small photographs in the box. I read the articles and looked at the pictures; however, I felt it was inappropriate to ask to read the letters, although Irma had been dead more than ten years.

Ofelia's room was next to the room with the desk. Placed beside a small bed near the window were a few portraits painted by Carlos Sáenz, the same artist who painted the indigenous man at the Cathedral. A glass cabinet was filled with dolls and small figurines. There were crucifixes and other religious objects. Next to the cabinet was a large photograph of Ofelia when she was a striking young woman. Above a wardrobe to the left of the bed was a very large painting of the Virgin of Guadalupe that was at least one and one-half by two and one-half meters meters in size. This painting was one of at least three Guadalupes that were in the house.

The rooms continued in the same manner. One painting, produced by a George Parsons in the early nineteenth century in Albany, New York, was a portrait of a young girl from Monterrey. In addition, there were other works by Sáenz, including a macabre-looking self-portrait that depicted the artist in the final stages of what Aquiles described as

Self-portrait of artist Carlos Sáenz, completed
in 1920 shortly before his death. Note the en-
largement of his forehead due to illness.
From the Sepúlveda family collection.

elephantiasis (the disease, however, may have been onchocerciasis, which
causes swelling in the head region).[1]

There were many other paintings. While some were on the walls,
many were lined up four or five in a row on the floor. There was antique
furniture, an upright piano, and antique lamps. There were the two
Renaissance-era paintings: one, as I have mentioned, of St. Joachim and
another of the Virgin Mary that Aquiles once told me came from a
Cathedral. Amid the paintings were more and more books, probably in
the thousands. Besides books that Ofelia and Aquiles collected, Aquiles
had published Irma's work and was continuing to sell the books on an

individual basis. He had also published and sold work by an obscure poet from Sabinas Hidalgo, a city 100 kilometers north of Monterrey. The author's name was Felipe Guerra Castro. Some months later Aquiles himself would read to me one of the poems from the book. The title of the poem was "Delirio."

Cannibalism

> . . . in the jeweled setting of the tale, native speech takes on the figure of a missing precious stone. It is the moment of ravishment, a stolen instant, a purloined memory beyond the text: "Such a joy it was [writes Léry . . .] hearing the beautifully measured rhythms of such a multitude . . . that I remained completely ravished . . . every time the memory comes back to me, my heart throbs, and it seems as if their music still rings in my ears." (de Certeau cites Jean de Léry 1988: 213)[2]

After my visit with Ofelia, I quickly returned home and could do nothing else but think about Ofelia's house. For the next several days I struggled to conceptualize what I had seen. It was as if I had entered another dimension that is rarely experienced in everyday life. I was afraid to tell anyone what was inside the house. I kept thinking of the value of the antiquities and art, the advanced age of Ofelia and Aquiles, and the possibility that someone could take everything. After all, some time before, Alvarado had told me that the house next door to his office, which is in the same neighborhood as the house on Arreola, had been abandoned for years after the residents, two elderly women, were robbed and murdered.

I was even afraid to tell Yolanda, which now seems odd, since she actually entered the house before I did. However, she had not seen the interior rooms. For days and days I kept going over in my mind each thing I had seen, how it could be there, what it meant to be there, and where it had come from. Most importantly, I wondered how Ofelia and Aquiles had all of these possessions related to Mexican, *nuevolenese,* and western history while the objects remained unacknowledged and sequestered in an unexplained, hermetic world.

De Certeau writes that Montaigne in the essay "Of Cannibals" ponders the "status of the strange." Who is "barbarian"? What is a "savage"? What is the place of the Other? (1988: 67). Ethnography's traditional focus on the primitive seems exceedingly simplistic at this point. What if a fantastic world is on the other side of the ethnographer's shadow? What if this fantastic is a collection of material objects that are actually representations of the "Age of Reason," the "crisis of conscience," and the "Enlightenment"?

At the moment when I entered the house on Arreola street, I was not only entranced by the aura of the space but also was overwhelmed with the excess. There was so much of everything. It was like a dream or the trance that de Certeau describes as *ravishment,* which is that moment when "the one possessed is unable to break through the aura of a trance 'evading legalities, disciplines of meaning'" (xvii). I could not transpose what lay in front of me into any coherent thought. I was utterly overtaken with so many incredibly interesting objects. Even more, the "hidden" quality of the place intensified my reaction. The experience was so unannounced and subtle; owned by a woman in a cotton housedress, the objects were kept in a house that was next to a toy store and a hair salon in a region known for its barbarians. The veritable existence of this space could not be explained.

Recalling the first time I entered the house, I imagined the painting by Sáenz of the indigenous man who worked at the Cathedral. When I first saw the painting, I was ashamed that for a moment I wanted that painting for myself. Many months later, Ofelia tells me in a telephone conversation that *El Indio* has been shipped to Mexico City for an important exhibition. The art world has discovered the long dead Carlos Sáenz. Yet the desire for the painting is only a substitute for the desire to write, to annotate, to transcribe what I have seen, to be the one who discovers. Conley, de Certeau's translator, writes: "Historiography traces an unending drama of encounters with the *réel.*" Entering the space of the house on Arreola street was much the same. There is no way to accurately describe that particular moment. It was an encounter with a repository for all that was civilized and erudite and what was seen as cultured and intellectual. For at least four decades, Ofelia, Aquiles, and Irma slowly brought these objects into their home. This collecting was done in a quiet manner through small purchases, chance encounters, and good fortune.

The conflictive aspect of the interaction between the Sepúlvedas and

Untitled work of *El Indio,* as Ofelia Sepúlveda calls the painting.
Supposedly of the man who rang
the bell of Monterrey's Cathedral,
painted in 1910 by Carlos Sáenz.
From the Sepúlveda family collection.

myself is highlighted in the issue of desire. Desire to own, yet more so,
desire to devour. De Certeau tells us that writing is cannibalistic. To observe, interiorize, and produce a text from a particular moment or vision
is to devour. The writing absorbs what is different about the event, di-
gesting the words to make them malleable for the reader. The narrative
is then fed away to the curious or those involved in the power of the production of the text. The result is tempered and transposed into a written
list of objects of an overwhelmed ethnographer. The question remains:
who is the barbarian?

The Repository

. . . writing constructs a *tombeau* for the dead (de Certeau 1988: 100).

The literal meaning for the French word *tombeau* is tomb. De Certeau, however, locates the word in its seventeenth-century meaning of a com- memorative genre of music, literature, or narrative. The blending of tomb, the place for the dead, with the artistic creation resonates with what is inside the house on Arreola street. The idea of a tomb is salient. The objects are hidden away, secretly placed in bookshelves, closets, dark rooms, and desk drawers.

Aquiles and Ofelia have never told me exactly when they started collecting art. As a young man, Aquiles studied painting with a well-respected teacher in Monterrey. In the 1960s he traveled to Mexico City with his sister, Irma, while she studied with Juan Rulfo. During that time Aquiles made portraits of the musicians from the Mexican National Symphony.

Periodically, people would arrive at the house asking Aquiles if he was interested in buying something. He often had a small amount of cash and would make an offer. He would also visit local antique shops regularly. He once showed me a small oil painting of a man that appeared to be from the Renaissance era. The painting was dark with variations of brown, gray, and red. Aquiles paid less than thirty dollars for the painting at a local antique shop. He believed it was a Titian. Unfortunately, he had no way of proving who painted the portrait.

Again, he told me that he was never able to go to Europe, but Europe came to him. As a younger man he was awarded a scholarship to study for two years in Italy. He said he did not go because he thought it would not be wise to be away from his mother for two years. He said that she was elderly and that later he might regret not having that time with her. In his sixties he said that he was glad he made that decision.

The story behind the Carlos Sáenz paintings was unlike the others. Ofelia befriended an elderly woman and cared for her closely while the woman was dying. In return, the woman willed all of her artwork and documents to Ofelia. While I only knew of a few items that came with the Sáenz works, even those few were marvelous. The portrait by Parsons came with the collection. A personal letter written by the girl in Parson's portrait was also included. The letter was dated 1815. There was also a letter written and signed by Guadalupe Victoria, the first Mexican president after Mexico's separation from Spain. Finally, there were numerous paintings and drawings by Sáenz. They had been acquired after Sáenz died in New York. His family did not want them and someone from the deceased woman's family made an overture to buy them.

As a boy, Aquiles said, he used to walk by a particular house day after day. Occasionally he could see inside. It was at these moments that he saw the paintings of Sáenz inside the house. When Ofelia finally acquired the paintings, it seemed so odd to Aquiles that in his house were the very paintings he had coveted thirty years earlier.

There were also a group of watercolors that Aquiles had acquired some eight years before I met him. A priest in Saltillo owned them at the time. They had been sent to England for sale but, for whatever reason, were returned to Mexico. Aquiles bought them all from the priest for less than 100 dollars. Aquiles believed that four of the paintings were by J.W. Turner and two were by John Constable. The paintings had arrived in the latter part of the nineteenth century. They accompanied the Purcell family from Great Britain. Purcell was affiliated with the northern railroad. He had an English mansion built next to the Alameda in Saltillo, a city which at the time was known to many people as the "Athens of the north," for it had a thriving cultural scene compared to Monterrey. Saltillo is a city with a high elevation and a very pleasant climate. Purcell had two daughters who also came to Saltillo. They never married and continued to live in the mansion next to the Alameda. They died in the early 1990s and, according to Aquiles, left no heirs. The state government of Coahuila confiscated the property and sold most of the artwork. Aquiles said these particular paintings were left behind because they were not framed "properly" and were thought to be worthless. One of the watercolors is still hanging above his bed in the back room of the house.

The Circulation of Culture

Gente Culta—Cultured People

. . . we can appreciate the pomp and circumstance of secret societies as merely carefully crafted caricatures of the skill essential to being a person, a social person, no less than a storyteller or poet knowing what not to know. (Taussig 1999: 195)

While mainstream descriptions of Monterrey usually focus on the industrial elite, like the Garza Sadas, there are many other facets of life in this city. There is the large contingency of the poor, who have substandard services and a minimal chance of escaping poverty. Tossed around with the unpredictable movement of the Mexican peso, a significant middle class live their lives as if they were always traveling on a roller coaster.

The Sepúlvedas are located on an indefinable periphery. They have consorted with the Garza Sadas. Several of the Garza Sada women attended Ofelia's Instituto. Yet the Sepúlvedas have never lived near the Obispado or San Pedro, which have been the homes of the rich for the past hundred years. The Sepúlvedas have not been allied with any industrial family. Their children did not study in a foreign country. Their ambition has not been to prosper in an outward material sense.

During one of my first visits with Ofelia and Aquiles, they sat next to me at the dining room table and were very direct: "Do not tell people what you know." "Do not tell people of your accomplishments." "Be subtle, keep things to yourself." "People are envious." "They will steal your ideas." This is when Aquiles first told me that Irma had been poisoned for reasons of envy.

In this way, they lived with all the treasure in their house. Yet they did not own a car. Their clothes were several decades old. Ofelia would wear the same housedress every time I visited with her. They lived very simply.

There was a feeling of loss about their wealth. Both Pepita and Ofelia repeatedly told me about the 620 hectares of land their father owned in Potrero and how it was taken away by Lazaro Cárdenas. Ofelia had been working with a lawyer for several years in an attempt to sue the government for compensation. She did not want Aquiles to know about her efforts because he would tell her it was hopeless and would scold her.

Pepita told me many times that she had to go to work after her father died; his death made it very difficult for her to marry. The older siblings encountered additional responsibility because Aquiles and Irma were small children when their father died. Yet, due to their concerted efforts, they always managed to survive comfortably. There was always "enough" for Aquiles and Irma to "create."

The sense of being "civilized" was felt in every interaction. Perhaps the "common description" of this feeling would be that of "old money." Jewelry and modern conveniences such as electronic appliances or a car were not important. The classical, the civilized, the cultured—the Titian, the Turner, the Carlos Sáenz, the square piano—were important. Their austere personal presence seemed to be related to a lack of obvious narcissism. There was no need to receive credit for any accomplishment. Internal satisfaction was sufficient. In tandem with this lack of narcissism was the sense of danger. The need to be noticed could bring death.

El Unico—The Only One

En el principio creó Don Eugenio la cerveza, y vio que la cerveza era buena, pero que algo le faltaba, y creó la fábrica de donde salieron las botellas para envasarla, y vio que era buena, pero que algo le faltaba, y creó entonces la fábrica de corcholatas para tapar las botellas, y vio que era buena, etcétera. (Nuncio 1982: 19) (In the beginning, Don Eugenio [Garza Sada] created beer, and saw that the beer was good, but there was something missing, and he created a glass factory that made the bottles for the beer, and saw that this was good, but something was also missing, and so he then created a metal factory that produced bottle caps, and saw that this was good, etc.)

In the year 2000, the economic focus of Latin America is Monterrey's economic success. The narratives surrounding this fabulous wealth locate the Garza Sadas solidly in the Forbes list of the world's wealthiest people.[3] They are considered the wealthiest family and the most powerful in all of Mexico. Abraham Nuncio notes that as recently as 1982 there had been no comprehensive biography of the Garza Sada dynasty. Their names had not even been listed in the *Encyclopedia of Mexico* (1982), which is considered quite unusual. Alex Saragoza, a historian at the University of California at Berkeley, published a book on the family in 1988 that covers their accomplishments and social activities. Perhaps after reflecting upon the experiences of other writers, Saragoza chose to be prudent in his analysis of El Grupo Monterrey.[4] There is no mention of the secrecy, ambiguity, and violence surrounding the Garza Sadas.

There is a common belief in northern Mexico, and perhaps in most of Latin America, that many people not only want to be the best or to have the most but to be "only." They want to eliminate the competition. This elimination has been accomplished in various ways in Monterrey.

The distancing of indigenous history has separated the northern elite from the "uncivilized, brown" masses of Mexico. The pairing with Jewish history has served as a safe vehicle for alignment with the erudite, white European. The ambivalent rejection of Jewish history has assisted in creating a separation from the endangered Other. In addition, the occulted nature of the house on Arreola street brings into play another dimension of historical elimination. To use a vulgar analogy, one could say there can only be one God, one king, one Queen, or one Emperor. The idea of a "kingdom" is similar to the world of the Garza Sadas. In a sovereign state, the subjects are required to be loyal to the monarch. As Foucault describes in *Discipline and Punish* (1977), the sovereign is the owner of his subjects. Breaking the law against the state is also an offense against the monarch. As Aquiles described to me in the story of Eduardo Rubio, the art dealer who was arrested amid spectacular media coverage, Rubio as "the sovereign subject" had fallen out of favor with the monarchy. His public punishment took the form of his entrapment and arrest.

In November 1999, Rubio's case was a "scandal" in Monterrey that was reported in newspapers around the world. An art collector, Eduardo Rubio Elosúa was arrested by federal agents in his home near the Obispado. He was accused of illegal trafficking in archaeological treasures. The house was stormed by nineteen agents dressed in black. The agents represented several federal and state law enforcement agencies. Rubio was forced to submit to incarceration (Alejo, Villasaez, and Ramírez 1999). Several months later he was exonerated. Rubio was the son of Aquiles's art teacher. Aquiles told me that the elder Rubio had been closely affiliated with the Garza Sadas. The elder Rubio was a courtier in the way de Certeau describes (1988).[5] The Museo de Monterrey, which was established on the grounds of Cervercería Cuauhtémoc, was initiated from the collaboration between the elder Rubio and the Garza Sadas. For reasons that Aquiles did not elaborate upon, he told me that the Rubios had fallen "out of favor." The arrest was an indication of disfavor.

The disfavor could emanate from any space, including the house on Arreola street. Aquiles had in his possession not only art that had traveled from Europe, but also probably one of the best collections of art from the northern region of Mexico. He told me that he had approached the large museums in Monterrey several decades earlier about exhibiting some of the work he had collected. They were simply not interested.

The disinterest Aquiles encountered is noted in an essay written by Abraham Nuncio in February 1999 in the newspaper *La Jornada.* Nuncio claims, ". . . *los pintores locales prácticamente no tienen acceso o éste es muy limitado. Es rara la inclusión de los artistas plásticos del estado en las exposiciones de MARCO del Museo Monterrey.* (. . . local painters practically have no access or very limited access [to public exhibition space in Monterrey]. It is rare for plastic artists of this state to be included in exhibitions at the MARCO or the Monterrey Museum)

The treasure of art and antiquities that Aquiles and Ofelia had in their home was based on a long-term cultivated knowledge, a careful study of who was selling the work, and a careful administration of the funds that allowed the purchases. The Sepúlveda collection is totally different from the flamboyant, new-money, Medici-like artistic interests of Monterrey's industrialists.

The need to repress what lay inside the house may have had numerous provocations. The public discovery of such a collection in the barbarous town of Monterrey would have certainly de-centered the idea of there being no culture in the north. It also would have taken the limelight off the Garza Sadas in their role as the Medici, as one *Los Angeles Times* reporter termed the family when he wrote on the opening of the fabulous MARCO (Museo de Arte Contemporáneo) in downtown Monterrey.[6]

While American perspectives may place nominal value on the need to be the "only" civilized and erudite group in a certain region, in numerous conversations I had with *regiomontanos* I found that the issue of *envidia* (envy) was salient and potentially dangerous. On many occasions I heard stories of problems within families or places of employment that emanated from issues of competition or *envidia*. Stories of black magic erupted in almost any environment, regardless of education or social class of those involved.

Erudition

Costa Lima writes of the predicament facing Latin American writers. He tells us that the writer is forced to make use of newspapers to display her work (1992). The institution of publishing in Mexico does not allow for the luxury of "reprints" or "second editions." The system of libraries is the same. Books cannot be taken off the premises at either the university or the high school level.[7] The circulation of knowledge and so-called "civilized" culture is limited to occasional moments and spaces. For this reason, there are often references to Hegel, Marx, Lacan, and other names from the occidental canon in editorial pieces in Latin American newspapers. The civilized have to be creative in finding where they can express their erudition. Yet, outside this domain, it is difficult to find a place to hear about "western civilization."

For the middle class, the public school libraries are nearly empty. There is little to read, and teachers establish few requirements to search out erudite authors. It is as if there is a counter-movement against intellectualism and artistic knowledge, which are only thrown about loosely in newspaper editorials and splashy exhibits at the city's museums. As described in a review on the MARCO, artwork on exhibit is placed in cramped and uneven spaces; the architect and the curator give little thought to the need for appropriateness of space.[8] In a superficial manner that betrays a lack of aesthetic knowledge, the western aesthetic is haphazardly displayed.

Yet instead of criticizing the lack of sophistication in Nuevo León, one must consider that this haphazard production of western culture could actually be a way of hiding erudition. It is safer for others to think that one does not know. Holding the secret of knowledge and art can be dangerous if the person owning such knowledge is exposed.

Aquiles used to tell me there was a paucity of understanding among the intelligentsia in the north. Always assuming there was nothing in Nuevo León worth looking at, they looked outside their region for knowledge. He said it was obvious in their indifference to the work of Carlos Sáenz and their hostility to the work of Irma, his sister. Feeling what he saw as their ignorance, he seemed to enjoy his own secret trove of paintings, documents, music, and musical instruments. If Aquiles could not speak what he knew, however, one assumes that no one else could either. While perhaps due to Aquiles's feeling of superiority, the reality is that he never knew what was outside his house. Everybody was keeping secrets.

The possibility of disfavor was almost everywhere. Aquiles said he once attended a meeting of the Communist Party, most probably in the late 1950s or early 1960s. He said he was identified and was subsequently blacklisted from artists' groups in Monterrey. Another story he told me was of a gifted Jewish pianist who "married the wrong woman." After the marriage, the pianist could no longer find work. All of his previous contacts had no interest in the pianist. Several years later, the couple divorced and, immediately, the pianist was contracted to perform. Aquiles said that the people in power, whom he assumed were the powerful Jewish groups, disapproved of the marriage and shunned the young pianist. I believe that his purpose in telling me this story was to teach me about the decisions people make regarding alliances and friendships. He saw risk involved in every interaction. The provocation of a certain displeasure in a person in power or the release of certain information could have drastic consequences.

In 1999, Aquiles experienced the greatest satisfaction; a retrospective of his work was exhibited at an important gallery near El Obispado. For several weeks, he was interviewed by newspaper reporters and museum representatives. He took the opportunity to discuss the status of the plastic artist from Nuevo León and explained that being from the same region made it impossible to be taken seriously by the local museums. He told me that several young men from El Museo Monterrey (the cervecería's museum) visited him on several occasions. He showed them the work of Sáenz and other regional painters. They were surprised. They had never heard of Sáenz. In the year 2000, as I mentioned previously, Sáenz's *El Indio* is in Mexico City along with his other work. The secret of Aquiles's treasure has been exposed. It is an interesting coincidence that Aquiles died only months after he told those young men what he had inside his house.

El Sueño—The Dream

Writing About Ghosts

A dream I had of Irma Sepúlveda came to mind months after I completed the first draft of this manuscript. I had the dream in the summer of 1998. There were aspects of the narrative that did not seem to have any association to my relationship with the Sepúlvedas. Now that I have re-read and re-worked this ethnography, the different images are beginning to achieve a type of coherence.

Two years after I have the dream, I am back in Houston; I am reading about secrets in Michael Taussig's book *Defacement* (1999). He tells about secrets that are familiar. The secrets are known but not told. More specifically, they are told but not publicly told, not "proclaimed" to be told. They are hidden or masked for reasons of policy or economics. As I am reading the chapter "Secrecy Magnifies Reality," I remember a mask in the dream I had of Irma Sepúlveda. I go through my notes and find an excerpt from an earlier essay I have written on Nuevo León that explains the day and the story behind the dream:

July 1998. I am staying at the home of the Gonzálezes, who live on El Cerro de la Silla. I have been traveling to Nuevo León for more than one year. I sit in a small bed near a large window overlooking Monterrey. At night there are many lights that give the view a surreal effect. I write how Alejandro Sepúlveda (Ofelia's nephew) has just told me of his aunt, Irma Sabina Sepúlveda. She wrote stories. He tells me that she was influenced by a Russian writer named Chekhov. Alejandro reads me a story and then lends me two of Irma's books. I tell him that I wish so much that I could meet her. He tells me I can't, since she died ten years ago. That evening I read stories of everyday life in San Isidro del Potrero, the town where the Sepúlvedas were born. Later that night I have a dream of a heavy-set woman who wears a white blouse and black skirt. She is standing to the right of my bed. She is fair-skinned with dark, straight hair that is not very long. Her eyes and face are covered by a lace fabric. She does not say anything to me. Days later, when I'm writing my notes on my encounters with Irma's sisters and brother, I think of the words, "The dead watch me as I write."

August 2000. As I re-read these words, I realize that in the dream Irma Sepúlveda could not watch me because she had her eyes covered by a lace fabric. I become aware of the association to Santa Lucía and her lost eyes. Yet, in the dream, Sepúlveda is present; she is watching without seeing. I am convinced there is something about seeing and not seeing that is of striking importance to Nuevo León and its people.

CHAPTER XI

Conclusion: *Delirio* and the Finality of Pragmatic Connections—a Paradox

El reflejo inquieto, descompuesto, del ángel de la melancolía, que es hijo de la locura que hizo préstamos a la razón para edificar este mundo [de Monterrey] lineal, abstracto, vacío. (Raúl Rangel Frias)[1] (The impatient reflection, undone, of the angel of melancholy, who is the son of the madness that mortgaged reason in order to build this linear world [of Monterrey], which is both abstract and empty.)

On Poetics

Meaning, I believe, is the foundation of ethnography. As we search the stories, practices, and histories of the people we "study," we explore the meaning of what we see and hear. The poetics of ethnographic writing blend with the poetics of the culture being represented. In the routine normalization of ethnographic description we expect uniformity in practices and "reporting." As I approach the end of this ethnography, I struggle to find a sense of coherence that will appeal to the reader of traditional ethnographic texts. The words of Chekhov assist me here. After all, there is a link between this writing and his own. As mentioned in a previous chapter, when Alejandro Sepúlveda first told me of his aunt, writer Irma Sepúlveda, he spoke of Chekhov's influence on her writing. In reading Chekhov's "The Steppe" (1970), I find numerous correlations to *Delirio* as a project. It is about a young boy, Ergorooshka, on his way to study in a gymnasium. He travels across the steppe of Russia. On the road and in village after village he listens to people tell stories. The stories are interwoven but seemingly distinct. Yet the final fabric produces a coherent whole. Michael Finke, in *Metapoesis* (1995), explores the poetics of Chekhov's first major work. In Finke's explication, I find a close analogy to the story of *Delirio* and Nuevo León. "The Steppe" is about a young boy's journey across the landscape of the Russian steppe. The story is about "life's critical junctures" yet is a juncture in itself (135). As I read Finke's citation of one of Chekhov's letters, I am reminded of *Delirio* as a text: "Each chapter is a separate story, but all the chapters are as interconnected and closely related as the five figures of a quadrille. All the pages come out compact, as if they had been condensed, and impressions keep crowding each other, piling up, and pushing one another out of the way."[2] Finke proposes that for the time it was authored, "The Steppe" had a number of characteristics that placed it "out of the norm." The story engaged in a "deliberate upsetting of the expected hierarchy of components" (136).

According to Finke, there are four "problems" in Chekhov's story. I believe they resonate with *Delirio*.

Non-Traditional Tropes: "The Steppe" contains a "variety in modes of writing, de-emphasis of plot, and a strange multiplicity of narrative voice" (ibid.). A similar situation occurs in *Delirio,* which transgresses the boundaries between literature and ethnography. The stories sound literary and fictive. The analysis at times seems more like literary criticism than ethnographic analysis. Moreover, the plot in *Delirio* is lost at times due to the many influences that are mentioned yet are connected to the story and its ultimate resolution (or lack of resolution). The "multiplicity of narrative voice" brings together the voices of the Sepúlveda siblings, the Gonzálezes, the people of Potrero, and Televisa's Alvarado. Throughout this text many people are speaking simultaneously. Multivoiced ethnography is spoken at different registers, more intense or less intense, depending on the situation of their elocution.

The Phantasmic: Finke continues by proposing that in "The Steppe" there is a "haunting, dreamlike repetition of certain motifs throughout the story" (ibid.). *Delirio* is about a haunting. In the repeated description of events in the history of Nuevo León, there are often moments that appear as if they were dreams. The stories, even if they are textual, have the flavor of fabulas.

"All Time at Once": According to Finke, in "The Steppe" there are many passages that find no place on even a warped time-line. The "time structure" of the story is complicated. "Fictions and tales of events long past affect the very movement" of the story (ibid.). "What happened once before occurs again now," giving a sense that everything is hap-

pening at one time (139). As explained in the introduction to *Delirio,* time is represented as a spiral, making an ever larger movement that is curved but not quite the perfect circle. It continues to evolve and move further out of its initial limits. Chekhov's ability to demonstrate that all time may happen at once resonates with my representation of Monterrey's history, which has been occulted inside its modern Macro Plaza, letting different eras cohabitate for the sake of maintaining secrecy.

If the reader/critic is seeking the normalizing gesture, the problems mentioned may create delirium in this text, as they do to a certain extent in Chekhov's story. "The Steppe" and *Delirio* are about junctures yet are junctures in themselves. They are junctures into other forms of writing and representation. In *Delirio,* the manner in which different events and people are associated is based on connections that do not necessarily emanate from traditional ethnographic writing. "The Steppe," according to Finke, does the same in the realm of literature. Lastly, "The Steppe" ends as Ergorooshka arrives at his destination. The end of the story brings on a dramatic thunderstorm. Ergorooshka becomes ill and is delirious for a time. Even so, he recuperates quickly and is soon taken to his new home to be with a childhood friend of his mother's. Here he will live and study. Here as in *Delirio,* the child realizes that there is no definitive conclusion. His old life is gone. There is no reductive ending in Chekhov's story or in *Delirio.* As "The Steppe" concludes, Ergorooshka realizes that he has no clue to what lies ahead of him.

Timing and Naming

> The full significance (not to mention validity) of each individual interpretation can emerge only in retrospect, after a complete set of such images accumulates and the scope of the story's metapoetic dimension reveals itself. (Finke 1995: 141)

The actual use of the term *delirio* does not make a significant entrance into this book until the "story" of Nuevo León has already been told. Again, as Finke argues, the "full significance" of the interpretations regarding "The Steppe" can form with some degree of coherence after the set of images are revealed and the "meta"-poetics of the story is uncovered. Finke's use of the term "metapoesis" relates to the overall meaning and composition of the text. I believe that *Delirio,* since its composition and complex meaning are produced with unconventional tropes, requires a full display of its images before the text can even be named. The sense of delirium within the space of Nuevo León is then manifested in the "multivoiced, multi-registered" narratives. These narratives parallel the work of Chekhov, who wrote about the juncture in a young boy's life as he literally moves across time and space. The parallels to Chekhov's story are the junctures or transformations of tropes, time, voice, and emplotment in Nuevo León. These types of changes, especially with their varying levels of volume and intensity, may believably create delirium.

The delirium becomes an aspect of the stories when they come together but only after the narratives have been laboriously described and told over and over again. At this juncture, the metapoetic distinction of delirium can be placed over the stories.

The specific choice of *Delirio* for the title of this book emanates from two sources. *Nuevolenese* historian Rolando Guerra argues that "*actualmente no existe solo una identidad norestense; sino que existe una multiplicidad de identidades norestenses*" (1997: 92) (actually there is no one northeast identity; instead there exists a multiplicity of identities). Taking it further than Guerra, I propose that there is not only a multiplicity of identities but also a constantly changing itinerary that provides simultaneous and contradictory expectations for those living in Nuevo León. Inside this complexity is the question of the occult, not necessarily in the sense of magic but in the sense of a secrecy that is rooted in the community or region. At moments this secret is formed like a lie the *norteña* has to wear as she proceeds through her everyday life. Here is the rule of the lie. Not a new phenomenon to Nuevo León, the lie has existed in many different forms since the beginning of El Nuevo Reino. Currently, it is embedded in the striking dichotomy between the fabulous wealth of Monterrey and everyone else in the city who is not on the list of the Forbes 500 wealthiest people in the world. Ultimately, it has located itself under the Macro Plaza and inside the walls of the old buildings that cannot speak.

Rolando Guerra describes identities that have been denied, eliminated, pushed to the foreground, and left holding onto the present as the future tries desperately to push them away. Providing a poignant backdrop to the men who have reached the distinction of being the richest in the world, these identities include the Jew who was executed and then banished, yet still exists; the indigenous person who was enslaved, poisoned, and barred from *nuevolenese* society, yet still exists; and the poor who are often dehumanized in their role as "servants." The idea of existing, yet not existing, eliminates the basis of reality. Such identities create *delirio* as the *nuevolenese* attempts to bring them together to form a desired identity that is only coherent in occasional fleeting moments. The Indian who does not exist comes alive when someone resembling Cristóbal López walks down a street of downtown Monterrey.[3] The Jew who was executed and banished reappears when someone's grandmother, who is living in northern Mexico, shows a family member a *yamaka* that has been in the family for generations.[4] The fabulously wealthy are not exempt. They are also placed within a paradox. The rich of Monterrey reach the pinnacle of success in being designated the "richest" by an American financial journal, yet they are still not of the First World. Their new Chevrolet Suburbans and their journalists who cite Nietzsche cannot compensate for their geographical location. They are still in Mexico.

Amor—Pasión—Muerte

Love—Passion—Death

The second reason for the choice of *Delirio* as a title is my acquaintance with the poem of the same name. Aquiles Sepúlveda read the poem to me in 1999. Several weeks later a historian at the library of the Universidad Autónoma de Nuevo León spontaneously recited "Delirio" after I told him it was the title of my project.[5]

In this text, the poem itself and the multiple identities join together. This myriad of *nuevolenese* identities in Nuevo León, which intersect, contradict, collaborate, confront, and hide each other, are left standing in the middle of this war of discourse that at times appears invisible. As Abraham Nuncio writes, "*En Monterrey opera, sutil pero férreo, el principio de que lo que no se dice no existe. Sobre todo respecto de ciertos hechos redeados de violencia*" (1982: 26–27) (In Monterrey, there operates, in a subtle but forceful manner, the principal that what is not said does not exist. Above all, it happens with respect to facts surrounding violence). *Delirio* "is" the language of the discourse.

An Exegesis of Delirium

If a formal definition is required of *delirio,* it may be located in the *Diccionario taxonómico de psiquiatría,* which was published by Mexico's federal publishing house in 1993. Twenty-one pages of description provide varying definitions of *delirio*. One mentioned is a definition from *Diccionario Robert*: "*Agitación, exaltación causada por las emociones, las pasiones, las tentaciones violentas*" (agitation, exaltation, caused by emotions, passions, and violent temptations). Other definitions include that of a Henry Ey: "*Palabra que . . . designa ya sea un estado (la experiencia del imaginario vivido automáticamente como en los sueños)*" (word that designates a state [the experience of a vivid imaginary automatically like in dreams]) (1993: 66–67).[6]

Delirio is created when reality cannot be placed in a coherent and stable location. This can occur when repeated moments in history are situated in hidden or inaccessible places. It is also present when history that is legitimated is inchoate and disjointed. The hope for a clarified origin is destroyed in the repeated stories that cannot be substantiated and in the living stories that continue to tell of barbarians in a space that is no longer barbaric. *Delirio* is located within the eye of the *norteño* who is constantly facing a de-centering and de-territorialization resulting from the convoluted and opaque nature of the region's written, oral, and occulted history.

It is a poetic existence that stirs passion and excitement. There is a certain sensuality to the state of *delirio,* which is actually the state of desire or *ravishment* as explained by de Certeau. In this trance state, the person is momentarily displaced and delimited because the limits are continuously fluctuating and moving from place to place. It gives discourse a plasticity that convulses the regulatory nature of society. In the state of *delirio,* rules are different, not what is expected. They adapt to the passion of the moment.

As shown in the following story, the ideology and acceptance of the *mestizo* origin, the joining of the Spanish and the indigenous, which is considered the heart of the Mexican nation-state, is negated in the search for whiteness. Enclosed in the story is the allusion to *delirio* as a form of madness from excessive endogamy or madness for the sake of madness. In the story, people from Cadereyta are sitting in trees; not interested in the goings-on of the world, they are living in a delirium created by an excess that has been hidden. The story alludes to the illicit narrative of the endogamous Jews that cannot be told. Although the story is supposed to be dead or non-existent, the madmen who are said to be their descendants continue to live.

White Skin as Protection

What haunts existence, now, in our time, is linked to the "domestic" dimension that can never be domesticated. (Ronell 1986: xviii)

Araceli Cantú sees the map of Nuevo León in my office and asks me if I am from General Bravo. She saw General Bravo on the map. She was born in China, which is ten kilometers from Bravo. As I tell her that I travel to Nuevo León for my research, she begins to describe her family, the Cantús. They are tall, fair, often blue- or hazel-eyed, and mostly from China and General Bravo, Nuevo León. She says that she doesn't really understand why, but there is a geographic area in northern Nuevo León where all the people are fair-skinned. She herself is fair, with a round, broad face and blonde hair. Although some people would say they are "pure-blood Spaniards," she tells me that no one around her has been able to say why the Cantús are so white.

The initiation of my acquaintance with Araceli seems to have been the process of delineating blood-lines. While the conversation continued for another half-hour, covering topics as varied as marriage, children, work, religion, witchcraft, and the wildness of northern Mexico, the initial theme was about the Cantús being white. Once my new acquaintance had told me of her heritage, she began to speak of her parents working in what is known as the "grape" in California (the grape fields), their contact with Cesar Chavez, and the conditions in the migrant worker camps. Painful to hear, the story involved many siblings, early marriage, and many children. Yet Araceli had laid the foundation for how she would present herself to me, since I am a person with some connection to her birthplace. The idea of the Cantús who do not appear indigenous sets her apart. Regardless of what else accompanies the declaration of "whiteness" or "pure blood," nothing can contaminate this position, which creates a liberating space in which a person can speak of her Otherness without being imprisoned.

I have known other Cantús, many of them fair like Araceli. I knew Oscar Cantú well. He was over six feet tall with a dark complexion. He smiled all the time and conversed like a child. For most of his life, he worked in the fields. Later, when he was past sixty, he would help people in town with odd jobs. His father was supposed to have been a ladies' man who left children all over northern Mexico and south Texas. His father may have been from Cadereyta. I have heard from several sources that Cadereyta is known for its residents who are insane. It is said that the insanity was due to excessive intermarriage and incest within families. Every year or so, Oscar would become very nervous. He would begin to hear things and see things. His family would then send him to the state mental hospital in Austin. He would return with his anti-psychotic medication that would help calm him until the next crisis.

The secret of Cadereyta's madmen proliferated throughout Nuevo León and traveled with its migrants into Texas. Yet it only appeared in the most intimate of conversations. The contamination of madness and incest were (and are) removed from public view. The camouflaged narratives of incest, barbarity, evil, and madness, combined with the trope of "whiteness," are part of a haunting that is inside of Nuevo León. There are stories in its past that have left reminders that continue to enter into interactions, conversations, and events.

One summer night in 1999, my landlord in Monterrey hosted a *carne asada* for his daughter Jenny and her fiancé, Lalo Cantú. Their family, the parents and three daughters, was present. Since we lived over their carport, my daughter and I were often invited to family events. My landlord, Raúl, was very pleased about his daughter's upcoming marriage. Lalo Cantú, an engineer who worked at the PEMEX refinery in Reynosa, drove a new car and often bought Jenny luxurious gifts. In jovial conversation, Raúl told all of us present that his future son-in-law's family was from Cadereyta. Their name was Cantú. Raúl said all of the Cantús from Cadereyta were said to be insane. Apparently not offended, Lalo agreed that it was a common story.

Curious about the story concerning Cadereyta, I asked Alvarado what he knew. Alvarado said there was a story about someone important who visited Cadereyta. The visitor was surprised to find many of the local people sitting in the trees. I pressed Alvarado for an explanation to see if his story referred to the endogamy that was said to have caused the madness. Saying the people from Cadereyta were simply crazy, he denied this part of the story.

Was the story of the insane, inbred people from Cadereyta a remnant of the stories of intermarriage between *nuevoleneses?* In General Terán in particular, I found that most married couples were at least second cousins. In searching for genealogical information on Nuevo León, I found remarkable connections, such as a family of five brothers marrying five sisters of another family. In Ernesto Tijerina's book, I found numerous instances of first cousins or double cousins marrying. In Latin American tradition, people from Mexico use the surname of both parents. There were numerous Garza Garzas, Cantú Cantús, González Gonzálezes and Tijerina Tijerinas. In Mexico, my own name would also be Hernández Hernández, although my parents say they are not related. In hearing about cousins marrying cousins, I wonder how this intermarriage is connected to the early stories of the Jewish settlers only marrying their kin (a story that is also documented in medieval Spain).

Telling of one's "whiteness" is a safety measure. It protects the speaker, removing the person from the danger of falling into the space of the Other, who is wild, indigenous, and barbaric. Ironically, the process of declaration is an indication of what cannot be said. The ghosts of the contaminated press the speaker to protect herself because the impurity cannot be removed. Traces of "bad blood" remain and are attended to "after" the narrator declares she is not contaminated. The force behind the narrative of "purity" is the haunting of the defiled.

Encountering *Delirio*

Haunting creates delirium. The *nuevolenese* is trapped. When sequestered inside delirium, the questions of life, rationality, and health are interspersed within the delirious moment. Is the vision only apparent because of a foreboding pathos within the person? Is the not-quite-so-rational entanglement due to a form of illness or ignorance? Is the word *delirio* a close relation to the word *delito,* which refers to an immoral act?

Who defines *delito?* As in the meaning of *delirio,* the rules of logic vary according to time and space. This observation is most significant in the world of Nuevo León, which is a space pre-destined to produce multiple *delirios,* for its punishing geography produces innumerable mirages. The time that travels from the pre-conquest settlements of what was/is termed *el indio bárbaro* (Cavazos Garza 1964) has not separated from the present moment. *El bárbaro* is present in the convenient Other that he represents; while eliminated in a material sense, he is continuously manifested in *los delirios del presente* (the delirium of the present).

Yet the devalued nature of "the Other" is not constant. Difference and Othering enter into many aspects of *norteño* life. The word *especial* (special), a word often used to indicate "difference," can be viewed as either negative or positive. *Norteños son especiales;* they are different, at times difficult, and at times strikingly amicable. Their beliefs intermittently enter into the liminal area of occidental logic. At times they place the divine above them and at other times position it laterally. At moments they even view their own lives as existing a priori to their gods. These positions may be seen as *delirio, rebeldía* (rebellion), or gnosticism.[7] While many persons in the north may deny this gnostic association, their forceful determination and their occasional reference to "the presence of the divine in each human being" corresponds to a form of gnosticism. It could be heresy. It could be *delirio*. It could be individuation.

A Different Kind of Speech

. . . a strange alliance joins the "mystic" spoken word to the "impure" blood. The meeting of. . . . two religious traditions, one removed to an inner retreat, the other triumphant but "corrupted," allowed the new Christians to become, to a great extent, the creators of a new discourse, freed from dogmatic repetition, . . . structured by the opposition between the purity of the "inside" and the life of the "outside." (de Certeau 1992: 23)

Delirio is produced by juxtapositions formed by mythical, mystical ideas/perceptions/practices that show themselves in the north. *Delirio* is created when a thought or query regarding a certain time and place is joined with widely disparate moments, events, and locations. Nuevo León is a world that seems to be punished by nature, theocracy, and secrecy; yet, ironically, Nuevo León creates abundance and thus evinces the inherent possibility of paradox. The past of Nuevo León that is contained inside anguish creates a "belated present" (Bloom 1975), which is tinged with pieces of memory that transform deprivation into moments of triumph. The space between these past and present responses of anguish and triumph contains the paradox. The transformation that creates this metamorphosis produces *delirio,* which is the location of the unknown, the moment that produces no rational explanation. While I do not claim that Nuevo León is the only place that contains this curious space, the language and feeling of this unknown have been central to the daily life I have experienced in the three years that I traveled into the region.

Poetic Mortality

As soon as I focus on the glyphs, my eye is captured and drawn in. The Frame flattens into a composition of multiple frames . . . images that spill over or push out, oriented in different directions and even upside down in relation to each other. The sense of perspective is lost, the cube disappears, and the eye is cast adrift, transported or seduced by the tracing through of a phantasmagoric landscape. (Pandolfo 1997: 18)

Stefania Pandolfo leads us into the world of everyday phantasms in *Impasse of the Angels* (1997), which tells of life and death in a Moroccan Qsar (village). Her description of that loss of perspective when viewing the landscape of the Qsar strikes one as similar to the poetry of Felipe Guerra Castro. As I first heard the words of the poem "Delirio," with Aquiles Sepúlveda reading this narrative of jealousy and death, I suddenly found myself entering into a "phantasmagoric landscape." Guerra Castro's words are real, yet not real. Concrete little images that create sounds describing a tragic event, they are written in a text. Yet the story lies in the realm of the fantastic. The poet describes how he murders the woman he loves. As he sees her lying on the ground with blood spilling from her wound, his love overflows. Warm from its confrontation with her body, the bloodied dagger is still in his hand.

Felipe Guerra Castro, the author of the poem "Delirio," was born in the nineteenth century in Sabinas Hidalgo, Nuevo León. He left for Spain as a young man. A friend, Eusebio de la Cueva, wrote that in Europe, the poet let his life get out of control. In another of Castro's poems, *Vaiven,* there is indication of this dilemma. Looking for a helpful God, the poet writes of being punished. He wonders if he should work toward purification. His tone is desperate.

Aquiles Sepúlveda is the person who tells me of this long ignored poet. Guerra Castro, he tells me, is buried in Monterrey. On the grave is a statue of a man killing a woman. Sepúlveda reads the poem to me. The story sounds fantastic:

DELIRIO

En un charco de sangre, allí estabas tendida
para siempre callada, para siempre dormida,
con los ojos abiertos, muy abiertos . . . abiertos
y mirándome siempre como miran los muertos,
sin amor y sin odio, sin placer de amargura,
con sútil ironía y a la vez con ternura.
El puñal en mi diestra todavía humeaba,
pero ya a mis oídos el furor no gritaba,
y crecía el espanto y la angustia crecía,
y humeaba en mi diestra el puñal todavía
con el vaho candente de tu sangre ardorosa,
de tu sangre de virgen, de tu sangre de diosa . . .

(FELIPE GUERRA CASTRO 1880–1923)

DELIRIUM

In a pool of blood you laid
always silent, always asleep,
with your eyes open, very open . . . open
and observing me always with the gaze of the dead,
without love, without hatred, without the pleasure of bitterness,
with subtle irony and at moments with tenderness.
The dagger in my right hand was still moist
yet now the furor of my hatreds no longer screamed
the fear grew larger, the anguish grew larger,
the vapor from the dagger in my right hand still
with the steady vapor of your arduous blood,
your blood of a virgin, your blood of a goddess . . .

There are no esoteric aspects to Guerra Castro's poem "Delirio." Yet the fantastic sensibility of the murder, the easy gaze of the poet, and the conflation of the dead woman as betraying lover, virgin, and goddess locate the narrative in the fantastic. The title "Delirio" places the reader in a moment of irrationality. Yet reason returns with the material presence of a statue commemorating the murder/poem over the poet's grave. The space between the delirium/murder and the building and placement of the statue situates the question of my work. "Delirio," the poem, concerns mortality, rage, and a certain attraction to the strange beauty of death itself.

As if in a delirium, the ethnographer enters a world that de-centers her American conceptions of the real. The varying forms of "the public" illuminate the secretive quality of "the private," in which the question is not seen as a question but as a statement. Or as a paradox to those foreigners who do not understand *delirio,* which is quotidian to *norteños.* The ever-present issues of delirium and mortality comprise the ethos of *el norte.* This ethos is *inquietud,* a form of impatience with the limitations of mortality. The poem "Delirio" best exemplifies the living state of Nuevo León. The man in love assassinates his lover because she loves someone else. The words are elevated, repeated, and commemorated by means of the poet's tomb, which provides a visual representation of the moment of murder. Yet the poem does not directly confront the issue of transgressing limits, breaking rules, or the horror of eliminating a human. The poem is about the poet's jealousy, his passion, and the lover's beauty, even in death.

Magical Theory

He distinguido dos procesos causales: el natural, que es el resultado incesante de incontrolable e infinitas operaciones; el mágico, donde profetizan los pormenores, lúcido y limitado. En la novela, pienso que la única posible honradez está en el segundo. (Borges 1997: 115) (I have distinguished two causal processes: the natural, which is the result of incessant, uncontrollable, and infinite operations; magic, where details are announced briefly and clearly by a prophet. In the novel, honor is only possible in the second process mentioned.)

Borges proposes that the novelist who retains her "honor" is one who incorporates an understanding of magic, magic as theory, and the magic of the quotidian in her writing. Such a notion provides an interesting paradigm for this research. The interlacing of logic and delirium assist in presenting this world, which Mexican social scientist Octavio Ianni describes as lacking a concept and a space for understanding and explanation (1993). The cosmos of Nuevo León is explained in this lack of concept.

Delirio has a semblance to the "marvelous real." Yet *delirio* attempts to remove the problematic that is related to an inherent lack of ability to reason. Clearly the incidence of the fantastic or the marvelous is not limited to the Latin American continent. Writers such as Alejo Carpentier and Gabriel García Márquez have stratified this location, taking the reality of fiction into the real of the Western world, leaving their readers and interpreters with an image of Latin America as the world of the fantastic, full of ghosts and strange incidents. These representations constrict the vast geography and intent of the fantastic.

Nuevo León is not such a place. The marvelous delirium found in many of the exciting stories that have been transposed in this text are related to a constantly fluctuating reality that cannot be centered. The Occident only names these practices as subaltern because they are leftovers from a previous era, and have no logical or respected place within the discourse of twenty-first century reason to locate themselves.[8]

The question remains: is the marvelous real defined by theory or by the "observed"? Is perhaps the ethnographer overtaken by *delirio*? Is *delirio* what de Certeau describes as *ravishment?* This complex situation prohibits the resultant use of meta-explanation or a holistic analysis of what *is* Nuevo León. It does however produce the opportunity for the exploration of more innovative analytic processes that do not synthesize, yet seek out traces and intermittent patterns that may provide a sense for the paradoxical, fluid world of *el norteño*. It is not an unknown word in Mexico, this delirium of life. In Nuevo León it is even more intense. The lie that stands inside the world of Nuevo León leaves the human carrier slightly off balance, not in the sense of being insane, although the reference to Cadereyta's madmen is most probably a reference to this imbalance. It leaves the definition of life in constant flux. The poem "Delirio" explains passion, love, desperation, and the elimination of another life without guilt. The murdering lover stands inside his own moment of *ravishment,* so thoroughly entranced that his logic is located outside the realm of rationality, again recalling de Certeau, in this moment the poet is "evading legalities and disciplines of meaning." Aquiles tells me to visit the grave of Guerra Castro in the old cemetery on Aramberri in Monterrey. Standing starkly above the grave is a large relief of a man holding a dagger. At the man's feet is a woman, sprawled on the ground. The relief is not painted, except for the dagger, which is painted red; yet the blood of the murdered woman remains the same color as the stolid gravestone.

I believe that the celebration of the passion and delirium of this poem encompass what the *nuevolenese* sees as himself and herself. The man is the impassioned lover, acquitted because his murder is for love. The woman is the goddess, killed for her sensuality, adored as a lifeless image. Only this can remain after the burial of so many stories that once existed as Nuevo León moves its way through modernity. There is no indigenous man here; there is no Jew. The barbaric man remains, yet the savage nature of his act is resurrected in the cemetery on Aramberri.

Conexiones Pragmáticas—Pragmatic Connections to Ethnography and History

Beyond the poetic descriptions of the unstable state of *delirio,* each moment of lost/hidden or fetishized history has its correlation in the varying aspects of what is said to be *nuevolenese* identity. The stories and the Macro Plaza itself fit like yokes around the necks of the *nuevoleneses,* at times wrenching them back in time and at other times pushing them forward with modernity. We return to Foucault's relationship between entities; the strategic placement of these identities/entities propels the movement of life in Nuevo León. The "reality" of their existence lies in the propensity of the stories.

The barbaric Indian. He is fetishized and sexualized. According to Alonso de León, he has no morals and no god. He is the worst of the Other: Abraham Nuncio notes León's emphasis on the Chichimecas' lack of deities (1997). He is cannibalistic and polygamous; as Montaigne describes in his essay "On Cannibals," the two criteria prove barbarity. *El indio bárbaro,* located in the baseness of living beings, has no soul.

This judgment upon the Chichimeca is pressed further than that of the indigenous people to the south because of the longstanding conflict between the Spanish colonists and the northern tribes. While both groups committed barbarous acts, the colonists were not described (at least at first) as barbaric; the label of *barbarian* was pinned to the Chichimeca. Through the process of Indianization, the southern tribes were resurrected in a move resembling what Hayden White describes as the evocation of the "noble savage." Creating the image of a civilized indigenous people who were capable of creating a civilization, the material remnants of the Aztec, Mayan, Olmec, and other indigenous cultures were used to implement this cleansing. Thus the idea of an indigenous (or at least *mestizo*) nation was made palpable to the structure of the nation-state and its populace.

There was no resurrection in the north. As Nuncio aptly states, the only monument to the Indians in Monterrey is a statue of Cuauhtémoc (1997), which is most probably related to the brewery of the same name that was founded by the Garza Sadas in the late nineteenth century. Nuncio attempts a resurrection in *Visión de Monterrey,* his small (four-by-six-inch) book of 136 pages, which although eloquent, comprehensive, and succinct, leaves the reader wanting to know more about the extinct *indio.* Hoyo and others protest the mistreatment of indigenous people in a scattering of comments in regional historical texts. The situation remains the same. Cristóbal López has come to be known as the local "expert" on the indigenous people of the north. He has published two books on the subject and has conducted several years of fieldwork without the benefit of a graduate degree. Even so, he was ousted from the graduate program in social sciences at the Universidad Autónoma de Nuevo León for verbally confronting a professor about favoritism. Although he is an adjunct at the prestigious Universidad de Monterrey, he has only a limited amount of the financial support that would allow him the opportunity to obtain the education needed to become an officially "authorized" voice. His predicament recalls de Certeau's claim that a text written by a person without status means nothing.[9]

With limited "authorized" discourse to stem the tide of public belief that the north is predominantly inhabited by "whites," little possibility exists that a more postmodern view of the conflict between northern indigenous people and "white" settlers can evolve.

Paradoxically, the separation and continued devaluation of the Chichimeca (and subsequent Comanche and Apache raiders) may have assisted in the development of Nuevo León's exceedingly successful industry. The industrialist's authority, which has been used internally within northern companies and also manifested in business with the United States and other First World nations, has been augmented and intensified by the industrialist's "non-indigenous" status. The "white" entrepreneur can more easily move among his American and European colleagues. Again, it is important to note that being "white" in this context relies upon the projection of whiteness rather than "whiteness" as a biological category. There is no way of informing ourselves of the actual percentage of *mestizaje* among the *nuevoleneses.* Yet, if people believe that the presence of indigenous blood is minimal, this belief has greater impact than any non-visual reality.

Narratives describing the contrast between the north and the evidently more indigenous south create a significant barrier between the two regions. The northerners are said to be more identifiable by their fair skin. A French engineer I know, who has worked internationally for Schlumberger and lived in Campeche for three years, told me recently that "everyone knew" that "*norteños* are taller and have fair skin" in comparison to the rest of the people in Mexico. This distinction assists in separating the "problems" of the south—extreme poverty, low literacy rates, high infant mortality rates, and indigenous uprisings. Otherness is contained in the region containing "dark" people, leaving the north "cleaner" and more salable to its Western trading partners. In addition, since the indigenous man is fetishized and stereotyped as oversexed, the "cultured" and well-bred northern industrialist is viewed as a safer "business contact." Being "white" reduces the anxiety between the groups who deal together in business, since social contact is made more acceptable. Moreover, because the possibility of marriage between a "white" *norteño* and a white American is less threatening, the fear of miscegenation is removed should a chance union arise from these business connections. Without the indigenous ancestor, there is no miscegenation.

The barbaric norteño. Once when I asked my father about Dionísio García, a wealthy, powerful man who lived near our home in southeast Texas, my father responded, "There is a little bit of larceny behind every fortune."[10] Although García lived in southeast Texas, he had migrated as a young man from Monclova, Coahuila, which is about 400 kilometers northwest of Monterrey. Dionísio García strongly resembled the "tough" *norteños* described in oral and textual narratives. Tall and very fair, he always wore a cowboy hat and cowboy boots. He had numerous businesses and owned a farm outside of town. What I remember most about him was what he did on New Year's Eve. Every year, his "very gracious" wife (who drove a Thunderbird convertible) would host a spectacular party. Everyone would dress up, including the children. In their elegant home, we would use their imported china and sterling silver flatware while we ate the most incredible food and homemade pastries. All this festivity happened while the hi-fi was turned full volume to Mexican music by Pedro Infante, Miguel Aceves Mejia, and others. Right at midnight my father's friend would pull out his gun and fire six shots into the air. A real gun with real gunshots going who knows where. I was only about five at the time, but I remember feeling the barbarity of the moment. A tall, fair-skinned man yelled at the top of his lungs as he stood on the porch facing Avenue B and shot a round of bullets to celebrate the New Year. In his tough appearance and intelligent business maneuverings, this man resembled the common image of the *norteño*.

In his book on the north, Hernán Solís writes that contraband and other illegal activities were not only tolerated but were seen as "respectable" during the latter part of the nineteenth and the first half of the twentieth century (1973). A man with a tinge of barbarism would employ larceny to amass a fortune. Such a man is cunning, negotiates lucrative business contracts, and sees through a dishonest business partner.

Most importantly, if the barbaric man is not defined by "color" per se, he can metamorphose himself into the "non-barbaric" man as needed. All he requires is a different set of clothes and a different type of education and demeanor. Such a metamorphosis was facilitated by the Garza Sadas, who ingeniously sent most of the their male children to college at the University of Michigan or the Massachusetts Institute of Technology. Thus, the barbaric *norteño* can turn into a civilized man when the occasion arises, since his transformation is not hampered by his color.

The issue of barbarity also gives "approval" to activities that normally would not be (or would no longer be) considered socially appropriate, such as dueling, importing contraband, extortion, murder for hire, and of course, larceny.

The clandestine Jew. While devalued for the negative stereotypes that have persevered regarding Jews, an inverted form of this label has provided numerous supports for the *nuevolenese* construction of identity. As Caro Baroja, Castro, and other historians have described, the Jews and their *converso* descendants in Spain came to amass significant power and wealth, which was obtained with the blessing of the monarchy. These texts assert that Jewish merchants and advisors to the Crown financed the voyages of Columbus and numerous others. Luis de Carvajal y de la Cueva actually bought his title and territory (as mentioned in Chapter II) for two million ducats. While Carvajal's project ended in disaster, Diego de Montemayor, his successor, was able to reestablish El Nuevo Reino de León, repopulate the area, and officially found the city of Monterrey. Castro writes (as cited in Chapter VII) that the Crown at the end of the fifteenth century commonly used Jews with close affiliations to the Monarchy for positions of leadership in La Santa Hermandad, the "official" policing arm of the King in Spain and all of its territories. In El Nuevo Reino, Capitán Joseph de Treviño, who was fabulously wealthy and, according to local texts, was said to be a *converso,* was responsible for the activities of La Santa Hermandad.

The originary positioning of the Jew as "financier" and "policing agent" has accompanied the narrative into the present day. The talk of Monterrey is that the local rich are really Jews. They became Christians some centuries before but have maintained the "Jewish attitude," which has influenced their ability to deal in business and commerce. This identification with a non-Christian tradition does not affect their alliance with the church. In his insightful research on Monterrey, David Snodgrass writes that the powerful industrial elites are strongly allied with the church (1998); an additional trope of the north, however, is that its people, who are not really very Catholic, use religion only for the sake of appearances. Although the collaboration between the industrialists and the church is often seen as a vehicle for both groups to increase and maintain their power, the affiliation does not enter into questions of belief or piety. In addition, any Jewish identification found within the discourse of *nuevoleneses* generally does not include the actual practice of religious rites, which avoids a confrontation with an actual religion. As de Certeau writes of the Jews of Paris, they no longer go to the synagogue but are forever "designated" as being Jews (1988). The mark of identification remains, although the structure of the world around the designation has drastically changed.

In addition to being endowed with the stereotype of the "moneymaker," the *nuevolenese* who sees himself as a Jew is also seeing himself as "white." The history of endogamy, which is (for once) evidenced in the regional archives and the image of the Jew protecting his/her own *limpieza de sangre,* preserves the "clean" status of the *norteño* who could be descended from Jews.[11] Paradoxically, the Jew who is seen as Other in many societies is no longer Othered for the *norteño* (unless the *norteño* is a historian). As discussed in Chapter VII, local historians continue relying on archives to prove the actual existence of the Jews, which is an impossible endeavor since many of the documents were purged during the Mexican Revolution.

The tunnels, the underground city, and Las Emparedadas. There is no question that the tunnels exist underneath Monterrey. They have been observed and filmed. The fabulous stories about their size and uses are not necessarily fictional. The Underground City is another matter.

273

These stories have surfaced in scattered places with no basis for their veracity. The stories of Las Emparedadas (women buried inside of walls) reside somewhere between fabula and truth. These stories are published as fiction, yet are more public. Lilia Villanueva de Cavazos, the wife of Monterrey's official historian, has written a story about a woman buried in a wall in Montemorelos (1988). Her name was Leonora and she was buried for having an affair with her husband's farmhand. On a more national scale, Vicente Riva Palacio wrote a novel titled *Las Dos Emparedadas,* which speaks of two women who were separately entombed (1985). A jealous rival placed the first woman in a wall. She was rescued alive but went mad. The second Emparedada was the rival herself, entombed by indignant friends and relatives of the first woman.

The three narratives of tunnels, the city, and women buried alive are about interiors. Spaces that are no longer accessible, these interiors are where the Other has been placed. Here the unaccepted past and present of the city can be held without anyone being accountable.

The tunnels have a dual purpose. They are safety valves where the civilized can escape from the barbarian in the city or at La Ex-hacienda de San Pedro. They are links between the citizen and the divine; using the tunnels, the people of Monterrey can arrive safely home to the house of God and be thankful for the massive doors placed on the Cathedral by Governor Martín de Zavala. There is also safety in the Cathedral itself; barbarity cannot enter.

According to José Cano from General Terán, he marched with his fellow soldiers through the "large tunnel" between the Obispado and the Cathedral sometime during 1914 or 1915. The tunnels were also used as travel ways; perhaps it was summer, and the unbearable heat outside made marching through the tunnels a palpable alternative. Perhaps the Generalissimo wanted publicly to show the city that he knew the secrets of the tunnels.

The altered purpose of the tunnels may be for clandestine practices. Aquiles Sepúlveda told me the story of priests meeting in a room off the tunnel, under the Cathedral, where they studied the Kabbalah and read about exorcisms. This is no ancient story; Sepúlveda said these meetings happened in the 1940s. Other comments are light speculation, mentioned in passing, that the tunnels are for escaping criminals or drug lords. In fact, a *narcotraficante* in a southern Mexican city actually escaped capture by federal police by leaving through a tunnel under his house.[12] These things can happen, people say. Drugs and contraband can be hidden in tunnels. Jews can practice forbidden rituals in tunnels. The tunnels are forbidden zones of desire and adventure. In the fall semester of 1999, a college student from the Universidad de Monterrey told Cristóbal López that he had located the entrance to the tunnel near the Obispado. What else does the student know that he has not said?

The underground city is the phantasm. There are no written "reports" and no "official" story, not even a denial. The city simply does not exist. It is talked about only in secret among friends and intimate colleagues. The bookstore owner, a friend of Aquiles Sepúlveda, whose shop is on Guerrero, says that "everyone knows" about the city, but the media cannot say a thing. The church and the industrialists have banded together to closet these narratives. Children are told these stories at home. The stories are written and submitted to teachers but are not published along with other "legends" of Nuevo León.

Some people say Las Emparedadas were nuns who had children by the priests.[13] Others say they were young girls who were hidden away from Pancho Villa. The *compadre* of a friend says deformed and mentally deficient children were hidden in these catacombs under the city. José Cano told his sister in General Terán that he saw them himself. The problem is that José returned to the Revolution and was never heard from again. There is no documentation or archive to report what José Cano saw the day he marched through the tunnel in which horsedrawn carriages easily moved through the passageway. At the side of the tunnels, he saw women dressed in nuns' habits standing in front of their homes, which were burrowed rooms in walls of stone. There were children standing next to the nuns. This account is what Artemio Villagómez told me, what his grandmother Lozano told him, and what José Cano told her sometime around 1914 or 1915.

The woman buried in the wall, or the woman buried in her house underground, is a captured narrative that cannot tell the secrets that she saw. One's imagination can escape with this thought. It can place two cities, parallel, one above ground and one below ground. Aboveground are moneymakers, industrialists, and bankers. Also aboveground are pretty wives and children in their school uniforms. As Abraham Nuncio aptly states (1997), these are blonde mothers with their dark-headed children. The mothers bleach out the darkness that the children cannot yet. Underneath lies the city that holds the darkness of clandestine relationships, inverted chastity, and the hidden *indio* who never really goes away. The city holds the woman who was sealed up for being impure, being sexual outside societal constraints, using her own will to seek money owed to her, and doing what a man did. The tainted honor of the men above is placed inside the walls or under the foundations of the old buildings of El Barrio Antiquo. The walls and foundations keep the darkness away from the truth/lie that "lies" above the concrete expanse of the modernistic Mexican Plaza, the Macro, the largest. The Macro covers everything in darkness.

De Certeau/Mystic Speech/the Truth and the Lie

In the *Writing of History,* de Certeau repeatedly confronts the reader with the idea that what is repressed always returns. What returns can be mystical, phantasmic, unreal, or exotic. What grows inside the constrained position that keeps the person tied to a falsehood cannot be peeled away. Within Monterrey's (and Nuevo León's) history, the Macro Plaza can no longer be shed. It is durable, built to last several centuries. It is the cover, the Other reading of the scene. It is the layer that man in Monterrey placed over nature, hoping to harness the darkness, the dark side of nature, and its troublesome presence in Nuevo León. After all, nature has inundated this dry city scores of times and killed thousands with the overflowing water from El Río Santa Catarina. It is nature that heats the concrete sidewalks of the Macro Plaza to 150° Fahrenheit even in May. It is nature that is wild and untamed by civilization. The phrase *barbaric by nature* may be a description of those *norteños* who negotiated with the wild nature of Nuevo León, took in some of the wildness, and formed a world that at times seems like reality and at other times seems like the *réel.*

Postscript

In November 1999, Aquiles Sepúlveda told me that he feared the new millennium. He was not usually superstitious. I was surprised at his concern. He sensed tragedy. I spoke with him by telephone from Houston on Christmas Day. He was in good health. He told me that his nephew had begun searching the web for information that pertained to "the Bible." On January 11, 2000, Alejandro Sepúlveda took a seriously ill Aquiles to the hospital. Aquiles went into a coma within twenty-four hours and died on January 14, 2000. Three months later I return to Monterrey. I search out Aquiles Sepúlveda's grave, which is within a hundred meters of the grave of Felipe Guerra Castro, the poet who wrote "Delirio." According to Ofelia Sepúlveda, her brother Aquiles is buried in the family tomb. Yet his name has not been engraved on the tombstone.

Notes

Introduction

1. *Regios* and *regiomontanos* are terms used to describe people who reside in Monterrey. The designation *norteño* is used to describe a person living in northern Mexico or Nuevo León. The word *north* also indicates northern Mexico or Nuevo León. Within this text, I will occasionally italicize certain passages in order to distinguish my own voice from that of my informants or of cited sources.

2. Abraham Nuncio (1999) writes that he perceives a significant amount of xenophobia among Monterrey's elite. From students, professionals, and middle-class people in Mexico City, I have also heard numerous verbal narratives that devalue the *norteño* for being ignorant, uncivilized, and over-materialistic. Many of these attitudes (on both sides, north and south) are exemplified in the movie *Pablo y Carolina,* which was filmed with Pedro Infante in 1955. The movie is about the grandson of the famous Monterrey industrial family, the Garzas, who established the Cuauhtémoc brewery, which began Monterrey's ascent to industrial success. This grandson falls in love with an upper-class blonde from Mexico City; the ensuing story describes his brusque manners. The stereotypical "laziness" of those from the south is located in his friend who is from Mexico City and shares Pablo's "adventures" in courting the upper-class "Carolina."

3. I thank Theresa May for guiding me toward this conclusion.

4. As reported on television, radio, and American and Mexican newspapers.

5. Steven Bunker discusses the concept of *educación* in "'Consumers of Good Taste:' Marketing Modernity in Northern Mexico, 1890–1910," *Mexican Studies—Estudios Mexicanos* 13 (summer 1997): 227–270. He relates the idea of an acceptable middle-class "social presence" that is accomplished by exhibiting certain "appropriate" behaviors that indicate *educación.*

6. A number of *regios* I spoke with, including Aquiles Sepúlveda, describe a *norteño* as being fair-skinned and taller than Mexicans from other geographic regions. This distinction seemed to be of importance in many social situations. According to what Sepúlveda told me and what I observed in numerous situations, these physical characteristics are

seen as "desirable" and "allow" a person to more easily become part of "the *norteño* group."

7. The protagonist in the movie *Born in East L.A.* is an American of Mexican descent. He is mistakenly picked up by the Immigration and Naturalization Service (I.N.S.) during a raid at his place of employment. Because he did not have his documentation that certified he was an American citizen, he was unable to return to the United States for several weeks.

8. Actually, while Aquiles and many others repeatedly said there was a solid group of *nuevoleneses* that originated from the area, there are numerous references to the majority of the population (at least in Monterrey) being from "outside" (the south, San Luis, Mexico City, etc.). Abraham Nuncio writes of this in his essay on Mexico City, "¿Ciudad de México o Chilangolandia?", *La Jornada* (Mexico City), 25 October 1999.

9. "Manners of Speaking" is a chapter title in Certeau's *The Mystic Fable* (Chicago: University of Chicago Press, 1992).

10. *La sultana del norte* is literally translated as a female member of the Sultan's family, most possibly his wife, who is from the north. The use of a Muslim title is interesting, especially in that the Arab influence in Spanish culture in the north has not been recognized despite numerous references to Jewish influence.

11. All translations are by the author unless otherwise noted.

12. An earlier version of the chapter on Alvarado was published in "Television, Technology and Myth in Nuevo León," *Para-Sites: A Casebook Against Cynical Reason,* edited by George Marcus, Late Editions 7 (Chicago: University of Chicago Press, 2000).

CHAPTER ONE. Don Gregorio Tijerina

1. The municipality of China, Nuevo León, was named after a priest who was martyred in the Far East. Actually, he died in Japan, but somehow the name was transposed to "China."

2. José Vasconcelos lived for most of his youth in northern Mexico in Piedras Niegras, Coahuila. He came to be known internationally for his writing and philosophical works. He coined the word *mestizaje,* meaning the blending between the Indian nation and the Spanish. This blending, he believed, was the "essence" of Mexico. This thesis has been accepted as canonical in the Mexican academy.

CHAPTER TWO. Before and After History

1. A common historical supposition is that the Aztecs actually originated in what is now northern Mexico.

2. According to Chapa (cited in Hoyos), there were about 250 northern tribes at the time of Monterrey's founding in 1596. One hundred years later, the number had been reduced to 160.

3. Nuncio's writing on the use of regional folklore for the purpose of making the indigenous "objects of phobia and prey" presents a striking contrast to the purported use of folklore in the *nuevolenese* television program, *Reportajes de Alvarado*. In this program the stories are said to be a way of keeping the history of Nuevo León alive. Other sources of "Indian Stories" also press the nostalgia in regionally published narratives on Nuevo León's folk history. Stories in these books include those of people who were told by Indians (when the narrator was a young child) that they would be eaten because the Indians were cannibals (López 1996, 1994).

4. In oral and written narratives, it is reported that the cemetery inside the Convento San Francisco was used to bury Indians. In her May 1999 lecture at the Museum, Lidia Espinoza stated that "everyone" was buried there, not only indigenous people.

5. *Indigenismo* or *Indianismo,* related to Vasconcelos's use of *mestizaje,* is a returning to the "roots" of Mexican history. It is a re-valuation of the indigenous history of Mexico. Although very popular and seen as the most important ideological premise of Mexican history, the "everyday" narratives are quite the opposite, as Lomnitz states and I repeatedly encountered in my work.

6. In Nuevo León, *matachines* dance at religious celebrations. Usually the dancers are from the working class and often they are young children from the ages of six to twenty. The costumes are a combination of what is documented as Aztec attire: feathers, colorful ribbons, and bells on their sandals. Yet they have also adapted to the present with "vests" often embroidered with sequins of St. Theresa or Our Lady of Guadalupe. They dance in groups as large as 100. They are often paid for their services and dance for miles to reach the place of the celebration. It is said (among the people) that the movements have very symbolic meanings and are related to early Aztec rituals.

7. This is in contrast to the appearance of television newscasters on Mexico's national networks and to Mexico's national politicians. In a recent collection of photographs of those designated by President-elect Fox for his "transition" team, only one man of eighteen chosen had "dark" skin. As a side-note, there were also only three women among the group. *El Norte* (Monterrey), 18 July 2000.

8. From the records of The Church of Jesus Christ of Latter-day Saints, International Genealogical Index ® © 1980, 1997, data as of February 1997.

9. Abraham Nuncio cites Cuauhtémoc Velasco Avila (gives no source).

10. Aquiles Sepúlveda and I discussed on several occasions the possibility that Luis Carvajal was murdered in prison.

11. Sepúlveda repeatedly encouraged me to read Carlos Fuentes's *El espejo enterrado,* saying that the text would give me a special understanding of Mexico's history and ties to Spain.

12. Zurbarán painted Santa Lucía and Santa Agatha both holding serving platters displaying their dismembered parts.

13. Viceroy's letters use the term Villa de San Luis y Los Ojos de Santa Lucía as late as June, 1591 (Archivo General de Indias, México 220, N27).

14. After a thorough search of historical texts and documents at the Archivos General

de las Indias, I did not find evidence of any other governor in New Spain being brought before the Inquisition on charges connected to Judaism. However, I did find narratives of a governor's wife in New Mexico who was tried by the Holy Office in the seventeenth century on charges of practicing Judaism.

15. Taussig is citing W.E.H. Stanner's description of *Aboriginal Religion* (1959–1963).

CHAPTER THREE. Televisa

1. "Distant relative" not in the literal sense but in the sense that my ancestors were also from Nuevo León.

2. *Reportajes de Alvarado* is now broadcast throughout North America through cable access. *La Frontera* is the "frontier," the border. It denotes a place unsettled, uncivilized, and still "wild."

3. A *molino* is a mill where corn and flour are ground. It is one of the main locations in a town where many people congregate. The owner of the *molino* is often the person with information regarding any news in the area.

4. *Cada ocho días* (every eight days) is a Mexican expression that means something happening every week. The phrase is often used in describing something that happens in a predictable and consistent manner.

5. *Pasaporteados* is a word for Mexican citizens that have migrated to the U.S.

6. Hernán Solís Garza describes this problem when he addresses the issue of *los despadrados* (those without fathers). According to Solís Garza, generations of *norteños* have left their families to work in the United States leaving their sons to be raised by the wives (*El mexicano del norte,* Mexico: Editorial Nuestro Tiempo, 1970).

7. Taussig is referring to filmmaker Jean Rouch's essay "On the Vicissitudes of the Self: The Possessed Dancer, The Magician, The Sorcerer, The Filmmaker, and The Ethnographer," *Studies in the Anthropology of Visual Communication,* 15 (1978), 2–8, p. 8.

8. Taussig writes that "nonsynchronous contradiction" was termed by Ernst Bloch. In nonsynchronous contradiction, Taussig quotes Benjamin, who "argued that the persistence of earlier forms of production in the development of capitalism, . . . corresponded images [exist] that intermingle the old and the new as ideals transfiguring the promise offered yet blocked by the present" (1973: 159).

CHAPTER FOUR. Spaces In-between

1. In 1999 *El Norte* published an article describing the numerous saints and their purposes.

2. As we traveled by a motel that seemed to be in the middle of nowhere, I wondered who stayed there. However, I did not want to broach that subject with Alvarado because

I know from previous experience that such questions prompted his frequent habit of teasing me. There were numerous moments when I had to tell him I was offended by what he was talking about. He would often see a young woman and start saying how sexy she was and that a person was never too old. I tried to take this talk in stride, knowing what I did about how men in Mexico deal with women. On several occasions while doing fieldwork in Mexico, I had been propositioned by men I was interviewing. Before I began traveling to my field site, anthropologist José Limón at the University of Texas suggested that I tell people in Mexico that I was married. I decided against this idea, believing that it was a misrepresentation. Yet, ultimately, I understood Limón's perspective. A woman who is not married is often perceived as "excited," ready to have a sexual affair. Even so, when I asked Alvarado to stop talking about the bodies of the women we encountered on our outings, he would stop for at least a moment. The issue did not become a point of contention between us, at least not for the first two years I knew him.

3. Espinazo is the same village I visited earlier with Alvarado and the film crew. It was the home of Niño Fidencio and was basically known as a "pagan" town, since they worship a folk saint who has significantly more importance than the church. I later found out that the young novice returned home because her father became ill. Four months later she had not returned to the convent.

4. In *Creer, beber, y curar*, López writes of a village near Iturbide in southern Nuevo León. In the 1960s, the village was taken over by a "shaman" who ordered that no one could enter the place. They supposedly began sacrificing people and committing other horrible acts; the local police from Ciudad Victoria attempted to intervene, but they were shot at. Finally the Mexican Army was sent in to "restore order." López found these stories circulating 20 years after the event occurred, while he was doing fieldwork in Iturbide.

5. Emma is mentioned in Chapter III as the "wife of the jeweler who designed the Virgin of Guadalupe pendant I wear . . . who drives a new Cadillac [and] is from Cadereyta Jiménez."

6. Conflict and censuring of the Catholic Church began in the nineteenth century during the presidency of Benito Juarez. It intensified during and after the Mexican Revolution in the early part of the twentieth century. The conflict climaxed in the 1930s with the War of the Cristeros, which was a reaction to continued censure of the church by president Lazaro Cárdenas. Although most of the populace of Mexico continues to show intense devotion to the church, the official position of the government is still one of distance. In 1998, during the visit of Pope John Paul II, significant progress was made in the fractured relationship between Mexico and the Vatican. President Ernesto Zedillo and the Pope appeared together publicly at a religious service. For the first time in history, a sitting Mexican president had openly "worshiped" with the Pope.

7. In *Estampas de Colonia* (1994), Solange Alberro describes the world of Mexican convents as places of culture and elitism. According to Alberro, during the eighteenth

and nineteenth century, nuns were known to be among the most educated Mexicans, frequently studying music and art while cloistered in the convent.

8. Solís Garza notes the distance between the *norteño* and the Catholic Church.

9. In a conversation I had in 1998 with a young seminarian who assisted at mass at the Santuario de la Medalla Milagrosa in Villa de Santiago, Nuevo León, we discussed the influence of Protestant groups. He was alarmed at their strong influence among the "formerly" Catholic people in northern Mexico. My landlady and a significant number of her relatives belong to a fundamentalist denomination, as do a large section of the González Villagómezes who still live in General Terán.

PART THREE. Ethnographic Imaginaries

1. In *The Writing of History,* Certeau discusses the connection/collaboration influence of one's patron (1988). He writes '"The . . . dedication . . . bestows upon discourse its status of being *indebted* in respect to the power that . . . characterizes the scientific institution of the state of its eponym, the *patron.*" He mentions "thesis director," yet I believe it could also be the university advisor, the editor of the academic press, or one's academic peers. There is constant pressure to conform to the demands of the academy.

CHAPTER FIVE. A Place of Origins

1. This is elaborated in Foucault's *Order of Things* and remains as one of the tenets that exemplifies how he revolutionized the concept of "history" (1970). His thesis, in contrast to the search for "cause," is focused on the principle of "rupture," in which the drastic changes and/or catastrophic events lead to responses that "create" history. He also sees that traces or pieces (perhaps remaining from the explosion/rupture) create the archaeological field that constitutes history. Thus Potrero, in a sense, is a site that contains scattered traces of the past. The village represents the "rupture," the collision between past and present.

2. "The *réel* . . . implies a world of unmarked space and time that cannot be mediated by language or signs . . . a primary world of forms resisting intelligible practices which would strive to make them recognizable" (Conley 1988: xvi–xvii).

3. According to records from the American Genealogical Index, Juan Vásquez married María Teresa Botello in Villaldama in 1833 (Batch M601404, Source Call 0605610). After searching through numerous genealogical records from this era in Villaldama, I found a number of Botellos married to Treviños. It is possible that Botello's mother was a Treviño, although I have not found records to substantiate this.

CHAPTER SIX. The Mystic and the Fantastic

1. A *diplomado* is a continuing education course in which a certificate is provided upon completion. In the culture of Nuevo León, those who complete *diplomados* seem to increase their professional status.

2. La Intervención Francesca occurred when Bonaparte arranged to have a Hapsburg, Maximilian, become Emperor of Mexico.

3. The Virgin Mary in blue, the Virgin of Guadalupe, Fatima, Lourdes, Medjugorje, and the Black Madonna are all considered Mary, the mother of God.

4. Novenas are formal prayers that are often printed so that people can recite them with certain frequency. The novenas are usually associated with a request for some type of divine assistance.

5. *Comadres* are two women who are joined together socially because one woman was the sponsor (godmother) for the other woman's child at christening. This is a common social tie throughout Latin America and for many Latinos in the United States. The traditional expectation is for the godmother to have the responsibility of raising the child in correct Catholic doctrine should the mother or parents not be available. *Compadres* are the godfathers. *Compadrazgo* is the state of being godparents.

6. The Imaginary, as used by Jacques Lacan, is "the world, the register, the dimension of images, conscious or unconscious, perceived or imagined" (Sheridan 1977: ix).

7. In 1998, Doña Pepita asked me to mail a Medalla Milagrosa to President Clinton. It was silver but edged in 14k gold. She wanted to send Clinton the medal because he had been impeached and she felt he needed divine intervention. As she requested, I mailed the package (overnight express mail) to the White House. The purpose of the medal is akin to protection from the evil eye. David Rheubottom explains in "The Seed of Evil Within" that a "temporary lack in resoluteness" (being vulnerable) creates a potential for evil (1985). President Clinton was vulnerable in this way during his investigation by Special Counsel Kenneth Starr. The medal Doña Pepita sent Clinton "sealed off" the domain of protection, keeping Clinton from being attacked by the counsel's "evil."

8. It appears that the "devil house" is associated with the wealth of Santiago. There is no talk of a devil house in the less affluent sections of the city. The success of the rich in Santiago and the speculation about devil worship correlate to Deborah Kaspin's description of a "Faustian deal" made by the elite of the Chewa Villages of central Malawi in "Chew Visions and Revisions of Power" (1993).

CHAPTER SEVEN. The Discourse of Illusion

1. The same statue is now located across the street behind the Museo de Historia. It stands next to a bridge and is hidden from view if a person is standing in front of the museum on the Macro Plaza. It appears that the current placement of the statue continues to show Monterrey's ambivalence towards del Canto.

2. After a period of time, anyone with *converso* blood could be executed by the Inquisition, regardless of whether they were practicing Judaism.

3. The discourse itself was not diabolical, yet it was labeled as diabolical. Any knowledge related to this discourse is organized by a looking over. This creates an inherent problem in that the need for secrecy has erased what can be seen. There is "nothing" left to look over.

4. I believe that in a subtle way, the crucified *cabrito* (baby goat) symbolizes numerous ambivalences. It is a way to mock the crucifixion of Christ, in addition to crucifying the Jews. In a recent conversation I had with a Russian Orthodox priest, he told me that the sign of the cross by their belief is done backwards from that of Roman Catholics. Catholics touch their left shoulder after the forehead. Orthodox Christians touch their right shoulders after touching the forehead. The priest said the left shoulder should be done last because it is considered the good, symbolized by the lamb. The right shoulder should be done first because it is considered the representation of evil, symbolized by the goat.

5. See José Limón's *Dancing With the Devil* (1995). In his book, Limón discusses the presence of the "devil" in border society. He indicates that the evil emanating from the devil is not necessarily located in the "villain." It often finds itself in the very world of the "innocent," having been evoked by the tension related to being oppressed and subjugated.

6. This is disputed by José Amador de los Rios in *Estudios históricos, políticos y literarios sobre los judíos de Espana* (1942), which states that Raquel was Alfonso's lover and not the mother of his heirs.

7. Kaimen was named Grand Rabbi in 1999.

CHAPTER EIGHT. Inquisition

1. Hoyo cites David Cossio's *Historia de Nuevo León*, Vol. II, page 275 (1924–1926).

2. In the 1970s a song titled "*Renunciación*," sung by Javier Solís, was aired frequently throughout Mexico and Latin America. The lyrics are as follows: *No quiero verte sufrir, No quiero ver que las penas se metan en tu alma buena, por culpa de mi querer. No quiero verte llorar, no soy capaz de ofenderte, si sabes que hasta la muerte, puedo ser solo de ti . . . Me voy mi vida, de tu presencia, aunque me duela en el corazón* (I don't want to see you suffer. I don't want the pain to enter your good soul because I loved you. I don't want to see you cry, I am not capable of offending you, as you know, until death, I can only be yours . . . I leave, my life from your presence, even though it hurts my heart).

3. The Bible had several chapters that mention the Jews. For example, it stated the following: ORATIO MANASSÆ, REGIS JUDA, CUM CAPTUS, TENERETUR IN BABYLONE (422). The title page listed the following: BIBLA SACRA, VULATÆ EDITIONIS, SIXTI, Pontificus Maximi, Jussu Recognita, Et Clementis VIII, Autoritatate Edita, Distincta Versiculis, Indiceque Epiftolarum and Evagelioum Auta. LUG-

DUNI, Sumpt. Petri Guillimin and Ant. Beau Jollin. MDC LXXXVIII. Cum Privilegio Regis. In communicating with Schulamith Halevy, a scholar who studies "Anusim (Jews who went into hiding)," I found that the Bible is most probably a Christian Bible from the fifteenth century. However, this information does not explain the worn pages in the section titled "Pentateuch."

4. *Abuelita* is a diminutive term for grandmother; however, in northern Mexico, it is not associated with a small, passive grandmother. One of the best examples of this "character" is the *abuelita* in the movie *La oveja negra* (*The Black Sheep*), which was filmed in Montemorelos, Nuevo León, in 1949 with Pedro Infante. The paternal grandmother is a very small woman, much shorter in stature than anyone else in the family. She wears her gray hair in the classic bun and walks slightly bent. However, she is actually quite ferocious. She hits her middle-aged son about the head with her cane when he stays out all night carousing. Her loud, shrieking voice keeps the family "under control."

5. In *Inquisición y sociedad en México* (1988), Solange Alberro relates the story of a young boy living in Zacatecas who was visiting a nearby family. When asked if he wanted to eat some pork he responded that his family did not eat pork. This set off a series of incidents that led his family to the courts of the Inquisition.

6. What Manuel Rodríguez would tell me in the 1970s. Manuel was born in 1951 in General Bravo, Nuevo León. He migrated to Texas in the mid-1960s. As a young man in his twenties, Manuel had a very strong resemblance to a young Albert Einstein.

7. Mora-Torres's observations are collaborated by a Los Angeles newspaper article written by Juanita Darling: "The Monterrey corporations also developed a distinctive labor policy, a paternalistic style that undercut labor unions affiliated with the ruling party. Companies offered housing and health benefits long before the government mandated them" (*Los Angeles Times*, 22 October 1991). Also see the work of David Snodgrass in "Deference and Defiance" (1998). Snodgrass writes extensively of the Monterrey Industrialists' use of "welfare capitalism" in building their economic empire in Monterrey.

8. Hoyo also writes about how the Jews changed their names for protection: "*Debemos insistir en que los resultados estadísticos que arrojan nuestras nóminas no pueden considerarse definitivos." [citing] Eugenio Asensio, "La peculiaridad literaria de los conversos," en que sostiene que "ni los apellidos, ni la profesión, ni los viajes, ni las banderías encierran fuerza probatoria," opinión con que estamos plenamente de acuerdo.*" (1972: 203) (We have to insist that the statistical results that list the names are not conclusive. Citing Eugenio Asensio, "The literary peculiarity of the *conversos* in which neither names, profession, travels or disclosure limit their legal force," an opinion with which we are very much in agreement.) Caro Baroja's conclusions corroborate the conclusions of Hoyo. Spanish and Portuguese Jews readily changed their surnames to avoid being confronted by the Inquisition (1961).

9. Diego de Montemayor established himself as governor without the authorization of the Viceroy (AGI, México, 24, N. 65, 1, Pg. 9, Letter to the Viceroy, June 8, 1599). The Viceroy designated a wealthy miner, Agustín de Zavala from Zacatecas, to be governor in 1612. De Zavala remained governor for twelve years but never once visited El

Nuevo Reino (Hoyo 1972). In 1624 de Zavala's son, Martín de Zavala, was appointed governor by the Viceroy upon the death of his father. At this time, the son established his residence as governor in Cadereyta, forty kilometers north of Monterrey.

10. There are two *autopistas*, both from Monterrey; one connects to Nuevo Laredo and the other to Reynosa. The toll to Nuevo Laredo is 133 pesos (slightly more than fourteen dollars); to Reynosa the toll is 179 pesos (eighteen dollars). In Monterrey, the salary of an office secretary is approximately fifty dollars per week, making a one-way trip on the toll road almost two days' wages. The alternative to this road is a very congested two-lane highway that cuts through a somewhat dangerous mountain pass and is almost double the travel time.

11. My placement of the *nuevoleneses* as "maybe" Jews, Mexicans, and Americans is based on the following: The "maybe" of the Jews is related to the lack of "official" documentation regarding their claims to a Jewish heritage. The "maybe" of being Mexican is related to their distance geographically and culturally from the national Mexican identity. The "maybe" of being American is a consequence of their constant interaction (emotionally, politically, and economically) with the United States due to their geographic proximity.

CHAPTER NINE. *La Sultana del Norte*

1. The "second Nuevo Reino" is a reference to Abraham Nuncio's argument that the Grupo Monterrey began to establish a "kingdom" in the 1970s after the death of its founder, Eugenio Garza Sada (1997).

2. Information provided by Servicio Sismológico Nacional, Instituto Geofísica, Universidad Autónoma de México. Mexico City (http://www.ssn.unam.mx, 9–8–1999). The state of Nuevo León *está en "una zona donde no se tienen registros históricos de sismos, no se han reportado sismos en los últimos 80 años"* (a zone which has no registered history of earthquakes, which has not had any earthquake activity within the past eighty years).

3. Certeau cites Sigmund Freud, from *Civilization and Its Discontents,* in *Gestammaelte Werke* (London: Imago Press, 1940–1968), 14: 427–28. In "diachrony within synchrony" it is suggested that the motion of "archeological spatial organizations . . . [is maintained] within the spatial structure manifest today" (de Certeau, 1988: n348).

4. Cristóbal López had spoken with people in rural areas of southern Nuevo León who had told him of the men buried alive after searching for treasure. See *Creer, beber, y curar* (1998).

5. Artemio Villagómez and Yolanda González told me these stories. They said this was also related to the fear many families had about their children being stolen. People from nearby villages would steal children for placement in the buildings or lake beds.

6. This story told to me by Alvarado is corroborated by Sara Aguilar Belden who references a conversation between Villa and Jesús Aguilar in Monterrey after a dinner held in Villa's honor. The General told Aguilar, "*¡Aaaah, qué prieta tan re guapa ésa que yo bailé*

con ella! ¡Me la voy a robar! . . . Pos ya veré cómo le hago, pero me la voy a robar! Oiga . . . pos usté me va a ayudar." (1971: 386) (Ah, that dark one is really pretty, the one I danced with! I am going to steal her—Well I'll see how I do it, but I am going to steal her! Hey, you will help me).

7. Certeau describes "making do" as a relationship between the strong and the weak. The purpose of a practice/rule/tradition is "diverted from its intended aims by the use made of it . . . something else [is made] out of the story; . . . they [are] subverted . . . from within—not by rejecting them or by transforming them . . . but by many different ways of using them in the service of rules, customs or convictions foreign to the colonization which they could not escape" (1984: 31–32). The Jewish narratives and the "original families" of El Grupo Monterrey conflate to create an acceptable story of origins for Nuevo León. According to local folklore, legend has it that the group who developed Monterrey's industry is said to be of Jewish origin.

8. This is probably in reference to Alvarado's television program, which was often praised for keeping Nuevo León's history alive.

9. My daughter attended a public high school in Monterrey in 1999. In journalism class the students talked about the "*casa chica.*" She was told that this practice is very common among affluent families.

10. As Dundes argues, "Folklore means something to the tale teller." He believes there is a quality of projection in folkloric stories (1976: 1500). Pertaining to the Sepúlvedas, the stories of Irma being poisoned also represented Aquiles's concern for his own safety.

11. Scores of newspaper articles and television reports covered the Massieu killing and suicide. It was of special interest to Mexico because Francisco Massieu was the brother-in-law of President Carlos Salinas.

CHAPTER TEN. *La Joya*

1. From *Webster's New Explorer Medical Dictionary* (Springfield, MA: Federal Street Press. 1999).

2. Certeau is citing the twenty-one-year-old Jean de Lery's travel account of his exploration of Brazil, entitled *Histoire d'un voyage faict en la terre du Bresil* (1578).

3. Forbes' 1999 list of the top ten includes three men from Nuevo León.

4. Saragoza's book was published after Nuncio's. The more intently he looked into the role of the Garza Sadas in the life of Monterrey, Nuncio stated, the more he seemed to be under suspicion.

5. Certeau describes the courtier, who is subject to the whim of the court (1988). In this sense, Rubio was a courtier to the Garza Sadas.

6. Knight writes that he hopes the Monterrey Industrialists (the Garza Sadas?) will do as well as the Medicis.

7. The libraries in Monterrey are not accessible. Books are extremely limited.

Artemio Villagómez told me that no one reads the books even if they are there. For class the students are asked to look for small entries in encyclopedia-like texts.

8. Knight implies that the exhibit was placed with minimal knowledge of how to manage curatorial space.

CHAPTER ELEVEN. Conclusion

1. Nuncio cites Raúl Rangel Frias's *El Reyno* (S/E, Monterrey, 1972). No page given.

2. Finke cites Chekhov's letter which appeared in *Anton Chekhov's Life*, 91–92; *Pis'ma* 2:173.

3. Cristóbal López frequently talks about how he is descended from indigenous people who lived near General Terán. He realizes that he has indigenous features and is one of the few people I met in Nuevo León that would discuss this fact openly.

4. George Bernard is married to a woman from Brownsville. Her family is originally from Monterrey. On a visit to her family he spent time with her grandmother, who gave him some family history. She showed him a photograph of her parents when they married in Monterrey. When he saw it he thought to himself, they look Jewish. Then she brought out some caps. She said the men used to wear these, but she did not know their purpose. George did not know the Hebrew term, but he was aware they looked very much like the caps used by Orthodox Jews. His wife's family is Catholic. They have no stories about Jewish ancestors.

5. Although Aquiles Sepúlveda described the poem "Delirio" as lost work, either other people knew of the poem or they soon learned of it after the 1995 publication of Felipe Guerra Castro's poems.

6. The dictionary gives information on Ey, but none on *Diccionario Robert*. I have not been able to find a source for the citation.

7. This is referring to the concept of man being a priori to the Divine, as discussed in the work of Elaine Pagels's *The Gnostic Gospels* (1979) and Jorge Luis Borges's "Una vindicación del falso Basilides" in *Discusión* (1997).

8. Certeau proposes that ideas that are considered superstitious have not moved into the language of modernity. It is not that they are "more primitive" but that the new language has not found a way to articulate the concept (1988).

9. Certeau writes of the status of the writer as related to the authority of the text. The writer without status has no authority (1986).

10. In this particular instance, I have changed the name of the person to whom I refer. Dionísio García is a pseudonym, as is the city of his birth.

11. A never-ending push to "clean" accompanies the *limpieza* that haunts the dirty blood of Nuevo León. This blood was proven unclean by the Inquisition's trial of the Carvajals. Nuncio reports that as late as the eighteenth century *limpieza* was considered important in Monterrey's most affluent educational institution (1997).

12. A former Citibank official in Mexico City, Jorge Lankenau, reportedly escaped

arrest by leaving his colonial home through a tunnel. (*New York Times,* 20 November 1997).

13. In a letter dated June 12, 1789, the Bishop of Guadalajara writes to the Viceroy regarding a *cedula* abolishing the use of concubines by the clergy. The Bishop admits to the common practice of "concubinage" among the clergy in New Spain (AGI, Guadalajara, 563). This information gives credence to José Cano's story about the nuns and their children in the tunnels of Monterrey.

Selected Bibliography

Alberro, Solange. 1994. *Estampas de colonia*. Mexico City: Editorial Patria.

———. 1988. *Inquisición y sociedad en México, 1571–1700*. Mexico City: Fondo de Cultura Económica.

Alvarado Ortiz, Horacio. 1995. *Textos para conocer la historia de Monterrey 400*. Monterrey: Gobierno del Estado de Nuevo León.

Aguilar Belden de Garza, Sara. 1970. *Una ciudad y dos familias*. Mexico City: Editorial Jus.

Arroyo Llano, Rodolfo. 1996. *Historia del barrio antiguo de Monterrey*. Monterrey: Impresora del Norte.

Bachelard, Gaston. 1964. *The Poetics of Space: The Classic Look at How We Experience Intimate Places*. Translated by Maria Jolas. Boston: Beacon Press.

Baudrillard, Jean. 1988. "Simulacra and Simulations." *Selected Writings*. Edited by Mark Poster. Stanford, Calif.: Stanford University Press. 166–184.

Benjamin, Walter. 1968. "The Storyteller." *Illuminations*. Translated by Harry Zohn and edited by Hannah Arendt. New York: Schoken Books. 83–109.

———. 1968. "The Work of Art in the Age of Mechanical Reproduction." *Illuminations*. Translated by Harry Zohn and edited by Hannah Arendt. New York: Schoken Books. 217–251.

Bennett, Vivienne. 1995. *The Politics of Water: Urban Protest, Gender and Power in Monterrey, Mexico*. Pittsburgh: University of Pittsburgh Press.

Bettelheim, Bruno. 1977 [1975]. *The Uses of Enchantment: The Meaning and Importance of Fairy Tales*. New York: Vintage Books.

Bloom, Harold. 1975. *Kabbalah and Criticism*. New York: Seabury Press.

Bonfil Batalla, Guillermo. 1996. *México Profundo: Reclaiming a Civilization*. Translated by Phillip E. Dennis. Austin: University of Texas Press.

Borges, Jorge Luis. 1997 [1932]. "El arte narrativo y la magia." *Discusión*. Madrid: Alianza Editorial. 102–115.

———. 1997 [1932]. "Una vindicación del falso Basilides." *Discusión*. Madrid: Alianza Editorial. 77–84.

Bunker, Steven B. "'Consumers of Good Taste:' Marketing Modernity in Northern Mexico, 1890–1910." *Mexican Studies—Estudios Mexicanos* 13 (Summer 1997): 227–270.

Carpignanco, Paolo, Robin Andersen, Stanley Aronowitz, and William DiFazio. 1993. "Chatter in the Age of Electronic Reproduction Talk Television and the 'Public Mind.'" *Phantom Public Sphere*. Edited by Bruce Robbins. Minneapolis: University of Minnesota Press.

Caro Baroja, Julio. 1996 [1970]. *Inquisición, brujería y criptojudaísmo*. Valencia: Circulo de Lectores.

———. 1961. *Los judíos en la España moderna y contemporánea*. 3 vols. Madrid: Ediciones Arion.

Castro, Américo. 1962. *La realidad histórica de España*. Edición Renovada. Mexico City: Editorial Porrua.

Cavazos Garza, Israel. 1964. "Las incursiones de los bárbaros en el noreste de México, durante el siglo XIX." *Humanitas:* Anuario del Centro de Estudios Humanísticos. Monterrey: Universidad de Nuevo León. 343–356.

Certeau, Michel de. 1986. *Heterologies: Discourse on the Other*. Translated by Brian Massumi. *Theory and History of Literature* 17. Minneapolis: University of Minnesota Press.

———. 1992 [1982]. *The Mystic Fable: The Sixteenth and Seventeenth Centuries*. Translated by Michael B. Smith. Chicago: University of Chicago Press.

———. 1984. *The Practice of Everyday Life*. Translated by Steven F. Rendall. Berkeley: University of California Press.

———. 1988 [1975]. *The Writing of History*. Translated by Tom Conley. New York: Columbia University Press.

Chekhov, Anton Pavlovich. 1970 [1915]. *The Steppe and Other Stories*. Translated by Adeline Lister Kay. Freeport, N.Y.: Books for Libraries Press.

Conley, Tom. 1988. Translator's introduction to Michel de Certeau's *The Writing of History*. New York: Columbia University Press. v–xxiv.

Cossio, David Alberto. 1925. *Historia de Nuevo León*. 6 vols. Monterrey: Editor J. Cantú Leal.

Costa Lima, Luiz. 1988. *Control of the Imaginary: Reason and Imagination in Modern Times*. Translated by Ronald W. Sousa. Theory and History of Literature, vol. 50. Minneapolis: University of Minnesota Press.

———. 1992. *The Dark Side of Reason: Fictionality and Power*. Translated by Paulo Henriques Britto. Stanford: Stanford University Press.

Díaz Avilez, Mónica. 1998. *Paisaje de Nuevo León en la literatura: visión de tres mujeres*. Mexico City: Fondo Estatal para la Cultura y las Artes de Nuevo León.

Dundes, Alan. 1976. "Projection in Folklore: A Plea for Psychoanalytic Semiotics." *Modern Language Notes* 91:1500–1533.

Esposito, Augustine M. 1990. *La mística ciudad de Dios (1670), Sor María de Jesús de Agreda*. Potomac, Maryland: Scripta Humanística.

Finke, Michael C. 1995. *Metapoesis: The Russian Tradition from Pushkin to Chekhov.* Durham, North Carolina: Duke University Press.

Florescano, Enrique. 1994. *Memory, Myth and Time In Mexico: From the Aztecs to Independence.* Translated by Albert G. Bork. Austin: University of Texas Press.

[Ford, Henry]. 1920. *International Jew.* 4 vols. Dearborn Independent.

Foucault, Michel. 1972 [1969]. *The Archaeology of Knowledge and the Discourse on Language.* Translated by A. M. Sheridan Smith. New York: Pantheon Books.

————. 1977 [1975]. *Discipline and Punish: The Birth of the Prison.* New York: Vintage Books.

————. 1990 [1978]. *The History of Sexuality: Volume I, An Introduction.* Translated by Robert Hurley. New York: Vintage Press.

————. 1974. *The Order of Things: An Archaeology of the Human Sciences.* New York: Vintage Press.

Fuentes, Carlos. 1992. *El espejo enterrado.* Mexico City: Fondo de Cultura Económica de México.

Garrabé, Jean. 1993 [1989]. *Diccionario taxonómico de psiquiatría.* Mexico City: Fondo de Cultura Económica de México.

Garza Guajardo, Celso. 1989. *En busca de Catarino Garza: 1859–1895.* Monterrey: Universidad Autónoma de Nuevo León.

————. 1993. *Reportaje a reportajes de Alvarado.* Monterrey: Hacienda de San Pedro, Centro Informativo de Historia Regional, Universidad Autónoma de Nuevo León.

Godzich, Wlad. 1994. *The Culture of Literacy.* Cambridge: Harvard University Press.

Guerra Castro, Felipe. 1993. *Poemas.* Monterrey: J. A. Sepúlveda.

Guerra, Rolando. 1995. "¿Cual cultura e identidad norestense?" *Jornadas de identidad nuevoleónesa: Cultura y sociedad civil.* Monterrey: Fondo Editorial Nuevo León.

Hecht, Johanna. 1990. "St. Lucy." *Mexico: Splendors of Thirty Centuries.* New York: Metropolitan Museum of Art. 436.

Hernández, Marie Theresa. 2000. "Television, Technology and Myth in Nuevo León." *Para-Sites: A Casebook Against Cynical Reason.* Late Editions 7. Edited by George E. Marcus. Chicago: University of Chicago Press.

Horkheimer, Max, and Theodor W. Adorno. 1972 [1944]. "Odysseus or Myth and Enlightenment." *The Dialectic of Enlightenment.* Translated by John Cumming. New York: Continuum.

Hoyo, Eugenio de. 1972. *Historia del Nuevo Reino de León 1577–1723.* 2 vols. Monterrey: Publicaciones del Instituto Tecnológico y de Estudios Superiores de Monterrey.

————. 1985. *Indios, frailes y encomenderos en el Nuevo Reino de León: Siglos XVII y XVII.* Monterrey: Gobierno de Nuevo León.

Ianni, Octavio. 1993. "El laberinto latinoamericano." *Hacia nuevos modelos de relaciones interculturales.* Edited by Guillermo Bonfil Batalla. Mexico City: Consejo Nacional para la Cultura y las Artes. 235–258.

Kaspin, Deborah. 1993. "Chew Visions and Revisions of Power: Transformations of the Nyau Dance in Central Malawi." *Modernity and Its Malcontents: Ritual and Power in Postcolonial Africa*. Edited by Jean Comaroff and John Comaroff. Chicago: University of Chicago Press.

Leal, Felicitos. 1993. Introduction to *Reportaje a reportajes de Alvarado*. Monterrey: Hacienda de San Pedro, Centro Informativo de Historia Regional, Universidad Autónoma de Nuevo León.

León, Alonso de. 1961. *Historia de Nuevo León: con noticias sobre Coahuila, Tamaulipas, Texas y Nuevo México*. Monterrey: Centro de Estudios Humanísticos de la Universidad de Nuevo León.

Liebman, Seymour B. 1970. *The Jews of New Spain: Faith, Flame and the Inquisition*. Coral Gables, Fla.: University of Miami Press.

Limón, José E. 1994. *Dancing With the Devil: Politics and Poetics in South Texas*. Madison: University of Wisconsin Press.

Lomnitz-Adler, Claudio. 1992. *Exits from the Labyrinth: Culture and Ideology in the Mexican National Space*. Berkeley: University of California Press.

———. 1999. *Modernidad indiana: nueve ensayos sobre nación y mediación en México*. Mexico City: Planeta.

López, Juan Cristóbal, Manuel Durazo, and Rebeca Moreno. 1998. *Creer, beber, y curar: historia y cultura en Iturbide, Nuevo León*. Mexico City: Gobierno de Estado de Nuevo León, Consejo Nacional para la Cultura y las Artes.

López, Juan Cristóbal. 1994. "Las pervivencias de los Chichimecas en la tradición oral de Nuevo León." *Tradiciones y costumbres de Nuevo León*. Edited by Francisco Javier Alvarado Segovia, Rogelio Velásquez de León, and Sandra Lara Esquivel. Monterrey: Gobierno del Estado de Nuevo León. 221–227.

Maravall, José Antonio. 1975. *La cultura del barroco: análisis de una estructura histórica*. Espulgues de Lobregat: Ariel.

Marcus, George E. 1998. *Ethnography Through Thick and Thin*. Princeton: Princeton University Press.

Mendirichaga Cueva, Tomas. 1982. *Origen de los apellidos Garza y Treviño en Nuevo León*. Mexico City: Editorial Jus.

Mitchell, W. J. T. 1994. "Imperial Landscape." *Landscape and Power*. Edited by W. J. T. Mitchell. Chicago: University of Chicago Press. 5–34.

Montemayor, Blanca. 1991. "Vida y obra de Irma Sabina Sepúlveda." *Antología de becarios del centro de escritores de Nuevo León, 1987–1991*. Monterrey: Instituto de la Cultura de Nuevo León. 245–254.

Mora-Torres, Juan. 1990. "Social History of Nuevo León, 1848–1920." Doctoral dissertation. University of Chicago.

Nichols, Bill. 1994. *Blurred Boundaries: Questions of Meaning in Contemporary Culture*. Bloomington: Indiana University Press.

Nuncio, Abraham. 1982. *Grupo Monterrey*. Mexico City: Editorial Nueva Imagen.

———. 1997. *Visión de Monterrey*. Mexico City: Universidad Autónoma de Nuevo León y Fondo de Cultura Económica.

Pagels, Elaine. 1979. *The Gnostic Gospels*. New York: Vintage Books.

Pandolfo, Stefania. 1997. *Impasse of the Angels: Scenes from a Moroccan Space of Memory*. Chicago: University of Chicago Press.

Paz, Octavio. 1993 [1950]. Postscript to *El laberinto de la soledad*. Mexico City: Fondo de Cultura Económica.

Peña, Aniano. 1975. *Américo Castro y su visión de España y de Cervantes*. Madrid: Editorial Gredos.

Reineri, Eduardo G. 1994. "Los dulces nombres." *Historias de barrios Nuevo León*. Monterrey: Gobierno del Estado de Nuevo León. 124–138.

Rheubottom, David. 1985. "The Seed of Evil Within." *The Anthropology of Evil*. Edited by David Parkin. New York: Basil Blackwell Ltd.

Riva Palacio, Vicente. 1985 [1869]. *Las dos emparedadas: memorias de los tiempos de la Inquisición*. Mexico City: Editorial Porrua.

Riva Palacio, Vicente, and Manuel Payno. 1989 [1870]. *El libro rojo*. Mexico City: Consejo Nacional para la Cultura y las Artes.

Rios, José Amador de los. 1942 [1848]. *Estudios históricos, políticos y literarios sobre los judíos de España, 1818–1878*. Buenos Aires: Ediciones Argentinas Solar.

Robles, Vito Alessio. 1938. *Coahuila y Texas en la época colonial*. Mexico City: Editorial Cultura.

———. 1938. "La judería de Monterrey." *Bosques históricos*. Mexico City: Editorial Polis.

Roel, Santiago. 1963. *Nuevo León: Apuntes históricos*. Monterrey: Ediciones Castillo.

Rojas Sandoval, Javier, and María Elena Rodríguez. 1988. "La industria siderúrgica en Monterrey: HyLSA (1943–1985)." *Monterrey: Siete estudios contemporáneos*. Edited by Mario Cerutti. Monterrey: Universidad de Nuevo León. 55–94.

Ronel, Avital. 1986. *Dictations: On Haunted Writing*. Bloomington: University of Indiana Press.

Salinas Rocha, Irma. 1970. *Nostro grupo*. Mexico City: Editorial Jus.

Saragoza, Alex. 1988. *The Monterrey Elite and the Mexican State, 1880–1940*. Austin: University of Texas Press.

Scholem, Gershom. 1965 [1960]. *On the Kabbalah and Its Symbolism*. Translated by Ralph Manheim. New York: Schocken Books.

Sepúlveda, Irma Sabina. 1970. *El agiotista*. Monterrey: Sistema y Servicios Técnicos, S.A.

———. 1963. *Agua de las verdes matas*. Monterrey: Editorial Vallarta.

———. 1969. *Los cañones de Pancho Villa*. Monterrey: Sistemas y Servicios Técnicos.

Sheridan, Alan. 1977. Translator's note to *ECRITS: A Selection*, by Jacques Lacan. New York: W. W. Norton.

Snodgrass, David. 1998. "Deference and Defiance: Workers, Paternalism and Revolution in Mexico, 1890–1942." Doctoral dissertation. University of Texas.

Solís Garza, Hernán. 1971. *El mexicano del norte*. Mexico City: Editoriales Nuestro Tiempo.

Stewart, Kathleen. 1996. *A Space on the Side of the Road: Cultural Poetics in an "Other" America*. Princeton, New Jersey: Princeton University Press.

———. 1988. "Nostalgia—A Polemic." *Cultural Anthropology* 3:227–241.

Stewart, Susan. 1983. *On Longing: Narratives of the Miniature, the Gigantic, the Souvenir, the Collection*. Durham, North Carolina: Duke University Press.

Stoler, Ann Laura. 1995. *Race and the Education of Desire: Foucault's History of Sexuality and the Colonial Order of Things*. Durham, North Carolina: Duke University Press.

Taussig, Michael. 1999. *Defacement: Public Secrecy and the Labor of the Negative*. Stanford: Stanford University Press.

———. 1993. *Mimesis and Alterity: A Particular History of the Senses*. New York: Routledge Press.

———. 1987. *Shamanism, Colonialism, and the Wild Man: A Study in Terror and Healing*. Chicago: University of Chicago Press.

Tijerina Cantú, Ernesto. 1996. *Familia Tijerina: China, Gral. Bravo, Dr. Coss y Los Herreras*. Monterrey: Grafo Print Editores.

Todorov, Tzvetan. 1984. *The Conquest of America: The Question of the Other*. Translated by Richard Howard. New York: Harper Perennial.

———. 1977 [1973]. *The Poetics of Prose*. Translated by Richard Howard. Ithaca, N.Y.: Cornell University Press.

Tyler, Stephen. 1986. "Post-Modern Ethnography: From Document of the Occult to Occult Document." *Writing Culture: The Poetics and Politics of Ethnography*. Edited by James Clifford and George E. Marcus. Berkeley: University of California Press.

Uchmany, Eva Alexandra. 1992. *La vida entre el judaísmo y el cristianismo en la Nueva España, 1580–1606*. Mexico City: Fondo de Cultura Económica.

Vasconcelos, José. 1937. *Ulises criollo: la vida del autor escrito por él mismo*. 7th ed. Mexico City: M. León Sánchez.

Villanueva de Cavazos, Lilia E. 1988. *Leyendas de Nuevo León*. Monterrey: Archivo General del Estado de Nuevo León.

Webster's New Explorer Medical Dictionary. 1999. Springfield, Mass.: Federal Street Press.

White, Hayden. 1978. "The Forms of Wildness: Archaeology of an Idea." *Tropics of Discourse: Essays in Cultural Criticism*. Baltimore: Johns Hopkins Press.

Archives

Archivo general de Indias, Sevilla.
American Genealogy Index, The Church of Jesus Christ of Latter-day Saints.

Newspapers and Magazines

Alejo, José Luis, Rodrigo Ramírez, and Jose Villasáez. "Rastrean en Monterrey tráfico arqueológico." *El Norte* (Monterrey), 16 November 1999.

Campoy, Ana. "Explica el origen judío del cabrito." *El Norte* (Monterrey), 3 December 1999.

Carrillo, Pablo Cesar. "Reclama herencia otro hijo de Paco." *El Norte* (Monterrey), 30 August 1999.

Darling, Juanita. "Mexico; Progress and Promise; Culture; Pragmatic Monterrey Provides Model for Modernizing." *Los Angeles Times*, 22 October 1991.

Kahn, Jeremy. 1999. "The Global Greats." *Fortune*, 20 December 1999, 222.

Knight, Christopher. "Monterrey's Grand Entrance; The First Show at a New Architecturally Impressive Contemporary Art Space in Mexico Displays the Museum's International Potential." *Los Angeles Times*, 21 July 1999.

Melo Ferreira, Rita de. "Gastronomic Gallery in Linares; Past and Present Meet in a Small Town." *News* (Mexico City), 13 May 1999.

Nuncio, Abraham. "¿Ciudad de México o Chilangolandia?" *La Jornada* (Mexico City), 25 October 1999.

Photographs of President-elect Vicente Fox's Transition Team. *El Norte* (Monterrey), 18 July 2000.

Preston, Julia. "For Citibank, A Problem Plum; Mexican Deal Survives, Despite Fraud Case and Political Turmoil." *New York Times*, 20 November 1997.

Films

Born in East L.A. Produced by Peter McGregor-Scott. Directed by Cheech Marin. 1988.

La oveja negra. Produced by Hermanos Rodríguez. Directed by Ismael Rodríguez. 1949.

Pablo y Carolina. Produced by Antonio Matouk. Directed by Mauricio de la Serna. 1955.

Index